HUMAN
SEXUALITY
OPPOSING VIEWPOINTS®

Other Books of Related Interest in the Opposing Viewpoints Series:

Abortion
AIDS
American Values
Child Abuse
The Family in America
Feminism
Homosexuality
Islam
Male/Female Roles
Population
Sexual Values
Teenage Sexuality

HUMAN
SEXUALITY
OPPOSING VIEWPOINTS®

David Bender & Bruno Leone, *Series Editors*

Brenda Stalcup, *Book Editor*
Bruno Leone, *Assistant Editor*
Karin L. Swisher, *Assistant Editor*

OPPOSING
VIEWPOINTS
SERIES®

Greenhaven Press, Inc., San Diego, CA

Greenhaven Press, Inc.
PO Box 289009
San Diego, CA 92198-9009

Cover photo: Rocky Thies

Library of Congress Cataloging-in-Publication Data

Human sexuality : opposing viewpoints / Brenda Stalcup, book
    editor, Bruno Leone and Karin L. Swisher, assistant editors.
        p.   cm. — (Opposing viewpoints series)
    Includes bibliographical references and index.
    Summary: A collection of debates about such topics as the
determination of gender identity, the establishment of sex
norms, and society's changing views of sexuality.
    ISBN 1-56510-246-0 (lib., acid free.) — ISBN 1-56510-245-2
(pbk., acid free.)
    1. Sex. [1.Sex] I. Stalcup, Brenda. II. Leone, Bruno, 1939–   .
III. Swisher, Karin, 1966–   .IV Series: Opposing viewpoints
series (Unnumbered)
HQ21.H744   1995
306.7—dc20   94-41913
                                                                   CIP
                                                                    AC

"Congress shall make no law . . . abridging the freedom of speech, or of the press."

First Amendment to the U.S. Constitution

The basic foundation of our democracy is the First Amendment guarantee of freedom of expression. The Opposing Viewpoints Series is dedicated to the concept of this basic freedom and the idea that it is more important to practice it than to enshrine it.

Contents

Page

Why Consider Opposing Viewpoints?   9

Introduction   12

Chapter 1: What Is the Purpose of Sex?
Chapter Preface   16
1. The Purpose of Sex Is Biological Advantage   17
   JoAnn C. Gutin
2. The Purpose of Sex Is to Develop Love Bonds   26
   Anthony Walsh
3. The Purpose of Sex Is Reproduction   33
   Paul Murray
4. The Purpose of Sex Is Sensual Pleasure   40
   Sallie Tisdale
5. The Purpose of Sex Is Spiritual Enlightenment   46
   Mark Gramunt
Periodical Bibliography   54

Chapter 2: What Sexual Norms Should Society Uphold?
Chapter Preface   56
1. Society Should Uphold Monogamy   57
   Sidney Callahan
2. Society Should Condone Nonmonogamy   62
   Deborah M. Anapol
3. Christians Should Renounce Divorce   67
   Tim Stafford
4. Christians Should Sometimes Accept Divorce   73
   Amy C. Gregg
5. Society Should Not Tolerate Homosexuality   79
   William Norman Grigg
6. Society Should Celebrate All Forms of Sexuality   86
   Terry Tafoya
Periodical Bibliography   93

Chapter 3: How Are Gender and Sexual Orientation Determined?
Chapter Preface   95
1. Gender Is Determined Biologically   97
   Jo Durden-Smith & Diane deSimone

2. Gender Is Determined by Social Practices   106
  Judith Lorber
3. Gender Is Determined Biologically and Socially   113
  Susan Golombok & Robyn Fivush
4. Evidence for a Biological Influence in Male
  Homosexuality   120
  Simon LeVay & Dean H. Hamer
5. No Evidence for a Biological Cause of
  Homosexuality   130
  Louis Sheldon & Chandler Burr
Periodical Bibliography   135

Chapter 4: What Constitutes Normal Sexual Behavior?

Chapter Preface   137
1. Homosexuality Is Normal Sexual Behavior   139
  Carlton Cornett
2. Homosexuality Is Not Normal Sexual Behavior   146
  Sy Rogers & Alan Medinger
3. Pornography Use Results in Abnormal Sexual
  Behavior   152
  Victor B. Cline
4. Pornography Use Does Not Result in Abnormal
  Sexual Behavior   158
  Martyn Harris
5. Prostitution Can Benefit Women   164
  Veronica Monet
6. Prostitution Harms Women   170
  Jane Anthony
7. Sexual Addiction Is a Serious Problem   176
  Mark Matousek
8. Sexual Addiction Is Normal Human Behavior   184
  Albert Ellis
Periodical Bibliography   191

Chapter 5: How Is Society's View of Human Sexuality Changing?

Chapter Preface   194
1. Americans Are Satisfied with Their Sex Lives   195
  Robert T. Michael et al.
2. Many Americans Are Unsatisfied with Their
  Sex Lives   203
  Lynn Rosellini

3. Sex Is Becoming More Intimate and Less Casual 212
   Mark Clements
4. Sex Is Becoming More Casual and Less Intimate 219
   B.K. Eakman
5. Many Americans Still Practice High-Risk Sexual
   Behavior 226
   Dore Hollander
6. Many Americans Are Trying to Abandon
   High-Risk Behavior 230
   Andrea Heiman
Periodical Bibliography 235

For Further Discussion 237
Organizations to Contact 240
Bibliography of Books 246
Index 250

Why Consider Opposing Viewpoints?

"The only way in which a human being can make some approach to knowing the whole of a subject is by hearing what can be said about it by persons of every variety of opinion and studying all modes in which it can be looked at by every character of mind. No wise man ever acquired his wisdom in any mode but this."

John Stuart Mill

In our media-intensive culture it is not difficult to find differing opinions. Thousands of newspapers and magazines and dozens of radio and television talk shows resound with differing points of view. The difficulty lies in deciding which opinion to agree with and which "experts" seem the most credible. The more inundated we become with differing opinions and claims, the more essential it is to hone critical reading and thinking skills to evaluate these ideas. Opposing Viewpoints books address this problem directly by presenting stimulating debates that can be used to enhance and teach these skills. The varied opinions contained in each book examine many different aspects of a single issue. While examining these conveniently edited opposing views, readers can develop critical thinking skills such as the ability to compare and contrast authors' credibility, facts, argumentation styles, use of persuasive techniques, and other stylistic tools. In short, the Opposing Viewpoints Series is an ideal way to attain the higher-level thinking and reading skills so essential in a culture of diverse and contradictory opinions.

In addition to providing a tool for critical thinking, Opposing Viewpoints books challenge readers to question their own strongly held opinions and assumptions. Most people form their opinions on the basis of upbringing, peer pressure, and personal, cultural, or professional bias. By reading carefully balanced opposing views, readers must directly confront new ideas as well as the opinions of those with whom they disagree. This is not to simplistically argue that everyone who reads opposing views will—or should—change his or her opinion. Instead, the series enhances readers' depth of understanding of their own views by encouraging confrontation with opposing ideas. Careful examination of others' views can lead to the readers' understanding of the logical inconsistencies in their own opinions, perspective on why they hold an opinion, and the consideration of the possibility that their opinion requires further evaluation.

Evaluating Other Opinions

To ensure that this type of examination occurs, Opposing Viewpoints books present all types of opinions. Prominent spokespeople on different sides of each issue as well as well-known professionals from many disciplines challenge the reader. An additional goal of the series is to provide a forum for other, less known, or even unpopular viewpoints. The opinion of an ordinary person who has had to make the decision to cut off life support from a terminally ill relative, for example, may be just as valuable and provide just as much insight as a medical ethicist's professional opinion. The editors have two additional purposes in including these less known views. One, the editors encourage readers to respect others' opinions—even when not enhanced by professional credibility. It is only by reading or listening to and objectively evaluating others' ideas that one can determine whether they are worthy of consideration. Two, the inclusion of such viewpoints encourages the important critical thinking skill of objectively evaluating an author's credentials and bias. This evaluation will illuminate an author's reasons for taking a particular stance on an issue and will aid in readers' evaluation of the author's ideas.

As series editors of the Opposing Viewpoints Series, it is our hope that these books will give readers a deeper understanding of the issues debated and an appreciation of the complexity of even seemingly simple issues when good and honest people disagree. This awareness is particularly important in a democratic society such as ours in which people enter into public debate to determine the common good. Those with whom one disagrees should not be regarded as enemies but rather as people whose views deserve careful examination and may shed light on one's own.

Thomas Jefferson once said that "difference of opinion leads to inquiry, and inquiry to truth." Jefferson, a broadly educated man, argued that "if a nation expects to be ignorant and free . . . it expects what never was and never will be." As individuals and as a nation, it is imperative that we consider the opinions of others and examine them with skill and discernment. The Opposing Viewpoints Series is intended to help readers achieve this goal.

David L. Bender & Bruno Leone,
Series Editors

Introduction

"Our sexual self is a complex combination of our social, cultural, and biological inheritance."

Pepper Schwartz, The Scientist, February 6, 1995

Human sexuality involves basic instincts—innate impulses and physical responses programmed into human biology over hundreds of generations to ensure the continuation of the human race. At the same time, however, human sexuality is also incredibly diverse, encompassing a wide spectrum of behaviors, customs, and beliefs. While in most other species sexual behavior is relegated to the sole purpose of reproduction, many humans regularly engage in nonreproductive sexual behaviors including oral and anal sex (either heterosexual or homosexual), masturbation (either mutual or solo), and sexual intercourse with the use of contraceptives. Unlike animals, humans entertain sexual fantasies, use pornography, and develop sexual fetishes or fixations. Throughout history and across the world, humans have debated sexual philosophies and values, prohibited certain sexual activities, and established social institutions in which sexual behavior is considered acceptable. For humans, the basic sexual instinct is only part of sexuality; cultural dictates and individual proclivities are major influences as well.

However, the outcome of this interplay of biological and cultural factors has varied greatly from society to society. For example, although many societies forbid sexual relations between parent and child or brother and sister, some cultures allow exceptions to the incest taboo. Among the Azande of Africa, chiefs are expected to enter into sexual partnerships with their own daughters; another African culture requires parents to teach their adolescent children about sex by being their first sexual partners. In the royal families of the ancient Egyptians, Incas, and Hawaiians, brothers and sisters were encouraged to marry in order to keep the royal line pure. Additionally, a number of ancient societies allowed marriages between half-siblings who had the same father but different mothers.

Because some cultures do permit incestual relationships, the question arises as to whether the widespread incest taboo has any biological origin, or if it is merely a cultural restraint. Incestual intercourse does occur in other species, including many primates, which suggests that an instinctive aversion to incest may not exist. Furthermore, although most cultures place strict taboos on incest, individuals within those cultures sometimes violate these prohibitions. Anthropologist Carleton A. Coon argues that incest taboos "are not based on instinct or the inductive experience of the genetic consequences." Rather, these restrictions serve to stabilize the family and society by clearly marking the "lines of authority . . . that hold the family together" and by encouraging the solidification of alliances between two families through marriage. On the other hand, there are also considerable biological reasons for preventing incestual relationships. Inbreeding substantially increases the probability that offspring will inherit two recessive genes, resulting in a high incidence of genetic disorders. According to H. Eldon Sutton, author of *Genes, Enzymes, and Inherited Diseases*, "the biological basis for taboos against marriages between relatives derives from this increased risk of producing offspring [who carry two copies of] rare recessive genes." Perhaps both culture and biology play a part in restricting incest, scientist David P. Barash, author of *Sociobiology and Behavior*, proposes: "Incest avoidance is cultural. . . . However, it goes further in being universal and therefore suggesting genetic predispositions." Even if both factors are involved, the question of whether cultural influence is more dominant than biological instinct in establishing the incest taboo—or vice versa—has yet to be resolved.

As evidenced by the disagreements surrounding the origin of the incest taboo, ascertaining which facets of human sexual behavior arise from innate biological tendencies and which result from cultural programming or individual experience can be a formidable task. That humans have a basic biological urge for sex has long been a scientific given, but the extent to which an individual's sexual behavior derives from biology or from environmental influences such as upbringing, early sexual experiences, or cultural values remains in dispute. Scientists disagree on the significance of biological or cultural influences on sexual matters such as gender, sexual orientation, mating behaviors, divorce rates, and transsexuality. These scientific debates often gain popular attention as well, since resolving the origin of controversial aspects of human sexuality could have a substantial impact on society's values.

The root cause of homosexuality, for instance, is a hotly debated topic among researchers and laypersons alike. A number of psychologists believe that homosexuality ensues from psychological trauma or developmental difficulties during early childhood. According to Joseph Nicolosi, a clinical psychologist and the founder of the National Association for the Research and Therapy of Homosexuality, "The homosexual condition is a developmental problem—and one that often results from early problems between father and son." However, recent research by neurobiologist Simon LeVay and by psychologist Michael Bailey and psychiatrist Richard Pillard has suggested a genetic origin for homosexuality. Bailey and Pillard's study found that when one twin is homosexual, the other twin is twice as likely to also be homosexual if the twins are identical (and therefore share the same genetic makeup) instead of fraternal. LeVay's findings located physiological discrepancies between the brain structures of heterosexual and homosexual men. Neurologist Dennis Landis noted that LeVay's findings, if accurate, "would begin to suggest why male homosexuality is present in most human populations, despite cultural constraints. It suggests it's a biological phenomenon."

Even though these recent findings do not conclusively prove that there is a biological origin for homosexuality, they are already affecting American society's view of homosexuality. Darrell Yates Rist, cofounder of the Gay and Lesbian Alliance Against Defamation, writes in *The Nation* of the change of heart undergone by a gay man's parents who after many years reconciled with their son: "'We could have never condoned this,' they told him, 'if you could do something to change it. But when we finally understood that you were *born* that way, we knew we'd been wrong.'" *Newsweek* reporter David Gelman notes, "In the gay community itself, many welcome the indication that gayness begins in the chromosomes. Theoretically, it could gain them the civil-rights protections accorded any 'natural' minority." Others, however, are concerned that the identification of a genetic basis for homosexuality might fuel discrimination and "prompt efforts to tinker with the genetic code of gay adults or to test during pregnancy and abort potentially gay fetuses," writes *Time* reporter William A. Henry III. If the root cause of homosexuality is ever determined to be either wholly biological or wholly environmental, the effects of this discovery will undoubtedly be felt far beyond the researchers' labs.

Indeed, one reason that issues about human sexuality can become so controversial is that they are concerned not just with a specific sexual behavior but with the way in which people use sexuality to define others, and themselves. Susan Ross, a professor of theology and the director of the Women's Studies Program at Loyola University, explains:

> People need to understand that in talking about sex, we're also talking about a lot of other things. We're talking about gender. We're talking about what it means to be a person related to other people. We're talking about how we understand our bodies. We're not just talking about this particular act.

The authors in *Human Sexuality: Opposing Viewpoints* examine these and other aspects of sex in the following chapters: What Is the Purpose of Sex? What Sexual Norms Should Society Uphold? How Are Gender and Sexual Orientation Determined? What Constitutes Normal Sexual Behavior? How Is Society's View of Human Sexuality Changing? As illustrated by the viewpoints in this volume, human sexuality encompasses far more than the physical act of sexual intercourse: It involves deep-set cultural and personal beliefs that affect the meaning and expression of sexuality in every society and for each individual.

What Is the Purpose of Sex?

HUMAN
SEXUALITY

Chapter Preface

The purpose of sex, it would seem, is obvious: Sexual desire is a biological instinct engineered in each human to ensure the reproduction of the species. On second glance, however, human sexuality is not so easily understood. Many aspects of human sexual behavior are unique to humans or are rarely seen among other species; some of these aspects are not essential to reproduction or would even appear, logically, to hinder it.

For example, the female of most species is receptive to sexual intercourse only during her ovulation cycle, when she is most likely to conceive. Anthropologist Meredith F. Small explains:

> Chimp females sport pink swellings on their hind ends for about two weeks, signaling their fertility, and they're only approachable for sex during that time. That's not the case with humans, who show no outward signs that they are ovulating, and who can mate at all phases of the cycle.

If the sole purpose of sex is reproduction, then why are humans not biologically limited to mating only during times when conception is possible? And what could be the reproductive value of the female orgasm—a trait that, as far as scientists have been able to ascertain, only occurs in humans?

Other behaviors found in human societies throughout the world, such as oral and anal intercourse and masturbation, would appear to have no reproductive value whatsoever. Evidence for the use of birth control—including recipes for herbal contraceptives—has been found in the earliest human civilizations. Undoubtedly, homosexual intercourse cannot result in a pregnancy, yet it is a behavior that has existed for thousands of years in many societies. However important reproduction may be, clearly it is not the only reason humans have engaged in sexual intercourse.

Humans, alone among the species, have a talent for embellishing basic instincts with customs, symbolic ceremonies, individual idiosyncrasies, and religious significance. Just as humans are the only species to surround the instinct of eating with intricate rules and rituals, so too have they imbued the instinct of sexual intercourse with multiple meanings and purposes. The primary purpose of sex differs from culture to culture and person to person; individuals may even find that the purpose of sex changes as they pass through different stages in their lives. A culture's definition of the purpose of sex can also affect sexual behavior: A society that believes the only purpose of sex is reproduction, for instance, might condemn intercourse for pleasure. The viewpoints in the following chapter present some of the theories that have arisen concerning the purpose of sex.

"The genetic variability afforded by sex gives us hosts at least a fighting chance against our various [pathogens], and the little breathing room it provides is what makes sex worth the trouble."

The Purpose of Sex Is Biological Advantage

JoAnn C. Gutin

There are two types of reproduction: Either an organism creates an exact clone of itself, or it mates with another organism to produce offspring that contain genetic material from both parents. At first glance, cloning may appear to be more efficient than sex, since organisms that clone can create exact genetic copies of themselves without expending valuable time and energy searching for a mate. Why, then, did humans evolve into sexual beings? In the following viewpoint, JoAnn C. Gutin examines current research that suggests that the genetic variety inherent with sexual reproduction helps the human race to survive. Gutin is an anthropologist and a writer for science magazines, including *Discover* and *E: The Environmental Magazine*.

As you read, consider the following questions:
1. According to Gutin, what led John Maynard Smith to question the established theory of the evolution of sex?
2. In the author's opinion, why can conjugation among bacteria be described as "proto-bad-sex"?
3. What is the Red Queen hypothesis, according to Gutin?

Excerpted from JoAnn C. Gutin, "Why Bother?" *Discover*, June 1992; ©1992 The Walt Disney Company. Reprinted with the permission of *Discover* magazine.

There's something about sex that seems to inspire whimsy. The scientific literature on how it all began is spiced with clever turns of phrase, witty asides, and the occasional risque double entendre. Perhaps the strain of accounting for such an absurd way of making babies goes to the heads of even the sober men and women of science.

You'd think there would hardly be cause for such exercise about the original reason for sex. After all, the problem was considered pretty well solved 30 years ago. "Sex was said to be good for the species," says Richard Michod, a 41-year-old professor of ecology and evolutionary biology at the University of Arizona in Tucson and one of the key figures in the current debate. By sex, of course, he means the mating of genetic material from two individuals to produce one with a new combination of genes. By ensuring that offspring were slightly different from their parents, sex increased the chances that a species would produce a new, improved model capable of surviving environmental changes or of getting the jump on a rival or predator. "It provided genetic variability, so sexual populations evolved faster, and that was that. It was in all the textbooks," says Michod.

In the mid-seventies, however, evolutionary biologists began to question that conventional wisdom. Chief among the worriers was John Maynard Smith, a professor of biology at the University of Sussex in England and, dare one say it, a seminal figure in the field. He was troubled that the standard explanation for sex invoked a slightly dubious mechanism (dubious in his view, anyway) known as group selection.

The classic example of group selection in action is the animal that gives a warning cry to alert the group to a dangerous predator and thereby puts itself at risk. Why does self-sacrificing behavior enter into a discussion of sex? Because no organism in its right mind would opt for sex with another organism as a way to create offspring. It's too darned expensive, genetically speaking.

Most higher organisms that go in for sexual reproduction package their genes into pairs of chromosomes (we humans have 23 such pairs). But any sexually reproducing organism throws half its genes overboard when it makes sex cells—that is, eggs or sperm—because its sex cells contain only one chromosome from each chromosome pair. (This is called the haploid, or halved, condition; the union of egg and sperm in sexual reproduction restores the diploid, or paired chromosome, condition.) Thrifty asexual organisms, on the other hand, transmit all their genes to the next generation.

Clones

This thorny fact of life presents a major problem for evolutionary theory. If natural selection acts on individuals, rewarding

18

those who get the most copies of their genes into the next generation, then sex would seem to make no sense. All organisms ought to opt for efficient cloning, not mad, untidy mating. Cloning—which exists in many single-celled organisms, some plants, and a few insects, fish, and reptiles—involves no apparently pointless halving of paired chromosomes, no compulsory union with other organisms in order to form a complete whole. Clones simply split in two or bud to generate identical copies of themselves, or produce self-sufficient diploid eggs that don't require fertilization by sperm.

Evolutionary Roots

Biologist Lynn Margulis of the University of Massachusetts at Amherst believes the evolutionary roots of egg and sperm cells can be traced back to a group of organisms known as protists that first appeared some 1.5 billion years ago. (Modern examples include protozoa, giant kelp and malaria parasites.) During periods of starvation, Margulis conjectures, one protist was driven to devour another. Sometimes this cannibalistic meal was incompletely digested, and the nuclei of prey and predator fused. By joining forces, the fused cells were better able to survive adversity, and because they survived, their penchant for union was passed on to their distant descendants.

From this vantage point, human sexuality seems little more than a wondrous accident, born of a kind of original sin among protozoa. Most population biologists, however, believe sex was maintained over evolutionary time because it somehow enhanced survival. The mixing and matching of parental genes, they argue, provide organisms with a novel mechanism for generating genetically different offspring, thereby increasing the odds that their progeny could exploit new niches in a changing environment and, by virtue of their diversity, have a better chance of surviving the assaults of bacteria and other tiny germs that rapidly evolve tricks for eluding their hosts' defenses.

J. Madeleine Nash, *Time*, January 20, 1992.

Furthermore, many organisms invest enormous amounts of time in pursuing mates, time that they might better spend on eating or on avoiding being eaten. Females end up paying a particularly high price for sexual reproduction; most females gestate and nurture their young, while males contribute nothing but their genes.

The group selection theory that worried Maynard Smith was a way to explain—or explain away—the toll that sex apparently exacted on the individual. According to the rules of natural selection, sex must be good because there's so much of it around. (Current estimates are that 99.9 percent of higher organisms are sexual.) Unfortunately, it looks very bad for the individual, so it must be the group that it's good for. Sex, the argument went, produces genetic variation by combining the genes of two individuals; very well, then, variation must be advantageous to the species.

Thus sex evolved to produce variation as a sort of group benefit plan, allowing groups that reproduced sexually to keep up with changes in their environment. It wasn't a pretty explanation, but it got the job done.

There things rested until the publication in 1978 of Maynard Smith's *The Evolution of Sex*, in which he wrote of his "distaste for the Panglossian belief that if some characteristic can be seen as benefiting the species, then all is explained." . . . Young researchers in the field recall being inspired by its puzzled lucidity. An important problem—maybe even *the* problem—in evolutionary biology had been put up for grabs again. Why bother with sex? . . .

There's a comedy routine beloved of Mel Brooks fans in which Brooks assumes his funniest persona, the 2,000-Year-Old Man. This ancient has been alive since the birth of Christ, and he's more than willing to editorialize on what he's seen in his long life. Asked to name the greatest scientific advance in his two millennia, Brooks promptly replies, "Saran Wrap." "Saran Wrap?" says startled straight man Carl Reiner. "What about the conquest of space?" "Oh," says Brooks, generously, "that was a good thing too."

Proto-Sex

Nowadays you could almost summarize the most influential arguments to explain the origin of sex as, "Oh, variability, that was a good thing, too." These arguments hark back to ancestral forms of proto-sex—the mixing of genetic material from two different organisms that paved the way for sexual reproduction proper. Researchers working at the molecular level regard these transactions as anything from a strategy for DNA repair to an accident, the consequence of a parasitic bit of DNA becoming especially persistent about getting itself copied. On one point, however, the newer views agree. All the genetic variability that sex affords is good, so good that it may well be what kept sex going once it got started, but it wasn't why sex evolved in the first place.

One of the arguments currently dominating the competition is championed by Michael Rose, a mathematical geneticist at the University of California at Irvine, and his colleague Donal Hickey of the University of Ottawa. Along with many others in their field, they believe that a bacterial phenomenon known as conjugation constitutes an ancient form of proto-sex. Conjugation is a property of some but not all bacteria in a given colony. It involves the extension of a projection called a pilus from one bacterium to another, and the journey along that bridge of a self-contained, parasitic loop of genetic material called a plasmid. ("There is a certain morphological similarity between conjugation and higher sex," notes Michod delicately.)

The bacteria seem to gain nothing from this transaction. In fact, if this is proto-sex, it's proto-bad-sex, because neither bacterium can be described as consenting. The plasmid contains the quintessential selfish gene, a bit of DNA whose only mission is to reproduce itself, thus driving the plasmid to distribute as many copies of itself to as many hosts as possible. In the process, bits of the original bacterium's genome occasionally cling to the plasmid like foxtails on a dog's coat and find themselves in the new host. Eventually, explains Rose, some hosts begin to use and benefit from the inadvertent gift of another individual's DNA.

Rose and Hickey have gone on to propose that selfish DNA could account for a primitive form of sex that's closer to sex as we now know it. In some early single-celled organisms, they theorize, selfish DNA didn't merely cause a bridge to form so that it could travel from one individual to another—it impelled the two organisms to actually fuse, in a primitive anticipation of what sperm and egg do during fertilization. This parasitic DNA could then spread contagiously until the whole population was committed to sex. . . .

Gene Repair

Michod's idea that the reshuffling of genes from two organisms originated as a mechanism to mend damaged chromosomes is another of the theories in current contention. Influenced by Maynard Smith, Michod refused to buy the argument that genetic variation was enough justification for sex.

"Look at us," he says, "adult organisms who have already passed muster, evolutionarily speaking. We've survived, so our genomes must be in reasonable shape." But what is the most striking effect of sexual reproduction? "It scrambles up that perfectly good genome. What are the odds that that will be an improvement? And even if it is, then what? You can produce a superkid, but she'll just reproduce and scramble the genome even more." Everything sex does, it partly undoes in the next generation.

Michod reasoned that since DNA is a way of conveying information, perhaps sex was initially a way of getting the message straight: it might be about error correction, not variation. In 1988 he and his team demonstrated sex-for-DNA-repair in a bacterium called *Bacillus subtilis*. These microbes engage in an activity called transformation, which involves incorporating bits of DNA floating in their environment. (Not to be too lurid about it, but this DNA originates from the disintegrating corpses of neighboring *B. subtilis*.) Michod believes that they use this "spare" DNA to repair breaks in their own chromosomes caused by exposure to environmental insults, such as excessive oxygen or ultraviolet light. The evidence? Damaged bacteria use more DNA than undamaged bacteria, and repaired bacteria replicate more successfully than unrepaired bacteria. (Comments Rose, "Sex with dead bacteria is apparently better than no sex at all.")

None of this means that either Rose or Michod underestimates the significance of variation. "Look," says Michod, "diversity is the fuel of evolution, and gene recombination produces diversity. We're just saying that recombination—proto-sex if you will—didn't come into existence to produce variation." Variation, in other words, is an effect of sex, one that's turned out to be extraordinarily useful, but it's not the original reason for sex. "There must be some short-term, individual benefit to recombination," says Michod, and in his view, it's DNA repair. . . .

Variation

The sex riddle is still only partially solved. Evolutionary biologists may have some idea of what made sex possible in the first place. But just because something is possible doesn't guarantee it will catch on. Why did so many organisms stick with sex after trying it? Why didn't they revert to cloning? This is where some researchers think variability really comes into play: it's what made sex such an *enduring* success.

On paper, clones look unbeatable. A clone wastes no time looking for a mate, runs no risk of scrambling a perfectly serviceable genotype, and can put more copies of itself into the next generation than a sexual organism. Yet while clones abound in the lowest ranks of life, they constitute a fairly exclusive club in the higher animal kingdom. True, some earthworms, spiders, and the water flea *Daphnia* can switch from sexual to clonal reproduction depending on environmental conditions. Certain all-female species of whiptail lizard have opted for total parthenogenesis—they have eggs that develop without fertilization—but they are nearly unique among terrestrial vertebrates. And quite a number of fish and amphibians come in sexual and asexual versions. But in all these cases the asexuals almost certainly had sexual ancestors, making them evolutionary backsliders. As a rule, the higher you go on the evolutionary ladder, the less likely a group is to have a clonal variant.

That's a puzzle: Why don't more organisms backslide and revert to cloning? Are we sexuals simply in a rut, so deeply invested in the visible and invisible machinery of sex that we can no longer throw it away? Actually, recent research suggests this may be at least part of the explanation for the persistence of sex. Mouse embryos in which both copies of a chromosome were engineered to come from one parent—rather than the standard, sexually obtained complement of one maternal and one paternal copy—died early in development. Somehow the sex of the parent does leave an indelible and absolutely necessary imprint on offspring. Thus males have become, once and for all, indispensable.

Of course, blinkered as we humans are by our own sexuality, we don't usually spare much thought for clones, let alone wonder why there aren't more of them. (Perhaps we're half afraid to. In the popular imagination—or is it the collective unconscious?—clones are the stuff of sci-fi nightmare. Who can forget the evil pod people overrunning San Francisco in *The Invasion of the Body Snatchers?*) But to a student of sex evolution, clones are a godsend. Commented one researcher, "To learn about health, you study disease. To learn about sex, you study clones."

In the first round of studying clones, researchers tried to discover if there were any consistencies in the habitat preferences of these organisms that had gotten off the sexual merry-go-round. The results of their experiments were, to put it mildly, surprising.

Earlier theorists had assumed that sex was advantageous in the long run because it produced variability in gross features like size and shape, thus equipping species to adapt and roll with the inevitable environmental punches. If that were the case, then sexual organisms ought to turn up in harsh areas on the frontiers of an organism's habitat, and clones ought to live only in cushy environments. In fact, nearly the opposite is true: clones tend to predominate in frontier settings, while sexual organisms fill the niches in environmentally stable zones.

It appears that in difficult habitats, or on the fringes of a range where populations are low and finding a mate may not be a trivial effort, clones do well. For one thing, they can reproduce quickly, which makes them excellent colonizers: they're homesteaders who don't need to wait for mail-order brides. But clones evidently falter in the dense jostling of stable ecosystems, which teem with life and where competition between and within species is fierce. . . .

Fighting Disease

Many researchers are coming around to the idea that all living creatures are trying to outrun pathogens just to stay in the evolutionary race. Pathogens, though tiny, have the advantage of speed and numbers: they can reproduce (usually asexually) in seconds and mutate many times while their hosts are held to slower reproductive timetables. The genetic variability afforded by sex gives us hosts at least a fighting chance against our various nemeses, and the little breathing room it provides is what makes sex worth the trouble. That idea stems from what has been dubbed the Red Queen hypothesis, after the irascible royal in Lewis Carroll's *Through the Looking Glass:* "Now, *here*, you see," says the Queen to Alice, "it takes all the running *you* can do, to keep in the same place. If you want to get somewhere else, you must run at least twice as fast as that."

It's nearly impossible to prove or disprove an evolutionary hypothesis like the Red Queen; the best that scientists can do is ask how organisms would behave if the Red Queen were running the show, and then see if organisms actually behave that way.

Let's suppose that organisms opted for sex to confuse pathogens by creating groups of genetically distinct individuals, each with its own uniquely challenging immune defenses. As the flip side of that idea, all sorts of enemies—viruses, bacteria, parasites— should be pretty adroit at infecting populations with whom they've coevolved and whose defenses they've had a chance to study, though they should be stymied by organisms they've never met. In other words, the bad guys should exhibit a sort of home-field advantage.

Experimentation

One researcher who is enthusiastically putting such ideas to the test is Curtis Lively, a 38-year-old population biologist at Indiana University in Bloomington. One of his first crucial experiments involved an old tussle between two species living in the lakes of New Zealand. The protagonists were an aquatic snail, *Potamopyrgus antipodarum*, and its parasitic nemesis, the rather unkindly named worm *Microphallus*. If the coevolutionary arms race between pathogen and host predicated by the Red Queen was occurring, Lively reasoned, you'd expect to see a genetic basis for parasite susceptibility in these snails. . . .

Accordingly, Lively drew snails and parasites from each of two lakes separated by some 10,000 feet of New Zealand alp—a barrier high enough to discourage even the most determined *Microphallus*. One lake had smooth-shelled snails, while the other had spiky ones, making it possible to put both snail types into the same containers and readily tell them apart. Lively then infected some containers with worms from one lake and some with worms from the other.

Just as the theory predicted, the parasitic worms showed a home-field advantage. They handily infected the snails with which they had coevolved and whose defenses they knew, but they were stumped by snails from the alien lake with an unfamiliar genotype. That suggests there could indeed be a pathogen-induced advantage to producing variable offspring, says Lively. His observation, moreover, meshed with a previous, more general survey of New Zealand snails. In lakes heavily infested with parasites, sexual snails, with their more variable genotypes, greatly outnumbered the clones; whereas in lakes with fewer parasites, clones formed a larger part of the population. Apparently, the more *Microphallus* there were nipping at the snails' heels, the greater the incentive for sex.

Lively has since participated in a study that clearly demonstrates the advantage of sex in a small Mexican minnow, *Poeciliopsis monacha*, which has both sexual and asexual variants. In rock pools where both coexist, the study found, parasitic worms made a beeline for the most common genotype—all those of the familiar-looking clones. The sexual fish outnumbered the clones by four to one.

"If there were no parasites in the world," says Lively, "a clone could take over in many species." The world being the pest-ridden place it is, sexuals predominate. By mixing up genes, sex produces variable offspring with rare genotypes that can stay one step ahead of their enemies. In contrast, clones are easy pickings for a parasite. (Seen one clone, seen 'em all.) "Clones," observes Lively philosophically, "pay a high price for being so uniform."

"The first human love bond was between mother and infant, and nature capitalized on this bond and on the sex drive to develop male/female love bonds."

The Purpose of Sex Is to Develop Love Bonds

Anthony Walsh

In the following viewpoint, Anthony Walsh examines the evolutionary link between human sexuality and love. Human sexual intercourse is distinct from that of other primates in several ways, Walsh suggests, and these differences are crucial to the ability of humans to form bonds of love with their mates. Walsh postulates that love evolved from sex in order to ensure two caretakers—father and mother—for a human infant and thus increase the chances for the survival of the human race. A professor of criminal justice and statistics, Walsh is the author of *The Science of Love*.

As you read, consider the following questions:

1. According to Walsh, what is the difference between uterogestation and exterogestation?
2. How do love bonds between a human mother and her infant increase the chances of the infant's survival, in the author's opinion?
3. Which evolutionary changes does Walsh believe contributed to frontal intercourse among humans?

Excerpted from Anthony Walsh, "The Biological Relationship Between Sex and Love," *Free Inquiry*, Summer 1991. Reprinted by permission of the Council for Democratic and Secular Humanism.

Philosophers have been debating the relationship between sex and love for centuries. The impression gained from perusing the history of the debate is that they always knew that sex and love somehow "went together," but also that they wished it were not so. Following Plato's example, the Christian church made a sharp distinction between sacred (agape) and profane (eros) love. The Church enshrined and blessed the former, but consigned wanton eros to hell. Poets waxed eloquently and freely about love, for it ennobled and elevated us, but the lusty bards of sex had to dodge the censor's wrath, for the rising penis had become a symbol for the fall of man. Many modern works also divorce love from sex, but aim to raise the penis rather than the spirit.

From the perspective of the individual human being, love and sex are certainly distinct phenomena (although a happy concomitance is often observed) that can be, and often are, pursued independently of one another. Taking a broad species approach rather than an individual one, the human sciences appear to be coalescing around the position that love is an epiphenomenon of sex, a position exemplified by Arthur Schopenhauer's statement that "Love is a snare set by sex to ensure the survival of the species." While I agree with the general thrust of this proposition, I view love as being much more than a simple derivative of sex. Love springs from sex, and thus shares with it a certain oneness of essence; but love pursues an independent existence, and in doing so elevates and ennobles that from which it sprang.

Mother and Offspring

Certainly our vaunted sexual appetites are enough to ensure ample pregnancies, but reproduction alone is not sufficient for the survival of a species whose young has a longer dependency period than any other. As we ascend the phylogenetic tree, infancy and childhood dependency periods become longer and increasing emotional attachment of mother and offspring is observed; mammals do not simply "lay 'em and leave 'em" as do the reptiles. We do not, however, observe a similar increase in emotional attachment among nonhuman adult males and females. No special affinity is observed among stallions, bulls, or dogs for the last mare, cow, or bitch mated with, and the feeling is mutual. For species with short-lived dependency periods, the only necessary male role is the provision of stud service. Thus, the "love as derivative of sex" proposition is not a general biological principle throughout the entire animal kingdom.

An emotional attachment between men and women that is qualitatively different from the frenetic mating of lower species had to evolve, not to simply attract them to one another, but also to keep them *attached* to one another sufficiently long to raise the vulnerable fruits of their passion. Human love in its

27

ideal form is attraction *plus* attachment. Anthropological evidence suggests an infant and child mortality rate of between 53 and 65 percent among Plio-Pleistocene hominids. It has been speculated that these rates would have risen to levels that would have spelled doom for the species had not some evolutionary mechanisms been selected into the human repertoire of traits to bond male and female together as a child-rearing team.

The evolutionary saga leading to the selection of biological processes coding for the emergence of the emotion we call love probably had a lot to do with the importance of intelligence for our species. We are a physically puny species with low fecundity. Such a combination of disabilities would have been disastrous for our hominid ancestors had they been as highly adapted to a particular ecological niche as many species are. The more a species is adapted to a particular niche, the more its responses to environmental stimuli are stereotyped. In essence, this means that the genes of such a species code for brains with neurons that are "hard-wired" (directly and permanently connected) to assure that species members will instinctively pay attention and respond appropriately to aspects of the environment that are vital to them.

Because of the vulnerability of our hominid ancestors to predators, they had to depend on guile to survive encounters with them, and had to frequently migrate to new environments to avoid them. Hard-wired stereotypical responses to stimuli would be counterproductive to organisms inhabiting highly variable environments in which new responses were constantly required. This meant that the genes had to surrender much of their behavioral control of proto-humans to a less rigid and fixed system for determining responses to stimuli—the plastic human brain.

Long-Term Development

Human infants take about one year to reach the stage of development at which other mammals are at birth, and their brain weights triple during this period. If the human infant were as developmentally precocious as nonhuman mammals, its head would be too large to pass through the birth canal. To accommodate natural selection for increasing human brain size, evolution settled on the strategy of human infants being born at earlier and earlier stages of development. Human infants are so developmentally incomplete that scientists posit a dual human gestation period: uterogestation (within the womb) and exterogestation (postnatal), the latter period lasting about ten months.

The importance of this observation in the present context is that such a developmental lag requires that the helpless infant have someone who will unconditionally administer to its needs. The selfless and unconditional care and regard for another human being is called "love." It is during this period of maximum dependency that the infant's brain is quite literally being "wired" (the process of synaptogenesis) by its experiences. Whether or not the neuronal pathways to the pleasure centers are sufficiently strong to enable the organism to love (as opposed to simply copulating) as an adult depends to a great extent on this early experience. Science has uncovered hormonal and neuronal substrates that cement mother/infant love. For instance, estradiol lowers the threshold for the firing of nerve fibers in the medial preoptic area of the female brain, an area associated with increased nurturing behavior in females. The male preoptic is insensitive to estradiol. It has been shown that progesterone and estradiol administered artificially to virgin rats will evoke maternal behavior, and that oxytocin, released in response to suckling, "intensifies" maternal behavior. There is an abundance of literature on the role of female hormones in evoking loving maternal behavior that cannot be addressed here.

A strong propensity to become emotionally attached to the mother and to other caregivers who provide food, protection, and a secure base from which to explore their environment has obvious survival value for the young of the species. As a child gets older, we may adequately account for his or her attachment behavior as a function of his or her history of operant reinforcement (well-loved children are strongly attached, neglected and maltreated children hardly at all). But something a lot more basic than a cognitive appreciation of rewards and punishments must provide the foundation for attachment. A biological system of internal rewards and punishments had to evolve.

The brain's natural opiates. the endorphin peptides, probably provide the chemical foundation of attachment. When an infant is snuggled in mother's arms, endorphins keep it contented. Separate the infant from its mother and endorphin levels fall, and levels of the stress hormone cortisol rise, triggering anxiety and crying. It has been shown that only the administration of exogenous endorphins will mollify separated infants in the same way that reunion with the mother will. Mothers are good for us, they keep us happy, they ease our anxiety, they make us feel warm and secure, and they keep our endorphins at pleasant levels and "high" on life.

Human Evolution

The intimate link between love and sex has its origins in the primary love bond between mother and infant, which is a function of the long human dependency period, which is in turn the result of evolutionary pressures selecting for intelligence. Two other evolutionary processes—the human female's loss of estrus, and the species' gradual development of upright bipedalism—

probably also contributed. Females have a large investment in parenthood. Males contribute a few pelvic thrusts, after which they can be on their way. Nature had to devise a system by which males could be persuaded to remain with females after copulation to provide food and protection for them and their offspring. Let us be aware that it was the *male* that nature had to capture in love. Strong evolutionary pressures had already awakened general feelings of attachment in the female by virtue of her motherhood role. These same nascent feelings were also present in the male by virtue of his early attachment to his mother. He now had to transfer these same feelings to other females, and sex was the vehicle by which this was accomplished.

Social Sex

On the ground, moving from fruit tree to fruit tree, bonobos [pygmy chimpanzees] often stand and walk on two legs—behavior that makes them seem more like humans than chimps. In some ways their sexual behavior seems more human as well, suggesting that in the sexual arena, at least, bonobos are the more appropriate ancestral model. Males and females frequently copulate face-to-face, which is an uncommon position in animals other than humans. . . .

Like humans but unlike chimps and most other animals, bonobos separate sex from reproduction. They seem to treat sex as a pleasurable activity, and they rely on it as a sort of social glue, to make or break all sorts of relationships. "Ancestral humans behaved like this," proposes Frans de Waal, an ethologist at the Yerkes Regional Primate Research Center at Emory University. "Later, when we developed the family system, the use of sex for this sort of purpose became more limited, mainly occurring within families."

Meredith F. Small, *Discover*, June 1992.

We know that most female members of nonhuman mammalian species are only sexually receptive during estrus, and are of interest to males only at that time. There was certainly a time in the history of our species when our female ancestors also went through estrus. Some hominid females must have enjoyed longer periods of sexual receptivity than others. Males would have naturally been more solicitous of such females, providing them with extra food and protection (it is often noted that other primate males are far more attentive and generous to females when they are in estrus). Females enjoying long periods of sexual receptivity would be more likely to survive, as would their offspring. Over time, natural selection would spread the genes for longer receptivity throughout the population, eventually leading to the disappearance of human estrus altogether.

Assuming that natural selection for upright bipedalism was taking place coterminously with the gradual loss of estrus, sight would have largely replaced smell as the impetus to mate. Upright hominids, with genitals now moved more toward the front, led to the uniquely human practice of frontal intercourse. Frontal intercourse involves far more skin contact than the old method of seizing the female from behind and staring off into space. Because of the intimate connection between the skin and the brain, formed as they are in utero by the same layer of tissue, humans find tactile stimulation most pleasing. Sexual intercourse began more and more to recall the pleasures lovers once found in their mother's arms. The sucking of the lover's breasts, the warmth of skin contact, eye gazing and nose nuzzling, and the feeling that all is right with the world (the endorphins in action), evokes deep unconsciousness memories of the mother/ infant bond. Frontal intercourse mimicked and capitalized on the primary mother/infant bond, and thus elevated the sexual drive above simple genital pleasure.

A Unique Individual

Frontal intercourse involves more of the human senses than the impersonality of belly/buttocks coupling. The evolution of intelligence and language enabled lovers to "know the individual" by translating their physical and visual pleasures into words. He or she is no longer simply a set of genitals that look and smell like every other set, but a unique individual who captures and holds the imagination. The imagination allowed our ancestors, as it allows us, to replay previous sexual encounters with their lovers, to anticipate future ones, and to come to value sexual intercourse as the ultimate celebration of love. Certainly, sex can be enjoyed without emotional elaboration, but who would deny that sex accompanied by love is infinitely more pleasurable than the grunting urgency of the casual hump? . . .

The link between sex (attraction) and love (attraction + attachment) is woman. . . .

Male/female love bonds are to a large extent governed by female reproductive behavior, which is governed by female regard for the survival of her offspring. Mother/infant and male/female bonds are biological; the infant/father bond is a purely human *cultural* concept. If the human male was to contribute something to the survival of the species other than stud service, the species had to become sufficiently intelligent to recognize and grasp the abstract concept of *relationship*. With the ability to grasp such a concept came the integration of the two biological bonds with the cultural fatherhood bond. The fusion of these basic bonds became a template for the evolution of ever more complex human relationships and bonds—kinship, family, tribe, and on up to the formation of society itself. The pivotal figure in the extension of basic biological bonds to cultural bonds is woman, for she is the only figure common to both biological bonds. . . .

The Joy of Love

There was certainly a time in our evolutionary history when love, the active concern for the well-being of another, did not exist. The mating of male and female genitalia was all that was necessary for species survival when our distant ancestors slithered around in the primordial mud. Proto-humans became increasingly intelligent as environments became more complicated, and the selection for human intelligence necessitated the selection for human love. The first human love bond was between mother and infant, and nature capitalized on this bond and on the sex drive to develop male/female love bonds. That scientists have discovered some of the chemical potions that nature uses to draw us together should not diminish the wonder of love one iota. Even a definitive understanding of the biology of love would leave us far from exhausting the richness of meaning contained in the sublime verb "to love." As far as we know, we are the only creatures in the universe who can grasp the meaning and joy of love: that love is what we give as well as what we get, and that it is the creative medium by which we and our lovers become more than we ever thought possible.

"We run the risk of trivializing sexuality when we . . . willfully isolate it from our procreative capacity."

The Purpose of Sex Is Reproduction

Paul Murray

Published in 1968, Pope Paul VI's *Humanae vitae* affirmed the Roman Catholic Church's stance against artificial contraception. However, not all Catholics agree with or follow the church's teaching on birth control, and this disagreement has led to much debate over the issue. In the following viewpoint, Paul Murray contends that sexual intercourse cannot be separated from its primary purpose of reproduction. To use artificial contraception to prevent reproduction, Murray argues, can only result in the devaluation of human sexuality. Murray is an elementary school teacher and an instructor of natural family planning.

As you read, consider the following questions:

1. In Murray's opinion, why is abstinence "utterly sexual in its nature"?
2. How does using contraception "limit the scope of our most intimate relationships," in the author's view?
3. On what basis does Murray describe the "contraceptive ethic" as negative?

Excerpted from Paul Murray, "The Power of 'Humanae Vitae,'" *Commonweal*, July 15, 1994. Reprinted with permission.

July 1993 marked the twenty-fifth anniversary of the publication of Pope Paul VI's *Humanae vitae*. The anniversary was marked by a flurry of correspondence which broke—should I say, interrupted?—the sullen stalemate into which many Catholics seem to have been frozen on the issue of church teaching concerning birth control. While twenty-sixth anniversaries don't usually lend themselves to commemoration, July 1994 provides the occasion to raise a useful question: What are we Catholics to do now? Ring out the old year, ring in the new, and be done with fruitless discussions of *Humanae vitae*? . . .

Initiating a Dialogue

I think that the process of resolution can begin only when partners speak positively for themselves, rather than merely react to the other. What do we want from our sexual relationships? What value do we seek to develop in them? How do the principles enunciated in *Humanae vitae* help or hinder us in that search?

I would like to speak for myself in considering these questions. Rather than run the risk of distorting the views of Catholics who disagree with me, I will as much as possible refrain from attempting to present them from my point of view. I will leave it to others to explicate the positive value in their own position, and I hope they do so.

I should also identify the perspective I bring to the issue. My wife and I have practiced Natural Family Planning (NFP) for all fifteen years of our marriage, having taken instruction during our engagement, in part to better understand the church's view of sexuality. We are now NFP instructors ourselves.

Yet the harmony that we enjoy with the church's position does not render us immune to the sense of dissonance that many Catholics feel about the question of contraception. Our personal experience is one of profound alienation from our popular culture on anything to do with sexuality and family planning. I am also uncomfortable with the way in which *Humanae vitae* is often—though not always—presented and defended. Little attention is given the holistic approach to sexuality to which the encyclical calls us.

So, without presuming to have composed a comprehensive discussion of it, I will examine some salient points . . . of *Humanae vitae* . . . and compare them with the sexual and cultural terrain I have been walking in my own marriage.

Humanae vitae *transcends conventional wisdom regarding sexual abstinence:*

> . . . this discipline [the observance of periodic continence], far from harming conjugal love itself, rather confers upon it a higher human value. It requires continual effort, but thanks to its beneficent influence husband and wife fully develop their personalities and are enriched with spiritual values.

In a culture that sneers at chastity, it is sometimes difficult to speak of abstinence as *good*. Yet it can be. We know that children often grow out of their egocentricity by coming up against the fact that they can't necessarily have what they want. We recognize the growth of maturity in children when they deal constructively and creatively with such deprivation. Conversely, we sense a lack of maturity when children go to great lengths to avoid it. The process of maturation does not end with childhood, and we don't foster it by contriving to have our way in this aspect of our lives.

Contraception Shuts God Out

It is precisely because man is not on the same level as animals that he is called to live in accord with a higher view of sexuality. Whereas animal sex is a fleeting union and results in simply another member of the species, human sex is meant to promote a profound bond and brings forth an immortal soul. . . . Contraceptive sex tends to foster fleeting and shallow unions more than the deeply intimate unions appropriate to human persons. Here let me briefly note that contraception does not merely thwart a purely biological capacity. God, loving creator that he is, chose to bring forth new human life through the loving act of spouses. The male provides the sperm, the female the ovum and God the human soul. Contraception allows couples to enjoy the pleasure God designed for sexual intercourse but shuts God out from performing his creative act in the arena he designed for bringing forth new human life.

Janet E. Smith, *America*, August 13, 1994.

On the contrary, we can avail ourselves of genital inactivity to construct a more varied sexual relationship. As we were all acutely aware before becoming sexually active with our spouses, periods of abstinence can be very sexually intense. Our conventional cultural wisdom cannot account for the sense of abandonment of self, the creative use of sexual energy in other aspects of the relationship, and the exhilaration experienced in a mutual decision to forgo sexual intercourse, when the desire to have intercourse is also mutual. If intercourse is intimate sharing, then a conscious decision to abstain under such circumstances is intercourse in all but the physical sense of the word, and is utterly sexual in its nature. . . .

Humanae vitae *challenges us to evolve personally as well as technologically:*

By safeguarding both these essential aspects, the unitive and the procreative, the conjugal act preserves in its fullness the sense of true mutual love and its ordination to man's most high vocation to parenthood. We think that men of our day are particularly capable of confirming the deeply reasonable and human character of this fundamental principle.

We of Western culture stand at a defining moment in human development. Through the application of sophisticated technologies, we have liberated ourselves from many of the material and time-space constraints imposed on people of the past (and in much of the world at present). We can now *choose to do* things which literally were not possible until recently, and can *choose not to do* things which have always been considered unavoidable. Our technological proficiency enables us to rule nature as we once were ruled by it. We now have the ability to exercise true responsibility in our sexual decision making.

The expectation of genuine, long-term sexual fulfillment is a relatively recent phenomenon. It has been greatly facilitated by the fact that we have time which need not be spent in the struggle to survive. We now have the power to pursue fulfillment of certain aspects of our sexuality independently of others, or to integrate them using natural methods of birth regulation that rival artificial means in their effectiveness. The way in which we choose to use this power will say much about how we define ourselves as human and sexual beings.

Is our capacity to make sexual decisions going to evolve as have our technological capacities? Will our understanding of our sexual nature grow as has our understanding of the world's nature? Are our sexual desires and motivations going to develop and become more comprehensive, or remain physically, sensually, and emotionally self-centered? Can we Americans ever transcend our "forbidden fruit" attitude toward sex, wherein we continually try to evade someone else's prohibitions? At a time in history when we have become able to accomplish it, *Humanae vitae* challenges us to a responsible integration of the unitive and procreative aspects of sexuality and so to a personal evolution that will undoubtedly be as painstaking, yet at least as consequential, as our technical development. . . .

Practice the Ideal

The encyclical confronts the sixty-four-dollar question, and calls us to seek the ideal in practice:

> . . . the church, calling men back to the observance of the norms of the natural law . . . teaches that each and every marriage act must remain open to the transmission of life.

> Similarly excluded [as a lawful means of birth regulation] is every action that, either in anticipation of the conjugal act or in its accomplishment or in the development of its natural consequences, would have as an end or as a means, to render procreation impossible.

This exclusion is often denounced as a harsh, intractable prohibition. I don't see any alternative but to agree, if we premise that the church should validate the attitude that conception is a complication of sex, rather than an immanent reality. It's that very attitude, however, that *Humanae vitae* sees as ultimately dehumanizing. Given the document's statement of the goods to be pursued in integrating the whole person in one's sexuality, and the evils following from the use of contraception, what other conclusion can be drawn?

Why is contraception to be evaluated differently from other moral shortcomings? I have to think there are exceptions to this enjoyment just as there are exceptions to, say, the Sunday obligation, or the Fifth Commandment. Yet somehow, when it comes to contraception, we seek to make the exception the rule, as if to justify a priori our failure to attain an ideal which we have deemed impossibly (or inconveniently) high. We seem to forget that the Commandments do not contain the words "if," "unless," or "try to."

It also seems to my layman's sense that most exceptions have to do with the imposition of circumstances beyond one's foresight or control. That isn't the case with contraception. We all know where babies come from. No one is forced to marry and make love. The difficulty involved in what the church defines as legitimate methods of birth regulation is something we ought to consider as we freely prepare to marry.

Disrespect and Hostility

Pope Paul VI was prescient about the consequences of contraception:

> Let [responsible persons] consider, first of all, how wide and easy a road would thus be opened to conjugal infidelity and to a general lowering of morality. . . . It can also be feared that the man who becomes used to contraceptive practices, may finally lose respect for the woman, and no longer caring about her physical and psychological equilibrium, come to the point of considering her as a mere instrument of selfish enjoyment, and no longer as his respected and beloved companion.

Enough said? We could perhaps contend that the frightening disrespect and hostility evidenced toward females in our time merely coincides with, and is not an effect of, the widespread use of contraception. That may be true, but I won't believe it until I see American society ridding itself of the one while maintaining the other. In the meantime, I think we are vainly trying to cling to both ends of a contradiction.

Humanae vitae calls us to a love that "is total . . . in which husband and wife generously share everything, without undue reservations or selfish calculations." In contrast, use of contraception implies that we have justified for ourselves the sundering of nature, the selection of certain aspects for our enjoyment, and the synthetic suppression or elimination of others as undesirable. This is ironic in a society which purports to be committed to sexual equality and dignity. We undercut our alleged commitment with our actions. On the one hand, we collaborate in surgically, hormonally, and chemically altering each other's natures; on the other hand, we denounce it when someone is denied the opportunity to fully develop his or her nature physically, professionally, educationally, or economically. Perhaps these two responses are variations on the same theme. They are behaviors by which we seek to manipulate and control the terms of our involvement with other persons. It is from this pattern of limiting the scope of our most intimate relationships that *Humanae vitae* calls us to free ourselves. . . .

Pope Paul VI apprehended the connection between fertility and the power of sexuality:

> Those who make use of this divine gift while destroying, even if only partially, its significance and finality, act contrary to the nature of both man and woman and of their most intimate relationship. . . .

Is there any doubt that the power of sexuality is inherently connected to the power to conceive? To the fact that sexual intercourse implies a union not just for one discrete moment, but forever, through our capacity to co-create another human being? Would we be held in such thrall by an act that did not contain within itself the same permanent ramifications?

Trivializing Sexuality

I am afraid that we run the risk of trivializing sexuality when we first willfully isolate it from our procreative capacity, and then disable that capacity. In fact, we seem to have succeeded in doing so: witness our culture's banal and superficial preoccupation with sex as reflected in the media, and the rising number of sexual partners with whom Americans have dallied as contraceptives have become more effective and available over the course of the last three decades.

It is an ever-growing sense of the deeply pervasive power of sexuality that convinces me of the basic truth of *Humanae vitae*. We are called to be in touch with that power at all times. I experience it in the unselfconscious beauty and desirability of my wife at her fertile time, the cyclical engagement in mutual courtship and consummation, and, yes, the frustration over sometimes long periods of abstinence and the apprehension felt when contemplating an unintended pregnancy. This life is, as Paul VI said, sometimes difficult but always possible, and it is never, ever, boring.

Isn't our ideal of sexuality something like that: something that has the power to transport us beyond ourselves? Something continually dynamic, through which we change and are changed, and *not* altogether under our control? My wife and I have found that our submission to the rhythm of fertility has made our way of birth regulation itself a medium of sexual interaction between us. It is a means of extending, deepening, and intensifying our relationship. Among the supposed benefits of contraception, this possibility seems conspicuously absent. Contracepting couples can seek to develop their sexuality *aside from* their particular contraceptive practice, but I don't see how they can do so *within* it. I perceive the contraceptive ethic, if one can be said to exist, as essentially negative. It seeks to justify a behavior which we will for ourselves. It does not define a value which encourages and allows us to transcend ourselves.

Humanae vitae calls us to transcendence, not by repressing or avoiding sexuality, but by entering more fully into it. *Humanae vitae* specifies how we can sanctify our sexual conduct within the context of our basic Christian call to sanctify the world. Ultimately, we must recognize that this call originates with God, and not with any individual pope. The call of God is often jarring, and the implications of following it sometimes seem incredible when considered through the eyes of the world.

A Challenge to Growth

Through the promulgation of *Humanae vitae*, the church challenges Catholics to grow simultaneously in both "sense and spirit," at some cost to our temporal comfort. That most Catholics don't agree with or abide by this summons is held to be evidence that the church has overstepped its authority or spoken erroneously. Yet I see it as altogether fitting and perhaps inevitable, that sexuality be the arena in which church and culture confront each other so explicitly.

In what other aspect of our lives are we so demanding of our autonomy and less open to another's questioning of our behavior? Given the prevailing level of sexual morality and its far-reaching consequences, it is not only appropriate, but essential, that the church address the issue directly. Would that she could do it without shaking us up so, but sometimes we need it. If that isn't what a church is for, then I don't know why we have one. If only we can bring ourselves to perceive the liberation that can be effected by our acceptance of this challenge.

"The ego is the selfish part of us that demands the pleasure of orgasm, that focuses self-centeredly on the body of another as a source of private pleasure."

The Purpose of Sex Is Sensual Pleasure

Sallie Tisdale

A contributing editor for *Harper's Magazine*, Sallie Tisdale is also the author of four books, including *Talk Dirty to Me: An Intimate Philosophy of Sex*, from which the following viewpoint is excerpted. Tisdale maintains that the pervasive desire for sensual pleasure and release is the moving force behind human sexuality. This desire encompasses not only physical release but also the loss of ego or self that can occur with orgasm, Tisdale asserts. Sexual passion, Tisdale concludes, is the key that separates humans from animals, that makes human sexuality unique.

As you read, consider the following questions:

1. According to Tisdale, what are the physiological results of orgasm?
2. What is the difference between the orgasms of masturbation and sexual intercourse, in the author's view?
3. How are sexual passion and fear connected, in Tisdale's opinion?

The human body in orgasm looks remarkably consistent—male or female, young or old. The rectal sphincter contracts between two and five times, each contraction lasting about 0.8 seconds; the neck, arm, and leg muscles cramp in involuntary spasms; the big toe juts out and the other toes bend back from the arched sole in a reflex called the carpopedal spasm; the skin turns red, almost rashy, in the "sex flush"; breathing speeds up to hyperventilation; the heart races at 110 to 180 beats per minute; the face is distorted by grimaces and contortions. Both sexes do "full-excursion pelvic thrusting." In women, the vagina and uterus contract at the same speed as the rectal sphincter, as many as ten to fifteen times; in men, the penis contracts at the same speed as the rectal sphincter, shooting semen out in several spurts, one to two feet away from the body. Women also sometimes ejaculate a clear and often copious fluid that used to be called "childish semen." Though Masters and Johnson noted it, female ejaculation is widely considered imaginary these days.

Sexual Release

What *is* an orgasm? In physiological terms, orgasm is the pleasurable, rapid release from vasocongestive and myotonic symptoms caused by physical and psychological sexual stimulation. In other words, orgasm, which feels so active, so much an *act*, is a kind of antiact after the action of foreplay—it is a letting go, a surrender and return to the normal. The build to orgasm is an awful joy, full of pleasure and tension in almost equal measure; orgasm is a cool bath bathing the burn. There are many mythic images of getting stuck in copulation, like dogs unable to separate, heroes and heroines in permanent, unceasing intercourse. To avoid getting stuck forever in coitus, the myths say, one has to die—that is, move forward, into orgasm. An orgasm interrupted is a peculiar and fearsome itch, every part of the body leaning into the halted drive. The testicles swell, the penis throbs. Something of the same happens to women, on a larger scale.

Masters and Johnson describe an experiment in which a woman was kept highly aroused for six and a half hours, during which she "underwent repeated pelvic examinations." Five times the woman was brought (exactly how is not explained) to a preorgasmic state without being allowed to climax. By the end of the experiment, her uterus was more than twice normal size, her vaginal barrel was "grossly engorged," her labia were swollen almost three times normal size. The pelvic exams had become painful. She then rested for six hours without any sexual stimulation, and this level of painful engorgement continued, along with cramping and backache. (She was also, we are informed in an aside, "irritable, emotionally disturbed, and could not sleep.") Finally, she was allowed to masturbate to orgasm and felt "immediate relief" from all symptoms.

In these simple physical terms, there is little difference between men and women, among different men, among different women, between one orgasm and another. Masters and Johnson studied men climaxing during intercourse and from masturbation, and women climaxing from penetration, from clitoral masturbation, from rubbing their breasts, and, in a few cases, purely from fantasy; in each case, the measured physical orgasm was essentially the same, varying only in the degree of tension achieved before relaxation. In other words, the worse it gets, the better it will be. That little blip is just a miniature version of the mind-blowing earthquake from last week, the only significant difference a difference of degree. But, of course, in our real lives this seems meaningless; what really counts about an orgasm takes place in our heads.

The move toward orgasm is a move toward preoccupation with one's genitals. Whatever the stimulus, sooner or later the conscious self gets shoved down into the crotch, nose to nose with desire. Premature ejaculation can be seen as nothing more than a sudden, unplanned relocation. But for all the similarities in muscles and sphincters, the male and female experiences of orgasm are markedly different. And who really cares about rectal-sphincter spasms when it's a rip-roaring, throat-splitting orgasm we want? The felt experience is what matters. . . .

I find myself thinking: Every orgasm is different. Then I must instantly amend myself, because every sexual event is different. Every point of arousal, every plateau, every intersection of desire with the desired is unique. The memory of sexual passion often feels as though it had been dreamed rather than done. As if it had happened to someone else, been told to us, or, more accurately, been witnessed. You, the other, catch me when I fall. I, the other, catch you.

Nakedness

To take one's clothes off at the beginning of the sex act is "a form of role removal," in the words of Murray Davis, author of *Smut*. (And putting on certain kinds of clothing at the beginning of sex is similar, a matter of putting on a role that isn't really yours.) By taking off our clothes in front of each other, we consciously take off our other selves, our relations to other people, the limits of our relations to each other. We become just a body, outside the normal strictures and plans of daily life. To be naked means to be seen, but below that, to be naked is to be emptied—blank. Taking off clothes is revolutionary, proletarian; stripping reduces and removes whatever status we rely on. And it makes us both more human and more like objects at the same time. In this sense, all sex is masturbation—the other person's body is an object by which we have intense but wholly internal pleasure, and our orgasm is a self-created and unshared universe.

As arousal increases, we imagine things not in the quotidian sphere of concern; we say and do things that seem then to be perfectly logical, correct—even necessary—but that are not planned, not even imaginable, in any other state. In fact, reason and logic are completely absent from this state. This was Thomas Aquinas's main objection to sex. If what distinguishes humans from animals is their ability to reason, then what could be more destructive to humanity than a force that steals reason away? Afterward, the next day, the morning after, when desire has been sated, there remains the shocked memory: "Oh, God, did I say *that*? Did I do *that*?" Yes, you did.

In passion, the body abstracts itself, is abstracted. Damp labia loom enormous, the wrinkled-apricot bundles of the scrotum grow in stature, a pearly drop of semen expands into a bell. The shapes turn alien and impressionistic, barely discerned in the chaos of color and line. They expand and ripple into something else, like a word said over and over for the sound of it until all meaning is lost and the syllables become foreign and new.

I catch myself talking about safe sex now and then, glibly, as though it had no psychic meaning. But for all the simplicity of latex, for all that protecting ourselves from sexually transmitted diseases is largely a matter of a few moments of forethought, there is a great price required. In the depth of sexual passion, the skin of the other has the quality of treasure; the mundane secretions our bodies make are honey, manna, light. To be cut off from each other's *fluids* is a terrible thing; our fluids are meant to mingle, and we long for this mingling that is both so outrageous and so pure.

No Turning Back

Tongues loosen during orgasm; things get said that would never be said otherwise. The Navajo thought one couldn't keep secrets, even the most important and magical ones, during intercourse. Certainly in a sexual relationship a moment arrives when you don't want to stop, you don't want to stop so much that your brain disengages and you would do anything to keep going—if you *could* do anything but this; all else disappears, the lover, the self, God; all other needs vanish, there are no other appetites or hungers left, everything is conquered and the land laid waste.

Orgasm is psychedelic; you can't describe it, but you can still understand if you've been there before. Two people on LSD; one says, "The rug!" and the other nods vigorously—"Yeah! The rug!" They have a kind of perfect understanding—both see the rug with ecstatic eyes. But they have no understanding at all, because they see the rug with separate eyes. Of course, some of us get more intoxicated than others, some days seem more reckless. We can't really explain how arousal feels, what an orgasm *is*, and the closer we get to one, the less value words have, the less we can use language at all. Reason doesn't just leave us when we enter orgasm; orgasm is antithetical to reason—orgasm destroys reason, and, conversely, a moment of reason can destroy an orgasm. A friend tells me that when he comes, he feels his penis enter his lover's vagina on Tuesday and emerge on Wednesday, eternally, endlessly, over in a few seconds. He is submerged in the ocean of the moment.

Greater Satisfaction

There is something really wonderful about orgasm, which is: the more you have it and the more different ways you have it, the more versatile you become! And it's hard to change; you really do cling to one particular pattern that will give you pleasure. But to find another way by which you can achieve that same satisfaction or even *greater* satisfaction—this only opens your body up to break the habit again and again. People who change their eating habits notice this too: at first it's so hard not to eat the same things, but once they start experimenting, then they want to try more and more!

Susie Bright, *Angry Women*, ed. Andrea Juno and V. Vale, 1991.

This is the most infantile state an adult can experience in an ordinary aspect of life, the moment when we are most outside the neurosis of self-consciousness, when we become only Mouth, Skin, Hunger, Cry, Smile. These are royal and holy seconds. The language of orgasm and the language of nirvana use the same words. The fear that keeps us from intimacy with others is the same fear that keeps us from religious fever, and this fear is pacified in arousal—sexual arousal or devotional arousal. Arousal begins in the moment when desire overcomes fear, and from then on, the course is happily, ecstatically, toward extinction. Naturally, this is a dangerous course; narrow roads usually are.

The merging of two into one in orgasm, this blending of identity, combines bliss and anxiety in a strange stew. This may be the best explanation for why the orgasms of masturbation can be more powerful and feel more physically whole than those shared. They are simply safer. Murray Davis uses the phrase "fear of ontological contamination" to describe how we can hold our inner self in check even when our body is fully engaged. But one of the great utilities of sex is to overcome this—to create a place of ontological surrender. The release is separate from the simply physical gratification, and yet it is felt physically and has physical effects. It is possible during sex—and not just in orgasm—to get out of one's head in a quite literal way. You lose *you* for a while and watch yourself go, and this as much as anything creates the almost total state of repose that follows. To lose oneself awhile can be such a relief. The odd thing about the human ego is how it both resists and longs for its own extinction; the ego is what gets us into bed in the first place, as much as our body; the ego is the selfish part of us that demands the pleasure of orgasm, that focuses self-centeredly on the body of another as a source of private pleasure; and it's the ego that, ultimately, is killed by the result. Orgasm is a version of the ego's death wish; it is the little death, a miniature reminder of the bigger one. Orgasm is an incandescent and inarticulate memory of the universe before birth.

The joke goes like this: When does the atheist pray to God? The cries of orgasm are curses as well as prayers—we call on God and Jesus and, for all I know, Allah and Muhammed and Moses as well, and we say Yes, and we say No. Another joke: Don't, stop, don't, stop, don't stop.

Human Difference

One of the unique human aspects of sex is our association of sex with fear, sex with power, sex with pain. And with death. We fear sex in a *psychic* way, which is often the way we desire it. This meld of fear and desire, writes William Irwin Thompson, is what gives human sexuality its obsessive quality. "Gone is the casual, ten-second coitus of the animal; present for good is the sexualization of human culture, and an association of erotic excitement with a thrilling sense of danger." Sexuality, not sex, is the new thing, the human addition. Sexual forms "unfold like the petals of shrapnel in an explosion. Sexuality explodes in every direction and will light upon any available appendage, orifice, or symbolic article. . . ." There's no safe place for the sexual human, no solid barricade behind which we can hide from sex, no defense so strong that the possibility of intimacy can't slip through. Sometimes I long for that release of the ego into the other, my lover, and I can't let go no matter how I try. But I remember more than once longing to be left intact, and being released against my will, like slipping at the top of an icy slide and knowing there's no way to stop until I come to the ground.

Desire is constant. . . . *It never goes away for long.*

"Tantra teaches us to move [sexual] energy inward and upward to regenerate and recreate ourselves."

The Purpose of Sex Is Spiritual Enlightenment

Mark Gramunt

In the following viewpoint, Mark Gramunt explores the spiritual and sexual teachings known as tantra, particularly as taught by yoga instructors Charles and Caroline Muir. The Western world has unnaturally separated spirituality from sex, Gramunt asserts, a separation that has had negative effects on human sexual experience. He advocates the practice of tantric sex in order to promote sexual healing and spiritual awakening. Gramunt is a freelance journalist in San Francisco, California.

As you read, consider the following questions:

1. What are some of the negative results of the division of spirituality and sexuality, according to Gramunt?
2. According to the Muirs, cited by the author, what is the reason for "our confusion about sex"?
3. In Gramunt's opinion, how does the exchange of energy during tantric sex benefit a couple's relationship?

Excerpted from Mark Gramunt, "Sacred Sex," *Yoga Journal*, no. 116, May/June 1994. Reprinted with permission.

Before you begin this viewpoint, I'd like you to take a test. Not some tabloid questionnaire to assess your level of sexual performance—how often you have an orgasm, for example, or (if you're a man) how often you have an orgasm before you're ready—but a kind of sexual Rorschach, an opportunity to reflect on some of your sexual attitudes and expectations. As you envision the following scene, pay attention to how you feel.

First, you enter a doorway into a candlelit bedroom where your beloved awaits. (If you don't have a beloved right now, imagine your ideal man or woman.) You begin by sitting quietly together, meditating or praying or simply opening to the sounds around you. Then you bow to one another, acknowledging the sacred or divine within you. As you embrace and kiss, you feel your throats, hearts, bellies, and genitals align and your breathing come into harmony. Lying down side by side, you begin to touch one another with utmost sensitivity, bringing all your presence and love into every caress.

With awareness, you help one another gently open to the places inside where you may feel fear, shame, or aversion. Looking deeply and soulfully into one another's eyes, you whisper endearments and tender words of love. As your passion increases, you touch one another with greater urgency, never losing your heart connection or the deep conviction that your lovemaking is a sacred activity. There's no performance anxiety because there's no particular goal you're trying to achieve.

As the charge between you increases, you experience a powerful current of energy connecting you at the genitals, rising up to the heart, bridging the space between you, and dropping back to the genitals again. Although your lovemaking continues for an hour or two, the energy between you continues to grow and expand, flowing from your heart like a never-ending fountain of love. At times, all sense of separateness dissolves, and you feel yourself to be one with everything.

Now take a moment to notice how you've responded to this vignette. Are you feeling uneasy or even annoyed at the juxtaposition of sexual passion and spiritual experience? Or maybe you long to achieve similar heights in your own lovemaking.

Perhaps you feel a nagging sense of shame about what you perceive to be your own sexual inadequacies. Then again, you may be inclined to dismiss the whole thing as some silly new age fantasy. "Who has time to make love like that these days anyway? With two jobs, the house, and the kids, we barely have enough energy at the end of the day to kiss one another goodnight."

The Mind/Body Split

Whatever your response, it's clear that many of us still feel uncomfortable when sex and spirit are mentioned in the same breath. Blame it on the body-negative values of our Judeo-Christian heritage or the ambivalent, do-as-I-say, not-as-I-do attitudes of certain Eastern gurus, but few of us have managed to forge a secure and fulfilling link between our sexuality and our spirituality. Although all of us have genitals, and most of us presumably use them, we have difficulty communicating openly about our sex lives, even with our closest friends, and we may be so confused and conflicted about sex that we seek asylum in spiritual teachings that counsel us to avoid it entirely.

Holistic Union

In Sanskrit, the word *tantra* means "expansion" or "weaving." When we weave other ways of giving and receiving sexual energy—expanding our sensual repertoire to include everything from bathing to gazing to bodywork to prayer to playful dialogue—we are invoking this ancient tantric spirit. . . .

Tantric yoga was a partnership practice that focused on health as much as spiritual and sexual intimacy. The word *yoga* means to "join together" self with the sacred. In other words, tantra has long been known as a holistic approach toward union—of bodies, minds, and souls.

Today we need an intimacy that involves all our senses, our science, our healing, and our health. Turning to tantra in a time of AIDS is one way we can heal the spirit-mind-body split that has harmed our bodies for so many thousands of years. Studying tantra together can offer couples, whether first-time partners or longtime companions, a new definition of lovemaking.

Brenda Peterson, *New Age Journal*, May/June 1993.

In the culture at large, of course, the split runs even deeper. Despite the sexual revolution, the women's movement, [sex researchers William H.] Masters and [Virginia E.] Johnson, and the [Shere] Hite's reports, [on male and female sexuality], sex for many remains a brief and loveless encounter, fueled by loneliness and lust but largely devoid of true passion, intimacy, or heart. Beneath our sexual impulse as a species lies a desire to penetrate the veil that separates us from one another. But rather than risk exposing our vulnerability, we hurry about in search of the right partner, or the right position, or a better vibrator, or a more titillating obsession.

If we choose to remain monogamous, we may simply fail to show up for sex, either emotionally or spiritually. (How often have you caught yourself planning your schedule or fantasizing about your favorite movie star in the midst of an ostensibly passionate moment?) Or we may respond to our sexual shame and confusion by shutting down and withdrawing from relationships entirely.

Those of us who are spiritually inclined are even more acutely aware of how difficult it is to bring our spiritual values, our hearts, and our genitals into harmony. "I'd meditated and practiced yoga for nearly a dozen years," reports one woman, "but somehow I couldn't bring the same depth and presence to my lovemaking. It was so hard to open up and let go." Or, as one man puts it, "No matter how much meditation I was doing, as soon as I'd become sexual, I'd become a different person. All the old conditioning and anxiety would come back about how a man is supposed to behave."

Ironically, many of us have glimpsed the possibility that lovemaking can be a gateway to a higher state of consciousness. We may have had peak moments in sex when all sense of separation fell away. Or we may simply have the intuition that our sexual longings have a higher purpose. As Georg Feuerstein points out in his book *Sacred Sexuality*, "sexual love is the most intense and tangible way that ordinary men and women strive for a union that transcends the boundaries of our everyday experience." For some people, notes Feuerstein, "sex—or to be more precise sexual love—can be a hidden window onto the spiritual reality." For the rest of us, without guideposts or role models, sacred sex remains little more than an empty oxymoron.

Of course, not everyone experiences such sexual frustration and emotional angst. Some of us have warm, supportive, reasonably fulfilling relationships in which we give and receive love freely. Or do we? "It's not that my husband and I don't love one another," explains one woman in her mid-40s. "We do. We still make love every week, and we even meditate together daily. But when he has an orgasm, which is generally within a few minutes, he abandons me emotionally. I lose him for several days. Of course, he makes sure I have an orgasm too—but it's not the same. I keep thinking there must be more to lovemaking than this."

Sacred Sexuality

If popular authors and workshop leaders Charles and Caroline Muir are to be believed, there can be more to lovemaking than this. The Muirs teach an approach to sacred sexuality they call the "art of conscious loving," a contemporary Western adaptation of the ancient spiritual teachings called tantra. With other well-known tantra teachers like Margo Anand and David and Ellen Ramsdale, they are at the forefront of a movement that invites its followers to approach sex as a sacrament, and sexual union as a sacred activity whose ultimate goal is self-actualization.

"The essence of tantra," the Muirs teach, "is to bring all of your consciousness and all of your love to the bedroom and to transform your lovemaking" from a brief and entirely genital encounter into an "extended meditation that affects you on every level of your being: physical, mental, emotional, energetic, and spiritual."

The reason for our confusion about sex, say the Muirs, is that we were never initiated into the mysteries of lovemaking by knowledgeable elders, but instead gleaned what little we know from sex manuals, women's magazines, locker-room banter, and limited personal experience. "The combination of our early conditioning and lack of formal education in this area leaves most people in an interesting predicament: We don't know how to feel or give love sexually or how to mix passion and intimacy in the beautiful blend that sexual loving can be."

Indeed, many of us, the Muirs note, are more than simply uneducated—we have been deeply wounded or even abused in our early sexual encounters and bring a history of pain into the bedroom with us. As a result, we've learned to split our hearts and our genitals, "having sex" without really "making love." Before we can become fully empowered sexual beings, they claim, we must heal this split through the practices that tantra provides. . . .

Exchanging Energies

At the core of the Muirs' work is the experience and cultivation of energy, which they teach—in a safe, supportive workshop setting involving no classroom nudity or other possibly intimidating sexual behaviors—through a series of exercises incorporating asanas [postures] and breathing techniques derived from hatha yoga. Sex is seen not merely as the rubbing of two bodies together, but as an energetic exchange in which two people nurture and empower one another.

In the traditional tantric view, the universe is the play of two polar energies (the masculine Shiva, pure consciousness, and the feminine Shakti, pure energy), and sexual intercourse is used to rouse the shakti, or kundalini (believed to lie coiled at the base of the spine), and thereby fuel the process of spiritual awakening. Adapting this view to more interpersonal ends, the Muirs teach that the energy generated by the polarity between the sexes—which often gives rise to misunderstanding and conflict—can be used to inspire, deepen, and sustain an intimate relationship. "The differences between men and women can be used as a positive force in a partnership," they write, "and the proper combination of these differences can produce a near-alchemical reaction, an ether in which everything flourishes, in which the garden of your relationship bursts with color and new life and growth, and you and your beloved thrive." (Although their workshops are addressed especially to heterosexual couples, singles are also welcome, and the same principles are applicable to gay and lesbian couples.)

Passion is a crucial component in an enduring relationship, the Muirs believe, and must be cultivated if the relationship is to survive. "When a couple lessens their lovemaking, they begin the not-so-slow process of starving their love. Love is nourished by the sexual energy a couple generates." Yet the generation of sexual energy need not involve intercourse, or even foreplay in the usual sense. . . .

Among the most powerful techniques the Muirs teach are those that enable a man to make love indefinitely by withholding his ejaculation and retaining and recirculating his sexual energy. Men who have mastered this process often report that their passion continues to build from one lovemaking session to the next, fueling the love they feel for their beloved. "Before I learned this technique," one man relates, "I found myself feeling a certain aversion toward sex, especially as I got older, because I knew it would take me several days to recover my energy. Now I feel endlessly attracted to my sweetheart—and perpetually in love."

When a woman realizes that her lover won't abandon her, she can relax and open to receive his love, opening more fully to her own deep sexual feelings as well. "When my partner contains the energy of ejaculation, his presence with me brings through a quality of maleness that supports me in experiencing the power of my deep feminine," reports one woman, a veteran of many workshops with the Muirs. "I often feel a primal sense of masculine and feminine coming together that makes me hopeful about the healing of gender conflict in our culture."

When couples come to realize that lovemaking can enhance their vitality and empower them in the rest of their lives, sex becomes much more attractive, and their sexual connection is renewed. "Right now we only have one avenue for this creative sexual energy," says Charles Muir, "it moves downward and outward to create a baby. Tantra teaches us to move the same energy inward and upward to regenerate and recreate ourselves. When people at our workshops unblock the conduits that carry this energy throughout the energetic and physical organism, they're surprised by its power, and they realize it has all kinds of creative uses that aren't sexual at all.". . .

God and Goddess

Couples are counseled to revere one another in their lovemaking as god and goddess, embodiments of the divine masculine and feminine. At one key moment in the workshop, the Muirs divide the men and women into separate groups and instruct them in the art of being fully present and attentive to their beloved as a sacred sexual being. In the event that culminates the workshop, called a *puja*, couples dress in their finest clothes and form two circles, the men on the outside and the women on the inside. As they slowly circle around, changing partners in a kind of tantric musical chairs, they draw on deep inner well-springs of love and nurturing to offer balm for the wounds of their brothers and sisters. . . .

Through exercises like the ones used in the puja, the Muirs give men and women an opportunity to act as sexual healers for one another—no small promise in this age of growing conflict and even violence between the sexes. One of the high points of this healing exchange is the sacred spot massage, which occurs as homework, on an evening halfway through the workshop.

The sacred spot, also known as the G-spot in Western sexology, is a little-known and widely misunderstood area of sexual sensitivity located on the front wall of the woman's vagina, just behind the pubic bone. According to the Muirs, this area is frequently the dark closet where a woman stores the shame, fear, and pain of past sexual experiences and conditioning. It may be painful to the touch at first and trigger powerful feelings when stimulated. But on the other side of this closet, as in C. S. Lewis's classic tale *The Lion, the Witch, and the Wardrobe*, lies a vast realm filled with secret treasures—powerful vaginal orgasms and the awakening of the goddess Kundalini Shakti. The key to entering this realm and liberating these treasures is the sensitive, skillful touch of a loving partner.

Because this area is excruciatingly sensitive in some women, the sacred spot massage is approached with utmost delicacy and respect. The men are instructed to transform the bedroom into a temple, to consecrate it with flowers and incense, and to be "saintlike" in the attention and presence they bring to their beloved. The women—some of whom have never even heard of their "sacred spot" before, let alone touched it—are encouraged to allow their lover to touch them more deeply than they've ever been touched before.

Sexual Healing

"I'd spent years in psychotherapy," reports one woman, "but it wasn't until I received the sacred spot massage from my partner that I finally felt I healed the deep pain I still carried from my earliest sexual experiences." Says another: "I would get to a point in my lovemaking where I'd be afraid to let go into the pleasure. The sacred spot work—and the support of the other women—empowered me to have all these incredible feelings." For women like these, the exercise is a transformative experience, in which they release old sexual conditioning and contact deep wellsprings of energy. For others, it's only the beginning of an extended journey of sexual healing. Whatever their initial response, however, couples usually report that regular sacred spot massage gradually releases a new level of orgasmic potential.

Aside from the increase in pleasure this affords, orgasm actually energizes and empowers a woman, claim the Muirs. "The shakti of men and women are complementary energies. While a man is empowered by controlling his sexual energy, a woman's energy is brought to fruition through release." By using the various methods taught in the Muirs' workshops, couples learn to circulate and share this shakti energy, thereby empowering each other. . . .

The quality of our practice of tantra will depend on the presence and intention we bring to it. Just as tradition holds that yoga can be used to achieve a variety of ends—physical health, psychic powers, spiritual realization—so tantra can be used to enhance our personal pleasure, heal our sexual wounds, strengthen our connection with our beloved, or fuel our spiritual awakening.

Periodical Bibliography

The following articles have been selected to supplement the diverse views presented in this chapter.

Rebecca Chalker   "Updating the Model of Female Sexuality," *SIECUS Report*, June/July 1994.

Stephen Jay Gould   "Freudian Slip," *Natural History*, February 1987.

Robert P. Heaney   "Sex, Natural Laws and Bread Crumbs," *America*, February 26, 1994.

Celia Hooper   "The Birds, the Bees, and Human Sexual Strategies," *The Journal of NIH Research*, October 1991. Available from 2101 L St. NW, Suite 207, Washington, DC 20037.

Jonathan Ned Katz   "The Invention of Heterosexuality," *Socialist Review*, January/March 1990.

June Kinoshita   "Swap Meet," *Discover*, April 1991.

J. Michael Miller   "Telling Lies with Our Bodies: What the Pope Thinks About Sex," *Crisis*, March 1991.

Madeleine Nash   "Is Sex Really Necessary?" *Time*, January 20, 1992.

Off Our Backs   "Sexual Reproduction: Not All It's Cracked Up to Be," July 1994.

John Rennie   "Trends in Parasitology: Living Together," *Scientific American*, January 1992.

Meredith F. Small   "Sperm Wars," *Discover*, July 1991.

John Welwood   "Sexuality: Making Love Heart to Heart," *EastWest Natural Health*, November/December 1992.

Karen Wright   "Evolution of the Big O," *Discover*, June 1992.

What Sexual Norms Should Society Uphold?

HUMAN
SEXUALITY

Chapter Preface

The sexual drive is a powerful force—so powerful that many civilizations have believed it must be regulated in order to avoid conflict. However, the laws and customs that establish proper sexual behavior have varied widely from culture to culture.

In ancient Greece and medieval Japan, for instance, men of the warrior class often maintained sexual relationships with young teenage boys, a practice that was sanctioned by their societies. Some present-day cultures, such as the Batak of Sumatra, not only approve of homosexual relationships between young boys but expect and encourage this behavior until the boys reach the marriageable age. Many Islamic civilizations allow a man to marry up to four wives, while Tibetan women are permitted to marry more than one man. In medieval Europe, divorce was considered sinful and was, except in rare cases, prohibited; in modern America, however, divorce is easily obtained and has lost most of its social stigma.

By establishing rules of conduct, a society sets up a standard of correct behavior, or morals, that every individual is expected to uphold. A society's sexual morals are often based on a religion or philosophy that is predominant in that culture. However, not all members of a particular society necessarily believe in the same religion or philosophy and, therefore, the same set of morals. For example, although polygamy has been outlawed in the United States since the 1800s, U.S. citizens who are Muslim or Mormon—religions that have historically allowed polygamy—may not agree that polygamy is wrong. A civilization's sexual standards may also change over time: The development of birth control pills contributed to a relaxing of sexual morals during the 1960s and 1970s—morals that may be tightening again in response to AIDS.

Although not every member of a society may agree on what constitutes proper sexual behavior, most societies do reach a general consensus on the sexual norms that will be upheld. Obtaining this type of societal agreement has grown more difficult in recent years as populations of countries become less homogeneous and sexual minorities become more vocal. In the following viewpoints, the authors debate what sexual norms society should uphold concerning monogamy, divorce, and homosexuality.

"Two persons can become united as one in a way that is impossible for three or four persons."

Society Should Uphold Monogamy

Sidney Callahan

Many cultures around the world approve of polygamy and other forms of nonmonogamous relationships. In the following viewpoint, Sidney Callahan expresses her concern that immigrants from these regions may influence Americans to repeal our laws that prohibit polygamy. Callahan argues that humans evolved in such a way to make monogamy preferable to any other arrangement. Unlike polygamous groupings, Callahan asserts, a dyad (a pair) form intimate bonds that ensure the greatest benefits to children and to society in general. Callahan is a psychologist and the author of *Parents Forever* and *In Good Conscience*.

As you read, consider the following questions:

1. In Callahan's view, how do monogamous dyads encourage equality in a relationship?
2. What evolutionary advantages result from monogamy, according to the author?
3. On what basis does Callahan object to group sex and casual promiscuity?

Sidney Callahan, "The Case for Monogamy," *Commonweal*, July 15, 1994. Reprinted with permission.

Polygamy is better than monogamy, said a fourth of the adult students in my Bronx evening class! The most vocal advocate of polygamy was an intelligent young woman who had immigrated from Nigeria. She was aided and abetted by male students who were sympathetic to Islam and the Muslim custom of allowing four wives.

As the in-class debate raged on, I saw a new challenge of multiculturalism before us. African bishops are not the only ones who must argue for the hegemony of monogamy. Here in the United States we may yet confront a resurgence of claims for group marriage. Some unreconstructed Mormons have never accepted imposed monogamy and a growing number of immigrants and homegrown secular liberals might agree with them. Could an ACLU-Mormon-Muslim coalition successfully challenge our civic and religious commitment to monogamy?

Defending Monogamy

How do we mount "a monogamy offensive" capable of convincing doubters? Or—to be more honest in the face of our terrible divorce statistics—how do we keep our present system of "serial monogamy" in place? Those like myself who favor monogamy and yet have been willing to extend marriage to homosexuals have a special challenge. Already several opponents (all male) have figuratively flung down the gauntlet at my feet. A gauntlet, you may or may not remember, is a medieval mail-male glove that was hurled at enemies to provoke combat.

"Well, Sidney," say my attackers, euphemistically called "conversation partners" in PC speak, "if you're ready to give up the traditional requirements of heterosexuality for marriage, how can you not allow marriage between three or four or more? Why only two?" Somehow these fellows think that once you breach the dike of gender, no pun intended, monogamous marriage itself will be swept away in a flood of permissiveness.

But I've never found unsupported slippery-slope arguments very convincing. Why should we absolutize traditional customs when so many of them, i.e., abortion, war, and exploiting the poor, cry out for change? More reasonable arguments for privileging monogamy in our civil society can be made, even without turning to Christian belief. Bottom-up arguments support the institution of monogamous marriage.

Social scientists, for instance, who study group process, find a vast difference between dyads and all other numerical combinations of human relationships. With each member added to a group there ensues a geometrical progression of potential interrelationships: with three there are nine, with four, twenty-four, etc. The really BIG move, however, is from a two-person relationship to three or more. Where there are only two persons in a relationship there exists only one symmetrical mutual relationship.

This boundedness as a unit is why dyads gain their strength and intensity as psychological bonds. There is no third party to break open or diffuse the one-to-one focus and mutual dyadic interaction. Two persons can become united as one in a way that is impossible for three or four persons. Attentional focus in a dyad cannot so easily be distracted from the other, nor in a dyad can two or more persons gang up on one party.

Equality

The symmetry of a monogamous dyad works toward the equality of those in the relationship because there must be constant give and take in a bounded unit, particularly if it continues over time. This is why feminists for the most part have advocated monogamy; women in this kind of marital unit have more of a chance to achieve parity when they do not have to compete with other wives, concubines, or lovers.

Monogamy and Values

Family values are basically the belief that monogamy is the most peaceful and progressive way of organizing a human society. Dislike and distaste for anything that challenges the monogamous contract . . . are not just narrow or prudish concerns. They come from an intelligent recognition that the monogamous contract is a fragile institution that can easily unravel if disaffections become too widespread. . . .

It is probably not too alarmist to note that societies that have been unable to establish monogamy have also been unable to create working democracies or widely distributed wealth. No society that domesticates too few men can have a stable social order. People who are incapable of monogamy are probably incapable of many other things as well.

William Tucker, *National Review*, October 4, 1993.

Of course some women within polygamous societies will defend their familiar system. My Nigerian student claimed that one of the advantages of polygamy was that your husband was more apt to leave you alone, and so be less of a bother! But she did admit the oppressive pressure on women to procreate in order to be validated, as well as the existence of other family tensions over whose children or which siblings will be favored. Cultural observers have always noted that any competition for resources works against women and children.

In the long run, taking into account some of the testimony of sociobiologists, I do not think it an accident that pair-bonding has been the winner in evolutionary selection when offspring require concerted care and parental altruism. Two bonded mates working full-time for their mutually shared progeny produce more survivors. And with *homo sapiens* you have an extended socialization period of dependency (thirty-plus years?) along with capacities for foresight, promises, imagination, language, and intense emotions. Love, intimacy, kinship, and attachment to others constitute the human condition. If the most intense and complete psychosocial bonding, attachments, and intimacy are made possible by pair-bonding, along with positive social consequences, then there will be a valuable species-specific predisposition for marriage and monogamy.

When two people are limited to a monogamous dyad in space and through time any emerging problems or challenges in the relationship cannot easily be avoided; they must be worked out within the union. But conflicts and challenges that are overcome can be incorporated into a single history or narrative that builds up strength and enduring stability—or at least increases the force of inertia.

Sex and Intimacy

Human sex also differs from that of other primates because self-consciousness makes it possible to integrate sexual drives for the pleasure with intense emotional attachments, intimacies of communication, and mutual social exchanges. One psychologist has even suggested that changes in evolution which afforded face-to-face postures during sexual intercourse helped human consciousness evolve, since being passionately aware of another increases awareness of one's self. Delighted mutual eye-gazing during face-to-face monogamous mother-infant nursing must serve the same purpose, say I, with a shudder at what it must be like to nurse twins or triplets.

Third parties not only diffuse intimate unions, but the sexual choice of one sexual partner means the rejection of sex with another. The intense jealousy that appears when one's partner sexually chooses another arises not only from sexual deprivation but from the fact that the beloved's gaze, interest, and desire are turned away toward the one preferred. Completely self-disclosing conversations or pillow talk cannot be held with two lovers at once. Someone will be relegated to the periphery.

Those who might aspire to the simultaneous couplings depicted in Indian temples or in open marriage orgies have other problems. Which partner(s) does one attend to? Group sex and/or casual promiscuity can only serve individual sexual pleasure that must be dissociated from mutual tenderness or loving social and personal bonds. These efforts to isolate and exalt sex-

60

ual pleasure end in emotional and erotic burnout as well as social debacle.

No, no. As embodied beings programmed for deeply intimate attachments and passionate bonding, we are made for marital monogamy and monogamy is made for us. Persons do not have to be sexually active or marry, but when they do it should be a face-to-face, one-on-one commitment with all group marriages forbidden. For the sake of human flourishing we should continue to privilege monogamous marriage. Two by two we go into the ark if we want to get a view of the rainbow.

"Responsible nonmonogamy can help create a world of peace and abundance where all of humanity recognizes itself as one family."

Society Should Condone Nonmonogamy

Deborah M. Anapol

Deborah M. Anapol is a clinical psychologist and the cofounder of the IntiNet Resource Center, a clearinghouse for information on responsible nonmonogamy. In the following viewpoint, Anapol defines responsible nonmonogamy as the creation of ethical, committed relationships among multiple partners. Anapol contends that responsible nonmonogamy can solve many of American society's problems, including family instability, insufficient child care, and overconsumption of nonrenewable resources.

As you read, consider the following questions:

1. What types of relationships are and are not included under the term responsible nonmonogamy, according to Anapol?
2. In the author's opinion, in what ways does responsible nonmonogamy benefit children?
3. How can changing the concept of family also alter the structure of society, according to the author?

What is responsible nonmonogamy? The *nonmonogamy* part of the equation, while difficult to name, is far easier to describe than the *responsible* part. Nonmonogamy used to mean having more than one spouse during your lifetime. Now it means having more than one sexual partner during the same time period. Whether the partners are married, legally or spiritually, and even how they interact sexually is not particularly relevant to our definition of nonmonogamy. We're simply speaking of all sexualoving relationships other than those limited to two people. Singles who are dating more than one person are nonmonogamous, and couples who are sexual with others with or without the knowledge and consent of their primary partners are nonmonogamous. Three or more people who consider themselves to be married are nonmonogamous. Anyone with a circle of sexual friends is nonmonogamous. People who resume a sexual relationship with an ex-spouse or lover after finding a new partner are nonmonogamous. Even people who choose to have no sexualoving partners at all and remain celibate may be nonmonogamous. . . .

We have . . . words to describe specific forms of responsibly nonmonogamous relationships. Some of these are polyfidelity, open marriage, open relationship, group marriage, multilateral marriage, intimate network, polyandry, polygyny and triad. Responsible nonmonogamy can include all of these, and it is not limited to any one of them. In fact, responsible nonmonogamy even includes couples who are currently monogamous, but who do not necessarily intend to remain exclusive forever. One thing all these types of relationships have in common is that they are *both* sexual *and* loving or *sexualoving* with *no separation between the sex and the love.* In other words, we're not talking about casual, indiscriminate sport sex. . . .

Responsible nonmonogamy is not philandering, and it is not a way to justify an uncontrollable urge to continually seek out new partners. Responsible nonmonogamy has nothing to do with proving that you're a real man or a real woman. It's not an excuse for having secret affairs or a means of establishing your independence. It is not simply sex for sex's sake, but an expression of your heart and soul. . . .

Benefits

If you find that loving more than one person at a time is the right choice for you, and you are willing to accept the responsibility for exercising this choice, then you deserve to know that, contrary to what you may have been told, responsible nonmonogamy is not only good for you, it is good for the planet! Here's why you should be proud to be a responsible nonmonogamist.

First of all, by committing yourself to responsible nonmonogamy, you are expressing a desire to become a more evolved person. Many people who were inspired by books like Robert Heinlein's *Stranger in a Strange Land* or Robert Rimmer's *Harrad Experiment* in the sixties thought creating a multimate relationship would be easy. Instead, twenty years of false starts and painful discoveries have taught them that responsible nonmonogamy exacts a price. The fact is that humans have many contradictory impulses that pull us in the direction of nonexclusive love and simultaneously push us in the direction of jealousy and possessiveness. These opposing forces must be reconciled before we are truly free to love.

By choosing a multiple partner relationship, you're placing yourself in the center of the cyclone, where you will have many opportunities to confront these opposing forces. You'll undoubtedly make many mistakes. And if you're able to learn from them, you will find that you've gotten the benefit of several lifetimes worth of experience in a relatively short time.

The Benefits of Polyfidelity

First, in polyfidelity, the relating is *inclusive* rather than exclusive. This means that the relationships are not kept separate and apart, but rather are seen as part of one relationship circle. No one is left out or abandoned. No one lacks their share of attention or companionship or sex. The shared desire is for all needs to be filled, for love to flow between everyone involved. Whenever this goal is not being met, the group consciously works to heal any blocks and to get back on track. Second, in polyfidelity, the group chooses non-preferential relating. This means that each relationship within the marriage is as important as every other relationship. None of the relationships will ever be the same, just as none of the individuals are the same, but each bond is intimate and equally essential.

Ryam Nearing, *Loving More: The Polyfidelity Primer*, 1992.

Once you get past the initial struggles, your personal evolution should really speed up. Intimate relationships at their best are a path to higher consciousness and greater self-knowledge, largely because of the valuable feedback—or mirroring effect—one receives from a beloved. Having more than one partner at a time not only increases the available quantity of feedback, it also makes it harder to blame your partner for the problems you might be creating in the relationship. In other words, multiple partners actually help you to become a more responsible person.

Because multiple partner relationships are inherently more complex and demanding than monogamous ones and because you choose to explore territory beyond the norms of our culture, you will discover that you're on a path which offers some valuable lessons. Lessons about loving yourself, about tolerance for diversity, about speaking from the heart and communicating clearly, about learning to trust an internal sense of rightness and to think for yourself rather than blindly relying on outside opinion are only a sampling of the lessons. These qualities are earmarks of an emotionally and spiritually mature person—the kind of person who makes a good parent, who can contribute to his or her community and who can help our crisis-ridden planet make the transition into the next century.

Secondly, responsible nonmonogamy helps create stable and nurturing families where children develop in an atmosphere of love and security. With the traditional nuclear family well on its way to extinction, we are faced with a question of critical importance: Who will mind the children? Neither two-career nor single-parent families offer children full-time, loving caretakers, and quality day care is both scarce and expensive. Even at its best, full-time institutional care (including public schooling) cannot provide the individual attention, intimacy, flexibility and opportunity for solitude that children need to realize their potential. Serial monogamy presents children, as well as parents, with a stressfully discontinuous family life. Meanwhile, an entire generation is at risk.

Shared Parenting

Perhaps you are concerned that nonmonogamy might be harmful to children. But in the case of *responsible* nonmonogamy, nothing is farther from the truth. Multiple adult families and committed intimate networks have the potential of providing dependent children with additional nurturing adults who can meet their material, intellectual and emotional needs. In other words, the child is not losing the attention of his or her biological parent, he or she is gaining new aunts, uncles and adopted parents. Meanwhile the adults can share parenting, and experience less stress and less burnout without losing any of the rewards. In a group of men and women, it's more likely that one or two adults will be willing and able to stay home and care for the family, or that each could be available one or two days a week. If one parent dies or becomes disabled, other family members can fill the gap. Children have *more* role models, *more* playmates, and *more* love in a group environment.

Third, responsible nonmonogamy is also ecologically responsible. Sexualoving partners are more likely than friends or neighbors to feel comfortable sharing housing, transportation, appliances and other resources. Even if partners don't live communally, they frequently share meals, help each other with household repairs and projects, and vacation together. This kind of co-operation helps provide a higher quality of life while reducing individual consumption. Multiple partners also help in the renewal of our devastated human ecology by creating a sense of community.

Fourth, responsible nonmonogamy can help us adapt to an ever more complex and quickly changing world. Have you noticed that life seems to speed up more with every passing year? Are you inundated with more information than you can absorb and more choices than you can evaluate? Do you see new technologies becoming obsolete almost before you can implement them? Yes, the future is here, and trying to keep up can be stressful if not impossible for a single person or a couple. But a small group of loving and well-coordinated partners can divide up tasks that would overwhelm one or two people. Multiple partner relationships can be an antidote to future shock.

Finally, responsible nonmonogamy can help create a world of peace and abundance where all of humanity recognizes itself as one family. Idealistic? Yes. Realistic? Also yes! Our exclusively monogamous culture enshrines jealousy and possessiveness. Instead of working to eliminate jealousy and possessiveness so that people can freely choose how they will mate, our civilization tends to establish cultural and moral barriers that eliminate legitimate alternative relationships. By drawing a line around the couple or the nuclear family and saying, in effect, "inside this circle we share love and selflessly look out for each other, but outside this circle we keep anyone and everyone from taking what is ours," we perpetuate a system in which artificial boundaries are valued more than natural affinities.

Responsible nonmonogamy breaks down cultural patterns of control, as well as ownership and property rights between persons, and by replacing them with a family milieu of unconditional love, trust and respect, provides an avenue to the creation of a more just and peaceful world. By changing the size, structure and emotional context of the family, we change the personalities of the children developing in these families.

Children learn by example. We cannot teach our children to share and to love one another when we jealously guard and covertly control our most precious possessions—our spouses. By making the boundaries of the family more flexible and more permeable to the outside world, we set the stage for a new world view in which we recognize our kinship with all of humanity.

"*Divorce should be a failure and an aberration
. . . in each and every case.*"

Christians Should
Renounce Divorce

Tim Stafford

Tim Stafford is the author of several books, including *Sexual
Chaos: Charting a Course Through Turbulent Times*, from which
the following viewpoint is excerpted. Stafford maintains that divorce contradicts the Christian teaching of lifelong marriages.
People whose marriages are in crisis benefit more from struggling through their problems than from divorcing because they
are unhappy, Stafford contends. Although he acknowledges that
divorce is a reality among Christians today, Stafford believes that
marriages are ordained by God and should not be dissolved.

As you read, consider the following questions:

1. What distinction does Stafford make between bad marriages
   and hard marriages?
2. On what basis does Stafford disagree with the idea that
   personal happiness is the reason for marriage?
3. According to the author, why does divorce constitute a failure?

Taken from *Sexual Chaos* by Tim Stafford. Revised edition ©1993 by Tim Stafford. Used by
permission of InterVarsity Press, PO Box 1400, Downers Grove, IL 60515.

"If I understand what the Bible says about sex," my friend Ruth says, "I'd sum it up by saying that sex is meant to be connected. It's not supposed to be isolated from the rest of life; it's an expression of the connection between two people. And marriage is the ultimate connection. But if that's so, why are so few Christians sexually happy? Why doesn't the theory match the reality I see?

"Every marriage that I'm close to is, under the surface, unhappy. In every one, both the husband and wife would say in their most honest moments that they would be happier married to someone else.". . .

Marriage is very near the heart of a Christian view of sex, so the truth of Ruth's observations is quite crucial. It is all very well to speak eloquently about the beauty of marriage. Just how beautiful are marriages in real life?

When I think about the marriages *I* know, I come up with a different view from Ruth's. I don't think many of my friends would say, except on a particularly bad night, that they wish they were married to someone else. But that doesn't mean they would jump to describe their marriages as happy. Happy? When so much time and energy goes into learning to live with each other? When so many nights one or the other of them is depressed, or angry, or uncommunicative? When the same problems that surfaced last year surface this year? An awful lot of married people I know are still grieving for their dying dreams. I would not describe most of their marriages as bad. But I would describe them as *hard*.

Hard Marriages

It is hard to be happy when one partner craves conversation and emotion while the other prefers solitude. How did two people so unlike in personality ever fall in love?

Happy? It is hard to be happy when one partner runs up credit-card bills without a shred of worry, while the other is a worrier who loses sleep every time he sees the VISA bill.

Happy? It is hard to be happy when one partner is depressed and agitated at least one day out of three, and keeps her husband awake by thrashing around in their double bed all night while grieving over lost youth or fading dreams or something—she usually only gets more agitated if you probe.

These are among the marriages I know well enough to have an idea what goes on under the surface. They are, in fact, from my list of "good" marriages. The spouses are fine people who really do love each other. They don't have what you would call "serious problems" from the three Big A's—adultery, alcoholism or abuse. None of them, so far as I know, suffers from deep sexual inhibitions or dysfunctions. These are not what I would call

68

bad marriages. They are merely hard.

Such marriages require compromise. They require sacrifice. A wife must, perhaps, endure her husband's moving from one job to another in a seemingly endless search for job satisfaction. A husband must, perhaps, endure his wife's deep, enduring depression, in which she tastes bitterness in everything.

Most Christians, and a good many non-Christians, would say that such compromises and sacrifices are the price you pay for a greater shared happiness. Overall, the satisfaction of married life makes it worth "working at"—even when the work is hard.

"The correct response is 'I do' — — not 'It's worth a try.' "

But how hard? There is a wide spectrum of troubles, from chronic messiness to chronic abusiveness. Just where does "hard" turn to "hopeless"? At what point do you say, "No more"?

People's answer to that depends a great deal on what they believe leads to happiness. Many people in our society believe happiness is an individual matter. They therefore have an easy conscience about divorce. If someone leaves a relationship but gains greater peace of mind, well and good. (There are regretful backward glances at the cost children must pay, but rarely the suggestion that an unhappy marriage should be preserved just for them.)

Conservative Christians, on the other hand, stress happiness gained through relationship—in families, in churches, in communities. Every enduring relationship requires commitment, and with that goes some sacrifice of individual freedom. Christians tend to think those sacrifices are worth it, at least in the long run.

Nonetheless, I believe most Western Christians agree with the rest of our society that happiness is the reason for marriage. We might differ from non-Christians in our assessment of the chances of happiness, or the path to achieve it, but our fundamental values don't really differ. If a marriage has no realistic chance of happiness no matter how long and well people tough it out, we wonder why it should be preserved. Maybe it should—we know what Jesus thought of divorce—but most Christians I know aren't very clear on why.

That leaves us with the problem of those hard marriages. Some of them, no doubt, will get through long rough periods and become happy. But will all become truly happy? Or to put the question more precisely, is their state the happiest they are likely to achieve—married, unmarried or married to different partners? If you're aiming at happiness, is staying married always the best way to achieve it? . . .

St. John of the Cross wrote that love consists "not in feeling great things, but in suffering for the beloved." Paul told husbands to love their wives as Christ loved the church, and Christ's love found its greatest expression on the cross. For many of us, hard marriages—our own or others'—are the closest we ever come to understanding God's stubborn, passionate love.

Marriages like these are not happiness, nor are they peace. But they are certainly a sign. Their persistence points beyond themselves. It points to God. We are loved that way by our Lord. He may not be happy with his marriage to us. But he is not about to quit.

When two people in a hard marriage stick it out, persisting and insisting that their marriage become what it was meant to be, they may or may not end up happy. They will certainly end up showing the world a sign of faith.

Divorce

Is there, then, no possibility of divorce? I grew up in an era when Christians didn't divorce, and I have had a hard time accepting it as Christian friends, for reasons good and bad, have lost their marriages. I have come to accept, however, that there is such a thing as a dead marriage which we do not have the power to revive, and that it is not sensible or possible to live indefinitely with a corpse. I believe with all my heart that any marriage can survive if both partners are willing to try, but I also know that sometimes one or the other simply cannot or will not struggle any longer. Jesus said that the law of Moses permitted divorce because of the hardness of people's hearts; and people's hearts have not grown any softer since Moses. Sometimes hardened hearts are an inescapable reality.

"In the beginning it was not so," Jesus told the Pharisees when they asked about divorce. Indeed, it is impossible to imagine divorce in Eden. God joins the two in delight—what could separate them? At best, divorce is an accommodation to the "hardness of heart" that has invaded Eden and forced us out. It was not meant to be so.

It was not meant to be so, but it is so. Partners abuse each other. Hearts are hardened. Marriages are destroyed. People lose hope. These are realities of human life. Christians differ in their thinking about how to respond to these facts. Some reject any compromise with defeat. They will never accept divorce. Others, myself included, will choose to accommodate the realities of failed marriages, out of pity for the people involved. Reluctantly, sadly, they will accept that the marriage is dead and cannot be revived.

Perseverance

Nevertheless, I also know very intimately people who have been willing to struggle and suffer and persevere through astonishing difficulties for years. They are better for it. And I am better for it. And the world is better for it, because it makes the sign of Christ.

Ruth, with whom I began this viewpoint, has been married for almost twenty years, and I have known her well through most of those. They have not been easy years. She and her husband are both intense, dedicated, complicated. What causes their troubles? Sex, for one. They often can't get their signals straight, and feelings are hurt over imaginary (or maybe real) rejections. They compete with each other. They hold grudges. But maybe greater than any other single problem is this slippery one: neither one of them knows how to encourage the other. They try, but their attempts are always prickly. When one makes an effort, the other often rebuffs it. You could spend a long time analyzing why, and maybe you would figure it out. But how they are supposed to change is a different matter.

They have gone to counseling, and they have found some other couples with whom to share a genuine and deep fellowship. I've watched and tried to encourage their attempts. Sometimes their marriage really has seemed to be better. Other times, it has slipped back into grudges and embittered silences.

71

If the purpose of marriage were purely to provide happy intimacy, their marriage might have been called purposeless. Oh, sure, it' s quite possible they would have been as troubled with other partners, or alone. But I suspect they would have taken their chances. They have stayed married largely because they were brought up to believe that marriage is for life, and that divorce is wrong. Also, I suppose, because they are stubborn people. They don't give up easily. They keep on trying.

And one more factor: they really do love each other. In their own tormented way, they do need each other. Their own personal legacy of Eden is not entirely used up.

Not long ago, when I was out to dinner with them both, Ruth looked at me and said she had an announcement to make. "Robert and I have been talking about our marriage, and . . . well . . . we think we have grown out of most of our problems." Tears came to my eyes, because I understood what lay behind her typical understatement. She is painfully honest in all she claims, and she wasn't claiming bliss. She was claiming that the struggle had, finally, led somewhere. They were glad to be married. The marriage was being saved.

For days, even weeks, I carried their happiness around with me, like a little ball of sunlight. As a friend I had suffered with them; now I was so glad to share their relief. I have never known anyone who struggled harder to make a marriage prevail over its difficulties, and it filled me with hope that they had at last seen success.

I will be very glad if I get to see them enjoy the kind of love that Eden knew: relaxed, joyful, passionate. I am very grateful, too, that I have been able to see their persistent love, love such as God showed to Israel. Such long-suffering love is a sign that has pointed me to something beyond myself. Fidelity in a hard marriage is a sign pointing to the long-suffering faithfulness of God himself.

Our society now treats divorce as an ordinary happenstance, like a car breaking down. These things happen; it's too bad. You try your best but sometimes it doesn't work out. But for Christians, divorce should be a failure and an aberration from Eden in each and every case. It is always a cause for mourning, not merely because of the personal distress the broken marriage has caused but because divorce communicates something to the world. It says the partners in the marriage have lost hope, lost faith, lost love, and have quit at something God ordained. People will quit, in a fallen world, and in some way or another we will have to recognize that. But let us not call it anything other than what it is. It is a failure to make the sign of God's kingdom.

VIEWPOINT

"It is possible to affirm God's desire for committed, long-lasting intimate relationship without concluding that every marriage is ordained by God."

Christians Should Sometimes Accept Divorce

Amy C. Gregg

Traditional Christian doctrine teaches that once a man and woman have had sex together, they become as one body, inseparably and eternally linked. In the following viewpoint, Amy C. Gregg examines how this belief has influenced Christianity's attitudes toward divorce, attitudes that she contends are faulty in their logic. Surely, Gregg argues, God does not sanction marriages that are unhealthy or destructive for one or both spouses. Rather than indicating society's moral decline, divorce may actually be God's way of leading Christians to a new, better pattern of marriage, Gregg contends. A graduate of Union Theological Seminary, Gregg lives in Hawaii and is a lecturer in religious studies and women's studies.

As you read, consider the following questions:

1. How does the concept of completion lead to unhealthy marriages, according to Gregg?
2. In Gregg's opinion, what structural elements of the church contribute to the perpetuation of unhealthy relationships?
3. On what basis does the author disagree with the idea that divorce is always sinful?

Amy C. Gregg, "Is Every Marriage God's Will?" *Daughters of Sarah*, January/February 1989. Reprinted by permission of the author.

"I was sorry to hear about your divorce." This remark from acquaintances who genuinely care about me put me in an awkward position. On the one hand, I wanted to acknowledge that deciding to leave my husband and get a divorce was one of the most difficult and painful decisions I ever made.

Yet this decision brought a deep sense of health and wholeness I had not felt for a long time. I wanted to communicate that too. I wanted to say that I even felt *joy* in the great relief I experienced—relief as from a heavy burden lifted from my shoulders.

Positive Feelings

These sensations of health, wholeness, relief, and joy in the midst of a painfully broken relationship confused me. They contradicted the tapes in my mind about divorce: lack of commitment, broken promises, guilt, sin. Why did I experience my divorce as a primarily positive process? Could I be Christian and feel this way?

Trying to understand my feelings, I began to research Christian literature on marriage and divorce. I reflected on how Christian teachings had affected my earlier attitudes toward marital relationships. My feelings and experience diverged significantly from assumptions in Christian literature about what divorce means and how we respond to it.

Gradually I came to understand the theological underpinnings of "mainstream" Christian perspectives on divorce. I also recognized that certain beliefs about the meaning of marriage were foundational to these attitudes. Then I realized that my new perspective required some rethinking of certain theological assumptions.

In the literature, the sayings of Jesus about divorce are often central to what is put forth as "a Christian view of divorce." A surface reading of Jesus' words reported in the Gospels suggests that dissolution of marriage is impossible—except perhaps for a situation involving adultery.

Jesus' sayings are also interpreted as communicating something essential about the will of God: God desires lifelong marital union unmarred by divorce. Underlying this interpretation is the belief that marriage is part of the order established by God in creation. Various Christian writers emphasize the principle of relationship in God's ordering of creation. But particular emphasis is placed on the "man-woman relationship" as "the right order for humanity." Whether explicitly or implicitly, each individual marriage is soon asserted *ipso facto* as being part of God's plan.

Sexual Completion

One reason for elevating the marital relationship and holding it to be indissoluble is the concept of "becoming one flesh." The sexual act between man and woman is seen as creating a "whole" from the union of halves, understood to have been separated at creation. By the special power attributed to this act of "reunion," woman and man are uniquely and *irrevocably* united and in some sense "completed."

This perspective is based on some important presuppositions: that male and female were created for each other sexually, that sexual union forms the core of the uniqueness of a marriage relationship, that sexual union creates a "whole."

Implicit in these presuppositions is the notion of complementarity: man and woman complement each other sexually. This is easily extended into nonsexual complementarity and ideas about "completing" each other. Indeed, both religious and secular culture highly value the notion of a couple "complementing" each other.

"Commitment" is another important term in discussions of marriage and divorce. In Christian literature, marital commitment is often viewed as part of Christian commitment. To "fail" in marriage is seen as failure in commitment to God and Christ. The marital covenant is likened to God's covenant with God's people and Christ's covenant with the church—eternal and unchanging.

Not a Failure

Marriage is wonderful when it lasts forever, and I envy the old couples in *When Harry Met Sally* who reminisce tearfully about the day they met 50 years before. I no longer believe, however, that a marriage is a failure if it doesn't last forever. It may be a tragedy, but it is not necessarily a failure. And when a marriage does last forever with love alive, it is a miracle.

Peggy O'Mara, *Mothering*, Fall 1989.

The concept of failing in a committed, covenantal relationship hints at the most prevalent theme in Christian writing on divorce: divorce is sin, stemming from evil. Since divorce is viewed as "never God's intention for a marriage," it is sinful. Divorce signals the presence of evil, representing a failure of commitment and a failure to live in God's will. Even when a permanent separation may be dictated by conscience, faith, and the facts of the situation, such a step is only to be taken—according to most authors—with a sense of sin and repentance.

These major, recurring themes raised several questions for me about theological presuppositions and practical implications. First, a literal approach to Jesus' recorded sayings is inadequate. In *The Mystery of Love and Marriage: A Study in the Theology of*

Sexual Relation (1952) theologian Derrick Sherwin Bailey cautioned against interpreting Jesus' words "anachronistically or in terms of contemporary non-Jewish usage." I would add that what Jesus said about divorce needs to be examined not only in its ancient Jewish context, but also within the context of his whole ministry.

Statements about God's intentions for a certain type of order within creation are, of course, always potentially dangerous and presumptuous. Regarding marriage, it is possible to affirm God's desire for committed, long-lasting intimate relationship without concluding that every marriage is ordained by God.

Right Relationship

The principle of relationship in creation is very important. But mainstream Christian writing about God's intentions for relationality all too often involve hierarchical, patriarchal, and domination-oriented approaches. Many feminist theologians, on the other hand, emphasize God's desire for *right relationship*—relationship based on mutuality and justice. Feminist theologians also tend to affirm a broad range of relationships as crucial to our lives in community and as arenas for justice-making and mutuality.

The idea of a man and woman completing each other is a highly problematic concept theologically and practically. I believe it contributes to unhealthy attitudes in intimate relationships. If a person must be linked intimately with another person in order to be complete, what is to be said about those who remain "single" or those who choose a celibate lifestyle?

Further, if we hold an ideal of complementarity, how exactly do we envision it working between two people? Is each "deficiency" or "weakness" in one complemented by a "strength" in the other? Can one person fully complement another? If this is not realistic, is it even a desirable goal?

I believe we can affirm our deep need for relationship with one another without perpetuating unhealthy notions of completion and complementarity. The ideal of complementarity in couples often relies on dualistic understandings of "masculine" and "feminine" traits or natures. The idea of two persons "completing" each other intertwines with the notion of "masculine" and "feminine" providing "balance" to one another.

Thus a single person is left with the impression of being incomplete and unbalanced. There may also be an emphasis on relative "strengths" and "weaknesses," creating an atmosphere of static definitions that inhibits growth. Foundations are then laid for unhealthy "dependent" relationships between men and women. From such relationships emerge sexist and heterosexist attitudes about intimate relationships.

Dualism, sexism, heterosexism, patriarchy, and hierarchy have been structured into the church as an institution. Likewise, these factors have undergirded much of the church's message, whether explicit or implicit, about relationships between women and men.

Our society as a whole is permeated by—and perhaps founded upon—these oppressive elements. Individual unhealthy relationships develop under the influence of these larger forces. But the church has not recognized the structural nature of such forces at work in the forming and perpetuating of intimate relationships. It has also failed, for the most part, to admit to and correct its own contributions to structures that maintain unhealthy relationships.

In addition, the church has tended to ignore wisdom from sociological and historical research. Such studies show that the forms of marriage and popular expectations about it have varied over the centuries. Marriage has not had a static function or form. The idea of companionate marriage, for example, is relatively recent. The longer life expectancy of people in Western countries is an important factor influencing the form marriage takes in contemporary life. Yet theological treatments of marriage tend to speak in terms of an unchanging, eternally valid *meaning* for marriage that suggests a static *form* as well.

Transitions

It is clear that our society is in the midst of major transitions in understanding sexuality, relationship, marriage, and divorce. Naturally our churches are also struggling with these issues. Change often frightens people, and transitions can be very uncomfortable. But rather than be threatened by the rising divorce rate, I have begun to look for the positive aspects—starting with what I learned from my own experience.

I have come to reject the notion of divorce as always sinful. Human brokenness—call it sin if you like—is a reality. But I see the connection between brokenness and divorce in a new way. It was brokenness that led me into and kept me in a destructive relationship. In my marriage I was guided by some ideas about complementarity, oneness, being "in love," acting "lovingly," and "God's plan for my life." On later reflection, I saw that these ideas were misguided at best and dangerous at worst.

My husband also operated from some seriously mistaken notions about how our relationship should work. An unhealthy relationship of dependency developed from the brokenness on both sides. But my gradual awakening to the problems and my tentative groping toward possible solutions were trivialized and largely unheeded by both my husband and my counselor. My decision to leave, therefore, constituted a conscious step *away* from brokenness *toward* health and wholeness. Therefore, talking of brokenness makes sense to me not in relation to my *di*-

vorce, but in the context of the foundations and development of my *marriage*.

I certainly do not believe divorce should be undertaken lightly. Obviously many divorces perpetuate brokenness rather than fostering healing. But I would suggest that many of our attitudes and assumptions as Christians entering into intimate relationships need to be reexamined. The *structural* nature of certain existing problems needs to be recognized, so that the church can contribute structurally to the formation of healthy relationships.

I highly value commitment in relationships. Intimate relationships take hard work, and commitment is key to any success. But there are times when commitment for commitment's sake—or for what is understood to be God's sake—can be a dangerous notion.

As a feminist theologian, my commitment is to well-being, mutuality, and justice. I believe those are among God's commitments as well.

Changing our understandings about marriage and divorce need not mean straying from God. In fact, we may be moving closer to God's intentions. Divorce can, I believe, be a positive indicator of a new pattern emerging for marriage. As we seek to form egalitarian, mutuality-based relationships, I do not believe that God is sitting afar off waiting for us to "discover" ways of justice. Rather, God is present in our processes, sharing our pain and conflict. God is there, sorrowing and celebrating, affirming our struggles as well as our goals.

5 VIEWPOINT

"History should dispel the impression that public tolerance of homosexuality is an index of a society's devotion to liberty."

Society Should Not Tolerate Homosexuality

William Norman Grigg

Every society that has accepted homosexuality as normal has suffered as a result, William Norman Grigg maintains in the following viewpoint. Examining several cultures of ancient and medieval Europe, Grigg argues that homosexuality invariably disrupted the family, promoted pedophilia and child slavery, and contributed to the moral decline of society. Grigg warns that America's increasing tolerance toward the homosexual lifestyle will lead to the destruction of the family. Grigg is the author of *The Gospel of Revolt: Feminism Versus Family Values*.

As you read, consider the following questions:

1. How was pedophilia institutionalized in ancient Sparta, according to Grigg?
2. How are young people being indoctrinated to accept homosexuality, in Grigg's opinion?
3. According to the author, why does the State encourage sexual libertinism?

Excerpted from William Norman Grigg, "Normalizing Perversion," *The New American*, January 25, 1993. Reprinted with permission.

The alacrity with which homosexuality has obtained the un-qualified approval of America's elites is stunning. The September 14, 1992, issue of *Newsweek* published a poll revealing that most Americans still regard homosexuality as unacceptable. Neverthe-less, the electorate conferred its favor upon Bill Clinton, who openly courted the homosexual lobby. One of Mr. Clinton's most nettlesome campaign promises was to allow homosexuals into the military. In December 1992, the *San Francisco Examiner* claimed that "Openly gay people are filling an unprecedented 13 spots on the Clinton transition team." If this is true, such a presence will no doubt have a tremendous influence upon the priorities of the Administration, and serves a significant symbolic function. . . .

Little more than a decade ago, the consensus among even the "progressive" elements of American society held that whatever one may think of homosexuality, a barrier should be placed be-tween the subject and impressionable children. But formidable pressures are being brought to bear upon the Boy Scouts to ad-mit openly homosexual men as scoutmasters. Even as the public is treated to accounts of pedophilia scandals in some churches, "progressive" religious leaders, such as Episcopalian Bishop John Shelby Spong, are ordaining homosexuals to church office; others have performed "marriages" of homosexual couples. Even more astonishing is the fact that in some jurisdictions ho-mosexuals are being permitted to adopt children. . . .

Clearly the pro-homosexual movement desires much more than simple tolerance; it pursues the comprehensive restructur-ing of society's basic institutions, particularly the family.

Historical Homosexuality

History does provide examples of societies that have toler-ated—and even encouraged—homosexuality. Furthermore, there is reason to believe that the distinction between "homosexual-ity" and "pedophilia" (sexual attraction to children) is an inven-tion of modern propaganda. Those who agitate against "discrim-ination" based upon "sexual orientation" generally mention ho-mosexuality and bisexuality, and insist that pedophilia is a sepa-rate category.

However, Dr. John Money, director of psychohormonal research at Johns Hopkins University, disagrees. Money's efforts have been invaluable to those who have re-cast homosexuality as an "orien-tation." It is difficult to find a text that makes that claim without citing Money as an "authority." Money is presently investing his prestige on behalf of pedophilia. In the August 21, 1992, issue of *New Statesman* magazine, Money is quoted as follows:

> In the adulthood of the true pedophile, parental love is hy-bridized with sexual love . . . pedophilia is not a voluntary choice and there is no known treatment. Punishment is use-

less. One must accept that [pedophilia] exists in nature's overall scheme . . . and, with enlightenment, formulate a policy of what to do.

Those societies that have embraced homosexuality have displayed the "enlightenment" coveted by Money. Some of them actually institutionalized pedophilia; all of them actively subverted familial relationships in order to amplify the State's claim upon the individual. Even a cursory examination of the relevant history should dispel the impression that public tolerance of homosexuality is an index of a society's devotion to liberty.

Britt/Copley News Service. Used with permission.

Plutarch records that Lycurgus, the "lawgiver" of the proto-fascist Spartan state of antiquity, abolished the family in his domain: Spartan children were the property of the state. The males were taken from their parents at a young age and bonded to older, experienced warriors for the purpose of a military apprenticeship; that "bonding" included a sexual relationship.

Richard Posner observes that Greek homosexuality could properly be referred to as institutionalized pederasty: "male homosexuality usually involv[ed] a man of 25 to 30 and an adolescent boy." The Greeks believed that homosexuality was a developmental phase for all males, rather than a permanent preference for some. Accordingly, Posner notes that "it was easy to be a successful married man in ancient Greece and chase young men on the side. . . ." Many of the male deities in the pagan pantheon of ancient Greece were sexually involved with young boys; this provided a religious sanction for pederasty.

The Etruscan forerunners of the Romans tolerated homosexuality, including Greek-style pederasty. But following the eviction of the last Etruscan king and the founding of the Roman Republic, the practice was suppressed. In the code of Justinian (the digest of Roman law), homosexuality was treated as a capital offense.

But as Rome bloated into an empire it lost its civic discipline and moral vigor; it began to absorb many of the vices of the societies it conquered. Tacitus, a Roman historian and social critic, lamented that by the seventh decade of the Christian era,

> Promiscuity and degradation throve. Roman morals had long become impure, but never was there so favorable an environment for debauchery as among this filthy crowd. . . . Here every form of immorality competed for attention, and no chastity, modesty, or vestige of decency could survive.

Among the pandemic vices of Imperial Rome was homosexuality, including pederasty. Many among the Roman elite justified pederasty by invoking the Greek philosophy of man-boy sexual "education." According to Tacitus, by the first century AD Roman consuls were pursuing free-born Roman boys. The Emperor Nero, who is infamous for his persecution of the early Christians, also practiced the crime against nature. Both Tacitus and Suetonius mention an incident in which Nero dressed as a bride in a "marriage" ceremony in which he was wedded to a male "lover."

The early Christian community (which was, ironically enough, frequently condemned by Roman rulers for non-existent sexual offenses) was mortified by the violent, exploitive nature of sex in Imperial Rome. There were also a few surviving republican critics of Rome's decadence. The satirist and social critic Juvenal saw the prominence of "socratic perversity" in Rome to be a symptom of irreversible decline. Petronius, a writer who was privy to the activities of Nero's court, produced a work entitled *The Satyricon*, that depicted the Roman elite exhausting itself in every variety of homosexual indulgence.

Sexual Victims

Greek and Roman sex "literature" (what the morally alert would refer to as pornography) was quite popular in the courts of the Ottoman Empire. Sociologist Parker Rossman notes that Sultan Mehmed II of Turkey, who conquered Byzantium in 1453, was a disciple of what was euphemistically referred to as the "Greek philosophy of love." The Sultan used promises of young captive boys to inspire his troops to new conquests. As his armies captured half of Europe, Janissaries were sent into Christian villages to conscript boys between the ages of 10 and 14 to serve in the Sultan's court; the ruler divided his sexual attentions between the hapless prisoners and his harem. Predictably, a market in young sexual victims sprang up to serve the appetites of the Ottoman elites.

During the Renaissance period, sexual predators in Europe went about their labors with utter indifference to the gender of their victims. This fact was recognized and celebrated (yes, celebrated) during a 1989 Berkeley Anthropology symposium entitled "The Invention of Heterosexuality." The March 19, 1989, issue of the *San Francisco Examiner* reported some of the conclusions presented in that symposium:

> Apparently, there was a lot more man-man and woman-woman [sex] in centuries past, except that people just didn't call it names. . . . "The 18th century rake could indulge as frequently in sex with boys as he could . . . with females—as long as the rake was the active partner," the report said.

Contemporary homosexual "rights" activists often speak of the medieval punishments inflicted upon homosexuals as outrages against humanitarian decency. However, in that era "homosexuality" and "pederasty" were recognized as separate manifestations of the same sexual aberration. Burning deviants at the stake, although a disproportionate punishment by modern calibrations, is seen in a different perspective when one realizes that many thus castigated were molesting children, and possibly trafficking in them as sexual hostages. . . .

The history of homosexuality suggests that the practice is not rooted in an immutable physical condition—rather, it is behavior that is both learned and optional, and it defies the tidy categories that are so commonly invoked in contemporary discussion. A survey conducted by the Kinsey Institute discovered that 84 percent of homosexuals had changed their "sexual orientation" at least once; 32 percent had experienced a second shift; and 13 percent claimed no fewer than five changes of sexual "orientation." Apparently sexual "orientation" is quite protean for those who have been sexually "emancipated."

Recruitment

Much of what is described as "education" about homosexuality is composed of undisguised efforts to recruit children into the "lifestyle." In the 1981 edition of his book *Boys and Sex*, Wardell Pomeroy, a former associate of Alfred Kinsey, urged young male students to believe that "From a purely biological standpoint . . . it's reasonable to wonder why all boys don't engage in homosexual behavior." He continues:

There are only two reasons why it might not always be desirable. One is that society disapproves of such behavior and a boy runs the risk of being censured or punished, perhaps severely. Privacy is essential.

Clearly, Pomeroy—who was quite familiar with Kinsey's findings—does not consider homosexuality to be an ironclad "orientation," but rather a supposedly healthy experimental stage for most young people. He asserts, "A common misconception about homosexuality, often heard, is that 'some boys are born queer.' That probably isn't true . . . when an individual is born, he has the ability to do anything sexually." In fact, according to Pomeroy, "All of us are potentially capable of doing every act imaginable. . . ."

Alyson publications, which offers such titles as *Gloria Goes to Gay Pride*, has also published *One Teenager in Ten* and *Young, Gay and Proud!* for use by high school students. *One Teenager in Ten* urges teens to rebel against the values of their parents and experiment with homosexuality:

> We human beings are more fluid and flexible than society allows. . . . For instance, you may spend the first thirty years of life in gay relationships. Then you find yourself falling in love with a wonderful person from the opposite sex. Don't fight it. Rejoice in it.

Such a suggestion is inexplicable if, as homosexual activists insist, sexual "orientation" is immutable.

In the revisionist history favored by many homosexual "rights" activists and anthropologists, the traditional or "nuclear" family is depicted as a development associated with the Industrial Revolution rather than a natural arrangement necessary for civilized living. The conclusions of anthropologist Richley Crapo of Utah State University are typical of this school of thought. In a newspaper account published on February 27, 1992, Crapo's views were summarized:

> All industrialized countries, as they have developed centralized governments, have written laws to promote procreative sex. Those laws were to attain an end result, not to forbid certain behaviors for their own sake. "It made a lot of sense," Crapo explains, because government leaders realized that they would benefit by legislating for large families and consequently, a larger population. More babies mean more consumers to buy business products, more taxpayers and a larger military force.

> So, laws have flourished to discourage even married couples from having non-procreative sex. Before 1890, there was no English word for homosexuality. But at that time, the birth rate in the U.S. had been steadily declining, so all states passed laws against non-procreative sex, resulting in the birth of homophobia. . . .

Crapo's conclusions are not unique; they represent the party line of his profession.

How do we account for the influence of the homosexual "rights" movement? By the most reliable estimate, homosexuals account for about two to three percent of the population. Even after one makes allowance for the fact that homosexuals as a group are wealthier and better educated than the general population, the sodomite lobby possesses little demographic clout. Therefore another explanation must be found for the steadily increasing influence of the homosexual "community."

The abstract State has a permanent interest in the dissolution of the family. G.K. Chesterton once observed, "The ideal for which the family stands is liberty. It is the only institution that is at once necessary and voluntary. It is the only check on the state that is bound to renew itself as eternally as the state, and more naturally than the state." Thus the State constantly seeks to disrupt the sexual ethic through which the family is renewed: marital monogamy. This disruption is accomplished when the State encourages sexual libertinism of all varieties—especially homosexuality, which is the most sterile of all sexual distractions.

"The Gay and Lesbian community informs the entire society of . . . directions for exploring and living life to its fullest potential."

Society Should Celebrate All Forms of Sexuality

Terry Tafoya

Terry Tafoya, a Native American of Taos Pueblo and Warm Springs heritage, is a professor of psychology at Evergreen State College and the University of Washington. In the following viewpoint, Tafoya asserts that before European contact most Native American societies viewed homosexuals as important members of their communities. Many modern Native Americans still accept homosexuality as natural and normal, Tafoya maintains, especially since Native people's definitions of gender and sexual orientation are vastly different than the dominant Euro-American concepts. Gays and lesbians are not only tolerated in Native culture but perform vital societal roles, Tafoya concludes.

As you read, consider the following questions:

1. In Tafoya's opinion, how does the concept of Two-Spirited People differ from the Euro-American definition of homosexual?
2. What are the six genders understood by Native Americans, according to Jay Miller, as cited by the author?
3. According to Tafoya, what special attributes of homosexuals are valued by Native societies?

Most Native communities tend not to classify the world into concrete binary categories of the Western world—Good/Bad; Right/Wrong; Male/Female; Gay/Straight, but rather into categories that range from appropriateness to inappropriateness depending on the context of a situation.

For example, a Navajo man asked a nonIndian man for food to feed his family including his wife, who was about to give birth. The nonIndian agreed, but asked why the man's family was going hungry when it was well-known what a good hunter he was. The Navajo replied, "Because it is not appropriate that I who am about to receive a life should be taking life at this time." In other words, hunting is not seen as right or wrong, but only understandable in the context of a relationship.

This worldview is critical in understanding Native concepts of sexuality and gender, which do not always fit comfortably and neatly into general American concepts of Gay/Straight, or Male/Female. Indeed, even the discrete categories that exist for social science research will not always make conceptual sense to Native people who may have a far more sophisticated taxonomy addressing spirituality and function, rather than appearance. For example, how does an Euro-American system of "Gay/Straight" classify a man who wants to be anally penetrated by a woman wearing a dildo?

European Intolerance

When Native American people discovered Columbus five centuries ago, they presented a unique conundrum of identity. Not only did most tribes not organize themselves by kings and queens in European tradition, but the majority classified members as having more than two genders. This radical (for Europeans) way of seeing the world brought swift and tragic responses. The Spanish explorer Balboa, for example, declared such individuals who were not considered male or female to be "sodomites", and literally had them torn apart by his dogs in the 16th century. Thus, from the very beginning of European contact, Native people learned not to openly discuss matters of sexuality and gender with the newcomers, because they could be killed for being "different". Most American citizens are unaware of Native history and reality. For example, American Indians did not become citizens of the United States until 1924. When the reservations were created by the federal government, the superintendents of the reservations were all appointed Christian missionaries of various denominations, with the mandate to "civilize" American Indians by converting them to Christianity, often by withholding food and starving them into submission. Federal Boarding Schools were set up for Natives (American Indians and Alaskan). Natives were not permitted to attend public school until the mid-1930s.

There are still a number of Indian Boarding Schools operating today. Children were forcibly removed from their parents, sometimes at gunpoint, to deliberately prevent them from growing up with the influence of their culture and language.

Ancient Ignorance

None of the Gospel writers, nor the missionary Paul, nor the formulators of the Tradition, possess the psychological, sociological and sexological knowledge which now inform our theological reflections about human sexuality. They knew nothing of sexual orientation or of the natural heterosexual-bisexual-homosexual continuum that exists in human life. They did not postulate that persons engaging in same-gender sex acts could have been expressing *their natural sexuality*. They *presumed* that persons engaged in same-gender sex acts were heterosexual, *presumed* only one purpose for sexuality (procreation) and *presumed* that anyone engaged in same-gender sex acts was consciously choosing perversion of what was assumed to be the natural sexuality (i.e., heterosexuality).

We now know that same-gender sex acts have been observed in a multitude of species from sea gulls to porcupines and that homosexuality justifiably can be considered a minority expression, but a natural expression nonetheless, within the created order. We know that there are three natural and normative human sexual orientations—heterosexual, homosexual and bisexual. We know that same-gender oriented persons can experience deep love with one another and can nurture meaningful, long-lasting relationships.

William R. Johnson, *Positively Gay: New Approaches to Gay and Lesbian Life*, ed. Betty Berzon, 1992.

This forced segregation and isolation had a devastating impact on Native communities as a whole. Critical teachings and attitudes regarding sexuality and gender that would have been provided at the time of puberty, for example, were never passed on in many families and tribes because the young person was away at Boarding School. Such things were not permitted to be discussed. In addition, there was an incredible loss of Native lives through exposure to European diseases to which Native people had no immunity (a situation that has a number of parallels to the AIDS epidemic . . . the newspaper editorials of the 1880s of the Pacific Northwest condemn Native Americans for having unacceptable sexual behaviors and multiple partners, and declared their deaths by infectious disease to be "God's punishment"). It is estimated that in the Pacific Northwest, 80% of the Native population died within two generations of European contact.

It is fascinating, in working with the Native "Gay and Lesbian" community, to discover how often even those individuals who were denied access to their tribal histories of alternative gender roles and identities manifest the "duties and responsibilities of office" that were an integral part of being "different" before and after European contact. These traditional roles include teaching, keeping the knowledge of the elders, healing, child-care, spiritual leadership and participation, herbal wisdom, interpretation, mediation, and all forms of artistic expression.

Of the 250 or so Native languages still spoken in the United States, at least 168 of them have been identified as having terms for people who were not considered male or female. In the anthropological literature, the most common word used to describe such an individual is "Berdache". This is an unfortunate historic choice, reflecting as it does an old Persian term for a male sexual slave. The word was picked up in the Middle Ages by Europeans during the Crusades and its pronunciation and spelling evolved into its contemporary form.

When the French fur traders, explorers and missionaries encountered Native people in North America who did not fit European standards of gender roles, they used the term "Berdache" to describe them. In the 17th century, the word in French implied someone who engaged in receptive anal intercourse. It also has a connotation of someone with a biologically male identity, and so tends to exclude Native people who are biologically female. Some modern writers suggest the term "Amazon" to discuss the biological females who take on an alternative gender role. Berdache also indicates a sexual behavior that may or may not be relevant to a particular individual. Neither of these foreign terms are well known to traditional Native people.

Two-Spirited People

In other words, asking a tribal member, "Do you have a Berdache or Amazon tradition in your community?" may bring about a confused stare. Asking a Navajo, "Do your people have Nadle?" or asking a Lakota, "Do your people have Winkte?" may get a very different response, as people recognize their own language's term for such people. Many contemporary Native people have difficulty in being comfortable with identifying themselves as Gay, Lesbian, or Bisexual, feeling as though they are "being herded" into such categories by the power of English. In response to this, the term "Two-Spirited" or "Two-Spirited People" seems to be gaining a greater acceptance for many of today's Native people, in lieu of "Berdache", "Amazon", or Gay/Lesbian/Bisexual. "Two-Spirited" indicates that someone possesses both a male and female spirit.

A number of non-Native Gay, Lesbian, and Bisexual researchers and writers have suggested the Two-Spirited tradition as an historic "Gay" role model since it often carries with it a sense of positive acceptance or even celebration within many Native communities. For example, a European-American gay male nurse reported being surprised and delighted to be visiting a Catholic priest on an Apache Indian reservation when a proud mother came in and told the priest, "My sixteen-year-old son is attracted to other men. We need to arrange for him to be initiated with the Medicine men". The nurse was amazed to discover that there was a respected and sanctioned role for such a young person among the Apache, and to note that the mother's response was somehow different than his own mother's had been when his own sexual orientation became known.

Unfortunately, the simplistic reductionism (Berdache-Gay) of many non-Native writers often fails to see that while the Two-Spirited People and Gay/Bisexual/ Lesbian people experiences and worldviews overlap, they are not the same thing. The Two-Spirited position is not one determined primarily by sexual orientation. The role is one of a spiritual/social identity for Native people, as opposed to psycho-sexual identity. Paula Gunn Allen (Laguna/Sioux) suggests seeing the Berdache as a gender role, rather than a sexual identity. Tribal concepts do not stress individuality in the manner of Euro-American concepts, but instead focus on relationships, contexts, and interactions. In short, "Gay" can be seen as a noun, but "Two Spirit" is a verb. (This is meant as a metaphoric statement, where a noun is person, place or thing, where a verb deals with action and interactions).

Transformation

The rigidity of the English language prevents even many self-identified Gay/Bisexual/Lesbian Natives from dealing with fluidity of gender and sexual roles, if the only categories that exist in a valued way are "homosexual/heterosexual". Native tradition emphasizes transformation and change, and the idea that an individual is expected to go through many changes in a lifetime. Indeed, many tribes anticipate that someone will change his or her name more than once, since a person at age 45 is not the same person he or she was at ten. Hence, a name change seems most appropriate.

While hardly identifying as "Asexual" (a lesser used category used by some researchers to indicate a Gay or Lesbian who is not active with males or females), some Two-Spirited People will not be involved on a sexual level with a biologically same-gendered partner, although an emotional/affectionate bonding can occur. This may be a matter of personal choice, an individual's medicine path (a traditional Native term that indicates one's spiritual behavior and connotes a combination of destiny and free choice), or a result of a specific spiritual vision/perception of their appropriate behavior. This should in no way distract from the fact that a number of Native people very strongly identify as members of the Gay/Lesbian/Bisexual community. But to see "Gay/Straight" as the only possible categories of sexual identity for Native people (and certain other ethnic groups in India, Burma, the Middle-East, etc.) is grossly misleading and out of touch with historic and contemporary reality. It is also seen as very reasonable that Two-Spirited People can be heterosexual, and one's partnering may change over a period of time. In many tribes, there was a history of polygamy, or polyandry— multiple spouses. This may still have an influence on how Native Two-Spirited People deal with relationships. . . .

Concepts of Gender

Native individuals may be quite comfortable with their presented identity shifting its emphasis on so-called "masculine/ feminine" behavior, depending upon social context and the behavior/identity of a partner. In other words, a Two-Spirited person may become increasingly "masculine" within a specific environment, or when in a relationship with a "feminine" partner, regardless of biological gender. This appears increasingly complex, simply because the English language does not permit this discussion in a useful manner, with its emphasis on gendered pronouns and fundamental categories of Male/Female. Jay Miller offers a six gendered Native model, of 1) Hyper-Masculine (warriors and athletes, often reared away from women), 2) Ordinary Males, 3) Berdaches, 4) Amazons (or biological female Berdaches), 5) Ordinary Females, and 6) Hyper-Feminine. This model would also take into consideration a very strong femininely identified (e.g., Hyper-Feminine) individual who would partner an Amazon. . . .

Yet another alternative would be to see European concepts of gender and sexuality as being polar opposites, or different ends of the same stick. One is either/or male or female; gay or straight. Native American concepts usually prefer circles to lines. If one takes the line of male/female; gay/straight, and bends it into a circle, there are an infinite number of points. Just so, there are theoretically an infinite number of possible points of gender and sexual identity for an individual that can shift and differ over time and location.

Historically, the status of the Two-Spirited person was valued in many Native communities, since an ordinary male sees the world through male eyes, and an ordinary female sees the world through female eyes. However, a Two-Spirited person (who possesses both a male and female spirit, regardless of the flesh that is worn) will always see further. For this reason, many Two-

Spirited People have become Medicine people, leaders and intermediaries between men and women, and between tribal communities and non-Native people. Their greater flexibility provides greater possibilities to discover alternative ways of seeing oneself and the world. . . .

The role of the Two-Spirited person is critical in its relationship to those who are not Two-Spirited. The alternative behaviors and creative option of the Gay and Lesbian community inform the entire society of what possibilities exist and . . . offer guidelines and directions for exploring and living life to its fullest potential. A man or a woman is more clearly and accurately defined by the existence of a Two-Spirited person, just as a straight person may more fully understand him or herself in coming to know and understand Gay and Lesbians.

Periodical Bibliography

The following articles have been selected to supplement the diverse views presented in this chapter.

John Balzar	"Why Does America Fear Gays?" *Los Angeles Times*, February 4, 1993. Available from Times Mirror Square, Los Angeles, CA 90053.
Barbara Grizzuti Harrison	"Nine Brides for One Brother," *Mademoiselle*, November 1991.
Franklin E. Kameny	"Deconstructing the Traditional Family," *The World & I*, October 1993. Available from 2800 New York Ave. NE, Washington, DC 20002.
Gerald M. King	"The Mormon Underground Fights Back," *Reason*, January 1987.
David Link	"Religion Has No Corner on Morality," *Los Angeles Times*, September 15, 1992.
Jo McGowan	"There's No Such Thing as a Trial Marriage," *U.S. Catholic*, December 1992.
Mark Matousek	"The Master Stroke," *Common Boundary*, November/December 1994. Available from 4304 East-West Hwy., Bethesda, MD 20814.
Fred Moody	"Divorce: Sometimes a Bad Notion," *Utne Reader*, November/December 1990.
David Neff	"Really Good Sex," *Christianity Today*, August 19, 1991.
Dennis Prager	"Homosexuality, the Bible, and Us—A Jewish Perspective," *The Public Interest*, Summer 1993.
Kathryn Robinson	"The Divorce Debate: Which Side Are You On?" *The Family Therapy Networker*, May/June 1994.
David Seamands	"A Marriage Counterculture," *Christianity Today*, December 14, 1992.
Joseph Sobran	"Liberalism, Hedonism, and Homosexuality," *The Human Life Review*, Spring 1993.
Joseph Stowell	"The Divorce Dilemma," *Moody*, November 1991.
George Weigel	"'Rights' Are Not Always Trumps," *Los Angeles Times*, September 15, 1992.
Martin King Whyte	"Choosing Mates—The American Way," *Society*, March/April 1992.

How Are Gender and Sexual Orientation Determined?

HUMAN
SEXUALITY

Chapter Preface

The issues of gender and sexual orientation are among the most problematic in the area of human sexuality. For one, they raise the factious specter of nurture versus nature: Do gender and/or sexual orientation develop subtly but surely during each individual's period of socialization or are they a prenatal legacy indelibly stamped on the developing fetus? For another, it is common for popular writers and even experts on human sexual development to differ, often significantly, over the appropriate use of the terms *gender* and *sexuality*. Susan Golombok and Robyn Fivush, in the introduction to their book *Gender Development*, offer psychologists Kay Deaux and E. E. Maccoby as examples of this. Deaux, in an article in the *Annual Review of Psychology*, argues that the term sex should be restricted to specifying one's biological maleness or femaleness, while *gender* should describe social characteristics associated with each sex. On the other hand, Maccoby, in an article in *Developmental Psychology*, suggests that "sex and gender should be used interchangeably because biological and social aspects of sex may interact with each other and it is difficult to distinguish between the two." Finally, there are those who would eliminate entirely all designations of gender (as a social appellation) or sex (as a biological appellation), suggesting that such designations are archaic and divisive. Sandra Lipsitz Bem, a professor of psychology and women's studies at Cornell University and the author of the critically acclaimed *The Lenses of Gender*, has argued in favor of this approach. Bem holds that if behavioral traits derived their meaning from the traits themselves, not from the gender of the performer, the ideas of masculinity and femininity and all they connote would become meaningless. For example, if playing with dolls was regarded as a sign of caring rather than as a precursor to or a preparation for the role of motherhood, then dolls would be associated with nurturance, not feminine behavior. If professionals like Bem are correct in their assumptions, in a very real sense society eventually would become androgynous.

As the following chapter deals with some of the issues noted above, it would be useful to be aware of standardized definitions. For the most part, social and biological scientists view "gender" as a socially derived distinction between people and "sex," a biological designation. Accordingly, *gender role* refers to behavioral traits and ways of thinking that a culture or society considers appropriate for males or females. *Sex* refers to the presence of sexual organs and hormones specific to the biological male or female. *Sexual orientation* refers to whether an individual's sexual interest is oriented toward the opposite sex, the same sex, or both sexes. Most people view themselves and are categorized by others as the gender congruent with their biological sex. As the viewpoints in this chapter illustrate, however, it is often those exhibiting an incongruence between their sex and gender who are best qualified to clarify the distinction.

"The case for the prenatal effects of . . . sex hormones, on gender identity and sexual behavior, . . . is supported by work done on both animals and humans."

Gender Is Determined Biologically

Jo Durden-Smith and Diane deSimone

Authors Jo Durden-Smith and Diane deSimone have collaborated on numerous science articles. "Man and Woman," a seven-part series published in *Playboy* magazine, provided a foundation for their pioneering study *Sex and the Brain*. The following viewpoint, excerpted from that book, presents a case study illustrating what the authors believe is compelling evidence of the prenatal influence of hormones upon postnatal gender identity and sexual orientation. Written in 1983, *Sex and the Brain* anticipated many of the more recent studies arguing that a contributory (some claim exclusive) relationship exists between genetic makeup and sexual orientation.

As you read, consider the following questions:

1. What led Günter Dörner to conclude that sexual behavior is the result of messages sent to the brain by the hormones during the prenatal period, as described by the authors?
2. Who was Amaranta Ternera and what is her significance, as related by the authors?
3. According to Durden-Smith and deSimone, are the Dominican children the only examples of the effects of prenatal hormones on sexual orientation?

"Mood. Aggression. Body size. Body shape. Use of energy. Behavior," says Günter Dörner in a borrowed student's room at Cambridge University in England. "We have all these differences that appear in human males and females, almost all of them during and after puberty. And that's what most people automatically think of when they think about the sex hormones. They are aware of *some*—at any rate—of what Bob Goy, for example, has called in his scientific writing the *activational* effects of these hormones—the way they set up the reproductive cycle in women and at puberty influence hair, breast and muscle growth and attraction to the opposite sex. What they *don't* know about, however, is what Goy calls the *organizational* effects of these hormones. The sex hormones, you see, don't just suddenly appear out of nowhere at puberty. Nor do they just meander about the body. *They know where to go.* The cells that are their targets have already been primed, in the womb, to respond to the hormones that are now being produced. They've already— long before—been *organized*—by the early production of the sex hormones *themselves*, in a masculine or feminine way. This is true of the body, of the reproductive organs, heart, lungs, liver and kidney. But it is also true of the *brain*. The tissues, neural circuitry and chemistry of the brain have already been stamped during fetal life by the sex hormones. The foundations have already been laid, before birth, for the range of behaviors that will characterize the organism as male or female in adult life."

Günter Dörner is director of the Institute for Experimental Endocrinology at Humboldt University in East Berlin. . . .

Dörner, like other scientists, has been working to find a way into the connections between motivation, brain and behavior. And, like other scientists, he has concentrated on the most basic motivation of all—the drive to reproduce—and on the different sexual behavior of male and female. When the scientific community began to understand that it is the hypothalamus that controls the output of the hormones and the different patterns of male and female reproduction, Dörner was quick to find in the hypothalamus of rats what he took to be different male and female sex centers. These centers, formed under the influence of the sex hormones at an early stage of development, were responsible, he believed, for male and female sexual behavior. And he showed that if the rats did not get enough of their appropriate sex hormones during development, then something would go wrong with the formation of the centers and with later sexual behavior. Adult rats would behave in certain ways like members of the opposite sex. They would become, in a sense, "homosexual."

From this Dörner argued that sexual behavior is also stamped by the hormones into the *human* brain while it is still developing in the womb, and that primary human homosexuality is the result of a sexual stamping that has given the brain the wrong gender. He quotes from a study in which male homosexuals obsessively attracted to children were "cured" by an operation on their brain's presumed *female* sex center. And he himself has performed a series of experiments that show, he firmly believes, that both male and female homosexuality are caused by the prenatal effect on the brain of either too little or too much of the main male sex hormone—testosterone.

"There's no doubt," Günter Dörner says in his fluent, accented English, "that this theory is controversial. And it's true we don't know everything we'd like to know about these hormones. We don't know much about the prenatal sex hormones produced by the ovaries. We don't know much about how the *mother's* hormones are involved. But my theory is consistent with what we *do* know from both animals and humans. In humans, monkeys, rats, guinea pigs, birds—practically everywhere we look in nature—the quantities of sex hormones available to the fetus during critical periods of early development stamp into the developing brain a variety of masculine and feminine sexual and social behaviors—usually, *but not always*, in accordance with the genetic sex. The whole story of male and female, you see— and your search for the effects of the sex hormones, if I may call it that—begins not outside, at puberty, but in the womb."

Male and female created He them. And that, of course, is what we see around us—men with testes, a penis and prominent body- and facial-hair display; women, relatively hairless, with ovaries, a vagina and the advertisements of breasts. Men are the male gender of the human species, and women are the female gender. And that is all there is to it.

Not quite. . . . Take the case of Mrs. Went, for example. Mrs. Went is an ordinary, well-adjusted English housewife, married and with adopted children. In England she is, of course, legally a woman. But if she lived in Scotland, no more than a few hundred miles to the north, she would be treated by the state as a man. She is in fact genetically male; all her cells contain both the female X and the male Y chromosome. But she suffers from a rare genetic disorder . . . called the testicular feminization syndrome. This causes a complete insensitivity to the main male hormone, testosterone. And, because of it, Mrs. Went was born with testes hidden in her abdomen and the external appearance of being a girl. She was raised as a girl, and she remained a girl, impervious to the rush of hormones produced by her testes at puberty. She only discovered her condition at age twenty-three when, anxious about her failure to menstruate or grow pubic hair, she consulted a gynecologist.

In Mrs. Went's case, gender identity—what sex she *feels* she is—has come unglued from her genetic sex. And there are other examples of this phenomenon. There are transsexuals. There is a subgroup of homosexuals and transvestites who identify strongly with the sex opposite their own, like the New York transvestite we tracked down who first fathered and then mothered—breast-fed—his own child. And then there are hermaphrodites. Hermaphrodites are true bisexuals, both male and female, born with one active ovary and one active testis and the ability, under certain circumstances, to impregnate themselves. Usually, however, they are raised as either boys or girls, in one gender identity or the other. And this is the gender identity they choose to keep, even when they have not been surgically altered in infancy, to reflect it.

In the late 1970s, for example, a shy eighteen-year-old Malawian who had been raised as a boy, but who was in fact the three hun-

100

dred and third true hermaphrodite known to medicine, entered Stellenbosch University Hospital in South Africa, where Willem van Niekerk had been conducting a special study of Bantu hermaphrodites. The young Malawian, named Blackwell, had both a penis and a small vaginal opening. But the main reason he sought medical help was the fact that, during puberty, he had developed two large and finely shaped female breasts. Certain that he was a man, and wishing to continue his career as one, Mr. Blackwell asked doctors to stitch up his vagina and remove his breasts. And they did so.

Mrs. Went, Mr. Blackwell, transvestites, homosexuals and transsexuals like Renee Richards, the doctor and tennis player: it is cases like these that have kept in place the conventional wisdoms that science delivered up to us in the 1960s and 1970s about sexual orientation and gender identity. First, say the axioms of these wisdoms, sexual orientation is not innate but *learned.* It can be learned in such a way that it is concordant with genetic sex (XX or XY) *or* with gender identity or with both, as it is in most of us. Where it is discordant—as it is in homosexuals and transsexuals, for example—it is the result of formative or disordering psychological experience during childhood and adolescence. Second, according to these wisdoms, gender identity is *also* learned. A child can learn to be either male or female quite comfortably, whatever its genetic sex. But after a certain age, after it has learned to be one or the other, it cannot then change its gender assignment without some sort of psychological upheaval. The work of learning, once done—once etched into the brain—cannot be easily undone.

The most famous case of the period underwrote these contentions; it seemed to give them the force of natural law. This case was not an accident of nature, like Mrs. Went and Mr. Blackwell, but an accident of man. In the early 1960s, in the United States, a male child, one of a pair of identical twins, had his penis severed, at seven months, in a circumcision accident. After a good deal of heart-searching, it was decided by the boy's parents and by a group of doctors that included John Money of Johns Hopkins University that he should be raised as a girl, his brother's sister. At seventeen months, then, his testes were removed and a vagina was given preliminary shape. Later he was put on an extensive program of female sex hormones to mimic the developmental events leading to female puberty.

The case was everywhere hailed as a triumph for science. "This dramatic case," *Time* magazine announced in 1973, "provides strong support for a major contention of women's liberationists: that conventional patterns of masculine and feminine behavior can be altered. It also casts doubt on the theory that major sex differences, psychological as well as anatomical, are immutably set by the genes at conception." Masters and Johnson called it "dramatic documentation of the importance of learning in the process of gender formation." And John Money, who originally reported the case, wrote: "The girl's subsequent history proves how well all three of them (the parents and child) succeeded in adjusting to (the) decision."

That seemed to be that. But then, in the early 1970s, away from public attention, the descendants of Amaranta Ternera were discovered. And the controversy in science began.

Amaranta Ternera—we have changed, by request, her name and the names of her relatives—was born 130 years ago in the southwest corner of the Dominican Republic. There was nothing wrong with Amaranta, so far as we know; she seems to have led a normal and ordinary life. But there *was* something wrong with the genes she left behind her in her children. And there *is* something wrong with a number of her descendants. Seven generations later, Amaranta's genes have been located in twenty-three families in three separate villages. And in thirty-eight different individuals in these families the strange inheritance that Amaranta passed down to them has been expressed. These thirty-eight were born, to all appearances, as girls. They grew up as girls. And they became boys at puberty.

Take the ten children of Gerineldo and Pilar Babilonia, for example. Four of them have been through this extraordinary transformation. The eldest, Prudencio, was born with an apparent vagina and female body-shape, just like his next sister-brother, Matilda. Prudencio was christened Prudencia. And he grew up, Pilar says, tied to his mother's apron strings, kept apart from the village boys and helping with women's work. But then something strange began to happen to his body. His voice began to deepen. At around the age of twelve, his "clitoris" grew into a penis and two hidden testicles descended into a scrotum formed by the lips of his "vagina." He became a male. "He changed his clothes," says his father Gerineldo, "which the neighbors just had to get used to. And he fell in love with a girl almost immediately." Today Prudencio is in his early thirties. Like his brother Matilda, now Mateo, he is a brawny, elaborately muscled man. He is sexually potent and he lives with his wife in the United States. Like seventeen of the eighteen children studied by a group headed by Cornell University's Julianne Imperato-McGinley— all of whom, she says, were raised unambiguously as girls— Prudencio seems to have had no problem adjusting to male gender, male sexual orientation and male roles.

It is this which makes Prudencio and the other Dominican children important. *They seem to have had no problem adjusting to male gender, male sexual orientation and male roles.* Like Mrs. Went, Prudencio and the others are genetically male. But what

102

they have inherited from Amaranta is not a general insensitivity to testosterone, like hers, but an inability to process it on to another hormone, dihydrotestosterone, which is responsible, in the male fetus, for shaping the male genitalia. In the absence of these, the Dominican children were born looking like girls and they were raised as girls. At puberty, though, their bodies were pervaded by a new rush of male hormones to which they, unlike Mrs. Went, were sensitive. Their male parts—which had been waiting in the wings, so to speak—finally established themselves. And nature finished the job it had earlier botched.

The children, though, did not have the psychological breakdown that the conventional wisdoms predict they should have had. This is crucial, for it *must* mean one of three things. *Either* the children were really raised as boys from the beginning. *Or* they were raised, at least, with a great deal of confusion about what gender they were, in which case one might expect them to have a disturbed sexuality as adults. *Or* they were born with a masculinized brain already established before birth in their "female" bodies, a male brain that slipped comfortably into male expressions when their bodies changed at puberty. By this argument, not only the body is sexed at birth but *also* the brain. And by this argument, nature, in gender behavior, is every bit as important as nurture. Learning, in fact, may have little to do with it.

The parents, as we have said—and Julianne Imperato-McGinley—insist that the Dominican children were raised unambiguously as girls. This means that the third hypothesis—that their brains were masculinized before birth by the main male hormone testosterone—must be taken very seriously. For the fetal effects of testosterone can not only explain the ease with which Prudencio, Mateo and the others passed into manhood, they can also provide a new sort of explanation for the gender identities of Mrs. Went and Mr. Blackwell. Mrs. Went, remember, has been from the moment of conception insensitive to testosterone and to its derivatives like dihydrotestosterone. Her body and brain were unable to respond in the womb to male hormones. The result was that she was born looking like a girl. She happily assumed a female identity, a female sexual orientation and female roles—genetic males with testicular feminization are usually very feminine, fully capable of orgasm and drawn to children and careers as housewives. Mr. Blackwell, meanwhile, *was* sensitive, as a fetus, to the testosterone his one testis was producing. And so, for all the external anomalies of his body, he took to the masculine upbringing he was offered without difficulty, and in adulthood settled for male gender identity and sexual orientation, despite the unsettling arrival of his female breasts.

This idea of the priming of the brain by testosterone can be extended, as Günter Dörner believes it should be, to what Kinsey called "primary" homosexuals—those who have had no heterosexual experience and do not respond to aversive therapy; and to transsexuals, who believe that they are imprisoned in a body of the wrong gender. For it may well be that in their case too, the brain, as it developed, was exposed in the womb to either too little or too much testosterone for the normal expression, in later life, of their genetic sex. They are not, then, in some sense "made" by the environment of their upbringing. Nor are they the product of a sexual choice, freely taken. Rather, they were *born* homosexual, in the body of one sex, but with the brain, to one degree or another, of the other sex. Dörner believes this to be true, especially of males. And he believes that society should now face the question of whether or not it wants to "cure" homosexuality in the womb by giving fetuses at risk male hormones.

Nature versus nurture: the question of free will in sex and behavior. This is one of the more intense theaters of conflict in the general war between the entrenched orthodoxies of psychology and sociology. . . . And it is no wonder that the constant scientific debate, especially about the curious fate of the Dominican children, is often so politically charged. For it threatens, in its spreading implications, the liberationist assumptions of feminists and homosexuals. And it undercuts the idea of absolute sexual equality for all.

The case for the prenatal effects of testosterone, and other sex hormones, on gender identity and sexual behavior, however, no longer rests simply on the Dominican children. It is supported . . . by work done on both animals and humans in clinics and laboratories all over the world. And it is supported, too, by other reports of bizarre human experiences that are just beginning to creep into the scientific literature. There is the patient, seen by Richard Green of the State University of New York, who was born with ambiguous genitals and raised as a girl, but insisted throughout childhood that she was a boy—she threw away her dolls and took up trucks; she formed a male peer group; and she was extremely tomboyish. There is the patient, seen by Bob Stoller at the University of California, who looked like a girl and was raised as a girl, but who, after a decade of demanding to be treated as a boy, was told at puberty that she was right—she had undescended testicles. And there is, too, an odd corollary to the Dominican children's story. Julianne Imperato-McGinley, from her base at the Cornell University Medical School in New York, has tracked down other instances of the rare Dominican syndrome. She has found that of the children born outside the United States, all seem to have made the transition from female to male relatively comfortably. In New Guinea, in a tribe where the sexes are segregated at birth and raised separately, two "girls" had suddenly to be rushed through puberty rites and initiated as men. But in the United States such children were recognized as anomalous soon after birth, and all traces of masculinity, including a relatively enlarged clitoris, were surgically removed. These eight children were *made* into girls. They are now [in 1983] in their late teens and consider themselves female. But five of them, says Julianne Imperato-McGinley, may have acute psychological problems. "It is not clear that they can make it as women." If they cannot, then the reason, quite simply, may be that their brain is the wrong sex for their body. Primed to be male, it finds itself in a female environment, encouraged in female behaviors and exposed to female hormones. And it cannot cope.

"The building blocks of gender are socially constructed statuses."

Gender Is Determined by Social Practices

Judith Lorber

Judith Lorber is professor of sociology at Brooklyn College and the Graduate School, City University of New York. The founding editor of *Gender & Society*, Lorber, a well-known feminist, views gender as wholly a product of socialization subject to human agency, organization, and interpretation. In the following viewpoint, the author states unequivocally that gender does not equate with the "biological and physiological differences between human females and males." Rather, she argues, the contributions genes and hormones make to human social institutions are qualitatively transformed by culture and social practices.

As you read, consider the following questions:

1. What does Lorber mean by the words "doing gender"?
2. According to the author, in what ways do humans differ from animals?
3. What does Lorber mean by "gender bending"? What examples of gender bending does she offer?

Talking about gender for most people is the equivalent of fish talking about water. Gender is so much the routine ground of everyday activities that questioning its taken-for-granted assumptions and presuppositions is like thinking about whether the sun will come up. Gender is so pervasive that in our society we assume it is bred into our genes. Most people find it hard to believe that gender is constantly created and re-created out of human interaction, out of social life, and is the texture and order of that social life. Yet gender, like culture, is a human production that depends on everyone's constantly "doing gender.". . .

Humans vs. Animals

In order to understand gender as a social institution, it is important to distinguish human action from animal behavior. Animals feed themselves and their young until their young can feed themselves. Humans have to produce not only food but shelter and clothing. They also, if the group is going to continue as a social group, have to teach the children how their particular group does these tasks. In the process, humans reproduce gender, family, kinship, and a division of labor—social institutions that do not exist among animals. Primate social groups have been referred to as families, and their mating patterns as monogamy, adultery, and harems. Primate behavior has been used to prove the universality of sex differences—as built into our evolutionary inheritance. But animals' sex differences are not at all the same as humans' gender differences; animals' bonding is not kinship; animals' mating is not ordered by marriage; and animals' dominance hierarchies are not the equivalent of human stratification systems. Animals group on sex and age, relational categories that are physiologically, not socially, different. Humans create gender and age-group categories that are socially, and not necessarily physiologically, different. . . .

Western society's values legitimate gendering by claiming that it all comes from physiology—female and male procreative differences. But gender and sex are not equivalent, and gender as a social construction does not flow automatically from genitalia and reproductive organs, the main physiological differences of females and males. In the construction of ascribed social statuses, physiological differences such as sex, stage of development, color of skin, and size are crude markers. They are not the source of the social statuses of gender, age grade, and race. Social statuses are carefully constructed through prescribed processes of teaching, learning, emulation, and enforcement. Whatever genes, hormones, and biological evolution contribute to human social institutions is materially as well as qualitatively transformed by social practices. Every social institution has a material base, but culture and social practices transform that base into something with qualitatively different patterns and constraints. The economy is much more than producing food and goods and distributing them to eaters and users; family and kinship are not the equivalent of having sex and procreating; morals and religions cannot be equated with the fears and ecstasies of the brain; language goes far beyond the sounds produced by tongue and larynx. No one eats "money" or "credit"; the concepts of "god" and "angels" are the subjects of theological disquisitions; not only words but objects, such as their flag, "speak" to the citizens of a country.

Socially Constructed Statuses

Similarly, gender cannot be equated with biological and physiological differences between human females and males. The building blocks of gender are *socially constructed statuses*. Western societies have only two genders, "man" and "woman." Some societies have three genders—men, women, and *berdaches* or *hijras* or *xaniths*. Berdaches, hijras, and xaniths are biological males who behave, dress, work, and are treated in most respects as social women; they are therefore not men, nor are they female women; they are, in our language, "male women." There are African and American Indian societies that have a gender status called *manly hearted women*—biological females who work, marry, and parent as men; their social status is "female men." They do not have to behave or dress as men to have the social responsibilities and prerogatives of husbands and fathers; what makes them men is enough wealth to buy a wife.

Modern Western societies' *transsexuals* and *transvestites* are the nearest equivalent of these crossover genders, but they are not institutionalized as third genders. Transsexuals are biological males and females who have sex-change operations to alter their genitalia. They do so in order to bring their physical anatomy in congruence with the way they want to live and with their own sense of gender identity. They do not become a third gender; they change genders. Transvestites are males who live as women and females who live as men but do not intend to have sex-change surgery. Their dress, appearance, and mannerisms fall within the range of what is expected from members of the opposite gender, so that they "pass." They also change genders, sometimes temporarily, some for most of their lives. Transvestite women have fought in wars as men soldiers as recently as the nineteenth century; some married women, and others went back to being women and married men once the war was over. Some were discovered when their wounds were treated; others not until they died. In order to work as a jazz musician, a man's occupation, Billy Tipton, a woman, lived most of her life as a man. She died recently at seventy-four, leaving a wife and three adopted sons for whom she was husband and father, and musicians with whom she had played and traveled, for whom she was "one of the boys." There have been many other such occurrences of women passing as men to do more prestigious or lucrative men's work.

The Power of Socialization

From the moment a girl infant is wrapped in a pink blanket and a boy infant in a blue one, gender role development begins. The colors of pink and blue are among the first indicators used by a society to distinguish female from male. As these infants grow, other cultural artifacts will assure that this distinction remains intact. Girls will be given dolls to diaper and tiny stoves on which to cook pretend meals. Boys will construct buildings with miniature tools and wage war with toy guns and tanks. In the teen and young adult years, although both may spend their money on records, girls buy more cosmetics and clothes while boys buy sports equipment and stereo components. The incredible power of gender role socialization is largely responsible for such behavior. Pink and blue begin this lifelong process.

Linda L. Lindsey, *Gender Roles*, 1990.

Genders, therefore, are not attached to a biological substratum. Gender boundaries are breachable, and individual and socially organized shifts from one gender to another call attention to "cultural, social, or aesthetic dissonances." These odd or deviant or third genders show us what we ordinarily take for granted—that people have to learn to be women and men. Men who cross-dress for performances or for pleasure often learn from women's magazines how to "do femininity" convincingly. Because transvestism is direct evidence of how gender is constructed, Marjorie Garber claims it has "extraordinary power . . . to disrupt, expose, and challenge, putting in question the very notion of the 'original' and of stable identity."

Gender Bending

It is difficult to see how gender is constructed because we take it for granted that it's all biology, or hormones, or human nature. The differences between women and men seem to be self-evident, and we think they would occur no matter what society did. But in actuality, human females and males are physiologically more similar in appearance than are the two sexes of many species of animals and are more alike than different in traits and behavior. Without the deliberate use of gendered clothing, hairstyles, jewelry, and cosmetics, women and men would look far more alike. Even societies that do not cover women's breasts have gender-identifying clothing, scarification, jewelry, and hairstyles.

The ease with which many transvestite women pass as men and transvestite men as women is corroborated by the common gender misidentification in Westernized societies of people in jeans, T-shirts, and sneakers. Men with long hair may be addressed as "miss," and women with short hair are often taken for men unless they offset the potential ambiguity with deliberate gender markers. Jan Morris, in *Conundrum*, an autobiographical account of events just before and just after a sex-change operation, described how easy it was to shift back and forth from being a man to being a woman when testing how it would feel to change gender status. During this time, Morris still had a penis and wore more or less unisex clothing; the context alone made the man and the woman:

> Sometimes the arena of my ambivalence was uncomfortably small. At the Travellers' Club, for example, I was obviously known as a man of sorts—women were only allowed on the premises at all during a few hours of the day, and even then were hidden away as far as possible in lesser rooms or alcoves. But I had another club, only a few hundred yards away, where I was known only as a woman, and often I went directly from one to the other, imperceptibly changing roles on the way— "Cheerio, sir," the porter would say at one club, and "Hello, madam," the porter would greet me at the other.

Gender shifts are actually a common phenomenon in public roles as well. Queen Elizabeth II of England bore children, but when she went to Saudi Arabia on a state visit, she was considered an honorary man so that she could confer and dine with the men who were heads of a state that forbids unrelated men and women to have face-to-unveiled-face contact. In contemporary Egypt, lower-class women who run restaurants or shops dress in men's clothing and engage in unfeminine aggressive behavior, and middle-class educated women of professional or managerial status can take positions of authority. In these situations, there is an important status change: These women are treated by the others in the situation as if they are men. From their own point of view, they are still women. From the social perspective, however, they are men.

Switching Roles

In many cultures, gender bending is prevalent in theater or dance—the Japanese kabuki are men actors who play both women and men; in Shakespeare's theater company, there were no actresses—Juliet and Lady Macbeth were played by boys. Shakespeare's comedies are full of witty comments on gender shifts. Women characters frequently masquerade as young men,

110

and other women characters fall in love with them; the boys playing these masquerading women, meanwhile, are acting out pining for the love of men characters. In *As You Like It*, when Rosalind justifies her protective cross-dressing, Shakespeare also comments on manliness:

Were it not better,
Because that I am more than common tall,
That I did suit me all points like a man:
A gallant curtle-axe upon my thigh,
A boar-spear in my hand, and in my heart
Lie there what hidden women's fear there will,
We'll have a swashing and martial outside,
As many other mannish cowards have
That do outface it with their semblances.

Shakespeare's audience could appreciate the double subtext: Rosalind, a woman character, was a boy dressed in girl's clothing who then dressed as a boy; like bravery, masculinity and femininity can be put on and taken off with changes of costume and role.

M Butterfly is a modern play of gender ambiguities, which David Hwang based on a real person. Shi Peipu, a male Chinese opera singer who sang women's roles, was a spy as a man and the lover as a woman of a Frenchman, Gallimard, a diplomat. The relationship lasted twenty years, and Shi Peipu even pretended to be the mother of a child by Gallimard. "She" also pretended to be too shy to undress completely. As "Butterfly," Shi Peipu portrayed a fantasy Oriental woman who made the lover a "real man." In Gallimard's words, the fantasy was "of slender women in chong sams and kimonos who die for the love of unworthy foreign devils. Who are born and raised to be perfect women. Who take whatever punishment we give them, and bounce back, strengthened by love, unconditionally." When the fantasy woman betrayed him by turning out to be the more powerful "real man," Gallimard assumed the role of Butterfly and, dressed in a geisha's robes, killed himself: "because 'man' and 'woman' are oppositionally defined terms, reversals . . . are possible." . . .

Gender Is Learned

Although the possible combinations of genitalia, body shapes, clothing, mannerisms, sexuality, and roles could produce infinite varieties in human beings, the social institution of gender depends on the production and maintenance of a limited number of gender statuses and of making the members of these statuses similar to each other. Individuals are born sexed but not gendered, and they have to be taught to be masculine or feminine. As Simone de Beauvoir said: "One is not born, but rather becomes, a woman . . . ; it is civilization as a whole that produces this creature . . . which is described as feminine."

Children learn to walk, talk, and gesture the way their social group says girls and boys should. Ray Birdwhistell, in his analysis of body motion as human communication, calls these learned gender displays *tertiary* sex characteristics and argues that they are needed to distinguish genders because humans are a weakly dimorphic species—their only sex markers are genitalia. Clothing, paradoxically, often hides the sex but displays the gender. . . .

For human beings there is no essential femaleness or maleness, femininity or masculinity, womanhood or manhood, but once gender is ascribed, the social order constructs and holds individuals to strongly gendered norms and expectations. Individuals may vary on many of the components of gender and may shift genders temporarily or permanently, but they must fit into the limited number of gender statuses their society recognizes. In the process, they re-create their society's version of women and men: "If we do gender appropriately, we simultaneously sustain, reproduce, and render legitimate the institutional arrangements. . . . If we fail to do gender appropriately, we as individuals—not the institutional arrangements—may be called to account (for our character, motives, and predispositions) (West and Zimmerman)."

The gendered practices of everyday life reproduce a society's view of how women and men should act. Gendered social arrangements are justified by religion and cultural productions and backed by law, but the most powerful means of sustaining the moral hegemony of the dominant gender ideology is that the process is made invisible; any possible alternatives are virtually unthinkable.

"Gender development is a complex interaction among biological gender differences; cultural belief systems . . . ; [and] the child's own developing understanding of gender."

Gender Is Determined Biologically and Socially

Susan Golombok and Robyn Fivush

In the following viewpoint, psychologists Susan Golombok of City University in London, England, and Robyn Fivush of Emory University in Atlanta, Georgia, argue that gender development is the result of a complex interplay of social and biological factors. The authors do maintain, however, that socialization plays an important role in gender development and identification. Tracing the social development of males and females from infancy through adulthood, they examine both overt and subtle influences affecting gender. Golombok and Fivush conclude by noting that traditional gender-related behaviors are currently experiencing change.

As you read, consider the following questions:

1. According to the authors, how do parents contribute to the development of gender roles?
2. As described by Golombok and Fivush, in what ways do boys develop differently from girls during puberty?
3. How do the career paths of men and women separate as they enter the workforce, according to the authors?

Gender development is a complex interaction among biological gender differences; cultural belief systems as expressed both in stereotypes and behaviors and in institutionalized structures such as school and the workplace; and, equally important, the child's own developing understanding of gender and what it means to be female or male.

Gender development originates from the moment of conception. When a female egg unites with a male sperm to form an XX or XY chromosome pair, males and females embark upon different developmental pathways. The most far-reaching effect of our genetic makeup is the determination of physical sexual characteristics. Our physical appearance as male or female has a powerful influence on how we perceive ourselves and are perceived by others, and it is central to the development of gender identity. Also beginning before birth is the production of sex hormones, which lay the foundation for some aspects of later gender role behavior. Sex hormones do not determine gender development, however. At most, it seems that prenatal sex hormones may facilitate the development of gender role behavior in a male or female direction when postnatal experiences are compatible.

Parental Influences

Once born, from the very first day of life, boys and girls are treated differently. Parents perceive boys to be stronger and rougher than girls, and girls to be more delicate and prettier than boys, although there is little evidence that infants vary along these dimensions. In fact, simply labeling an infant as male or female elicits somewhat different interpretations of the very same infant behavior from an adult. Parents hold boys closer to the body than they do girls, and they spend more time verbalizing and cooing to girls than to boys. Although parents may be acting on their stereotypes of male and female behavior, they may also be responding to temperamental differences between male and female infants. Because males are somewhat more irritable than girls, they may need closer body contact for comfort. Because girls can stabilize their state a bit better than boys, parents can hold them cradled along the forearm, a position ideally suited to face-to-face communication. So here we see how parental beliefs and biological differences combine to produce differences in parent-daughter and parent-son interactions.

Interestingly, infants begin to show preferences for sex-typed toys as early as 12 months of age, although the research on parental sex typing of toy play during infancy is somewhat mixed. Again, although parents are most likely engaging in some sex typing of their infant's play behaviors, many of these preferences seem to come from the infant's own temperamental disposition. These early emerging differences, which are already an interaction between biology and culture, set the stage for what is a critical period in gender development, the preschool years. It is during this time that children first begin to understand for themselves what it means to be male or female, and gender concepts become increasingly important and increasingly stereotyped from age 2 through 5.

In addition to learning the physical differences, by age 3 children already know many of the cultural stereotypes associated with gender. This is probably not too surprising given how pervasive gender stereotypes are in our culture, permeating children's literature, television, and, of course, parents' and teachers' beliefs. Preschool children are usually extremely stereotyped and rigid in their beliefs about gender, and this seems to be true regardless of family values. It seems that at this point in development, the child's own need to make sense of the world overrides other information. And because preschool children are not yet capable of sophisticated and flexible thought, they are only able to understand gender in rigid fashion.

Hormones and Environment

Individual differences in sex hormone levels may result from processes largely controlled by a person's genetic make-up. But the environment can also exert important influences on hormone secretion. For example, emotional stress causes marked reductions in the levels of both male and female hormones in human beings and other mammals, and in several species of mammal the male responds to the presence of a sexually receptive female with a rise in testosterone secretion. Measurements carried out on a human male subject also showed that testosterone levels increased during and immediately after intercourse.

John Archer and Barbara Lloyd, *Sex and Gender*, 1982.

It is also during the preschool years that gender differences in play begin to emerge more consistently. By age 3, most children greatly prefer to play with same-sex peers when given a choice, and play patterns of female and male groups diverge. We see large differences in toy choice, and parents' differential reinforcement of their children's sex-typed toys and activities is strongest at this age. Peers also become important socializing agents, and peers, because they are so gender typed in their beliefs, strongly reinforce gender-typed behaviors. It is almost as if once the child realizes that gender is an important way of categorizing individuals, gender becomes extremely important.

There is little doubt that parents interact with their preschool daughters and sons differently. Parents engage in more face-to-face, communicative play with daughters and more rough-and-tumble play with sons. Again, this develops from earlier patterns of play and communication, which, in turn, result from interactions between biology and culture. Parents also subtly reinforce girls for staying close to adults and for helping around the house. In conversations with their preschool children, parents talk more about sadness with girls and more about anger with boys, although they talk more about emotions overall with girls than with boys. Through all of these avenues, girls are learning to stay close and emotionally related to other people, and boys are learning to be independent and emotionally less open.

The Middle Childhood Years

These patterns continue through the middle childhood years. Friendships between girls tend to be close and intimate, involving one-on-one communication, whereas boys tend to play rule-governed games in large groups. As children begin to think about moral issues, we see the influences of these patterns as well. Girls are more relational and care oriented in their moral reasoning than are boys, especially when thinking about moral issues in their own lives. Boys tend to think about moral issues in terms of individual rights and principles of justice. These patterns have their effects in the classroom. Boys are somewhat more competitive than girls. Teachers also respond to boys and girls differently, praising boys for getting the right answer, but praising girls for being obedient and working neatly.

Further, once gender identity becomes firmly established in middle childhood, the modeling of same-sex individuals as a process for acquiring sex-typed behavior takes on greater importance than during the preschool years. Preschool children do not necessarily imitate models of the same sex as themselves. Instead, they learn the behaviors that are typical for both males and females through observation, and model only those behaviors they consider to be appropriate for their own sex regardless of whether they are performed by a woman or a man. So preschool girls are more likely to imitate a male model who behaves in a traditionally feminine way than a female model who behaves in a traditionally masculine way. By the time children reach middle childhood and understand that gender will not change as a function of behavior or time, they begin to show an active preference for models of the same sex as themselves so as to learn behaviors that are consistent with their gender identity.

Intriguingly, girls know more about gender than do boys, yet boys are more sex typed than are girls. Girls not only know more about gender in general, they know more about the male gender stereotype than boys know about the female gender

stereotype. At the same time, girls are more flexible in their beliefs about gender than are boys and will imitate male role models to a greater extent than males will imitate female models.
Gender differences in gender knowledge can be partly attributed
to differences in socialization and prevailing cultural values. It is
simply more acceptable for girls to engage in cross-sex-typed behaviors, such as playing with cars and trucks, than for boys to
engage in cross-sex-typed behaviors, such as playing with baby
dolls and dressing up. There is no simple explanation for this.
But certainly males, and by extension, stereotypically male behaviors, are seen more positively in our culture. And males also
hold more power than females. Therefore, it is more advantageous for females to know about males than it is for males to
know about females.

The Advent of Puberty

With the advent of puberty, biological factors again come to the
forefront. Along with the physical changes that take place at this
time, adolescents begin to experience sexual feelings and to form
intimate relationships. Although the development of sexuality is
an important feature of adolescence for both boys and girls, the
beliefs and expectations that govern sexual behavior are different
for the two sexes. Greater social sanctions operate against girls
engaging in sexual relationships. Girls are also thought to be less
interested in sex and to experience sex differently. The research
evidence suggests, however, that in the absence of social constraints, women's and men's interest and involvement in sexual
relationships would not be substantially different.

Adolescence is also a time of forming close, intimate friendships, and the relational patterns of interacting that females
show through childhood continue through this period. Female
friendships continue to be deeper, more intimate, and more
emotionally disclosing than male friendships. Males, who tend
not to engage in intimate relationships in childhood, now begin
to have more emotionally disclosing relationships as well, but
most often these relationships are with females.

During adolescence one also begins to consider one's future
role as an adult. Most adolescents are still fairly traditional; females tend to aspire to home and family and, if a career is considered, it is most often a traditionally female career. Again,
these choices may stem from females' concerns with caring for
other people. Males are also gender typed in their career aspira-
tions, almost always selecting traditionally male careers. It is
also at this point in development that we begin to see diver-
gence in academic performance. Although females are equally
able to perform mathematics as males, females begin to select
out of mathematics courses, and believe that they are not capa-

ble of mathematical reasoning. These choices will later limit females' career opportunities.

As men and women enter the work force, career paths continue to diverge. Traditionally female work is less valued than traditionally male work, and even when women are performing the same job as men, they are evaluated more negatively and paid less money. Although a growing number of women are now in management positions, it is still the case that few hold top jobs. Moreover, women and male managers experience organizational life rather differently. Being in the minority often excludes women from informal communication networks that benefit their male colleagues, and additional domestic responsibilities place greater demands on women than on men.

It seems to be the case that the increasing number of young women entering the work force has been accompanied by a shift toward more egalitarian roles within heterosexual relationships. However, when women and men become mothers and fathers, differences in family roles and responsibilities clearly emerge. Although men are just as able as women to care for their children, mothers are more involved in parenting than fathers. And even when fathers are at home with their children, they interact with them less often than do mothers.

Interestingly, although motherhood is greatly valued by women and contributes toward a positive sense of identity, the restrictiveness of the traditionally female roles of wife and mother puts women at increased risk of psychiatric disorder. In spite of the pressures involved in combining work and family life, women who are employed benefit from social relationships in the workplace and experience greater emotional well-being than women who do not work outside the home.

Overall, then, the patterns of interaction we see emerging in infancy are maintained throughout the life span. Females are more relationally oriented than are males, and this orientation affects virtually all aspects of development. Moreover, although females and males do not differ greatly in terms of basic cognitive abilities, it may be the case that a relational orientation will lead females to select into or out of particular cognitive domains, such as mathematics and science.

Biology and Culture

Given the evidence that gender differences are at least partly biologically based, is it the case that these differences are inevitable? We think not. First, although there are slight biological differences between infant males and females, it is certainly true that these differences can be exaggerated or diminished by the prevailing cultural beliefs. That is, cultures determine which aspects of behavior will be deemed important, and through socialization and institutional structures, will communicate to each developing member of the culture the appropriate norms of behavior.

Second, we are already seeing many changes in gender-related behaviors, especially since the early 1970s. More women are entering the work force, and more women are entering traditionally male jobs. Family structures are changing as well. Families today encompass a much broader range of relationships and roles than the more traditional families of the past. It is no longer the norm for children to be raised by a mother and father who are married to each other or who remain married until the children leave home, and where the father goes out to work while the mother stays at home. Instead, children are being raised in a variety of family types, including dual-career families, one-parent families, and stepfamilies, and may move from one type of family to another as they grow up.

Does this mean there might come a time when gender is not an issue? Probably not. Although the stereotypes about what it means to be female or male may evolve and change, it is the case that females and males are somewhat different. Different cultures and different times may note and value these differences in different ways, but all cultures in all times have categorized people by gender.

"A brother of a gay man had a 14 percent likelihood of being gay as compared with 2 percent for the men without gay brothers."

Evidence for a Biological Influence in Male Homosexuality

Simon LeVay and Dean H. Hamer

In the August 30, 1991, issue of *Science*, Simon LeVay claimed that a quantifiable difference existed between the brains of heterosexual men and of homosexual men. LeVay, who earned a doctorate in neuroanatomy at the University of Göttingen in Germany, hypothesized that that difference accounted for the sexual orientation of gay men. In the following viewpoint, LeVay and coauthor Dean H. Hamer reiterate LeVay's earlier argument and offer additional support for the thesis that a biological basis for homosexuality exists. Hamer is currently chief of the section on gene structure and regulation at the National Cancer Institute. LeVay heads the Institute of Gay and Lesbian Education, which he founded in 1992.

As you read, consider the following questions:

1. Why do the authors believe that the Roger Gorski study of rats is "of particular importance"?
2. What three possibilities do the authors say might explain the correlations between sexual orientation and brain structure?
3. What statistical evidence from twin studies do LeVay and Hamer offer in support of their thesis?

Most men are sexually attracted to women, most women to men. To many people, this seems only the natural order of things—the appropriate manifestation of biological instinct, reinforced by education, religion and the law. Yet a significant minority of men and women—estimates range from 1 to 5 percent—are attracted exclusively to members of their own sex. Many others are drawn, in varying degrees, to both men and women.

How are we to understand such diversity in sexual orientation? Does it derive from variations in our genes or our physiology, from the intricacies of our personal history or from some confluence of these? Is it for that matter a choice rather than a compulsion?

Probably no one factor alone can elucidate so complex and variable a trait as sexual orientation. But recent laboratory studies, including our own, indicate that genes and brain development play a significant role. How, we do not yet know. It may be that genes influence the sexual differentiation of the brain and its interaction with the outside world, thus diversifying its already vast range of responses to sexual stimuli.

The search for biological roots of sexual orientation has run along two broad lines. The first draws on observations made in yet another hunt—that for physical differences between men's and women's brains. As we shall see, "gay" and "straight" brains may be differentiated in curiously analogous fashion. The second approach is to scout out genes by studying the patterns in which homosexuality occurs in families and by directly examining the hereditary material, DNA.

Researchers have long sought within the human brain some manifestation of the most obvious classes into which we are divided—male and female. Such sex differentiation of the brain's structure, called sexual dimorphism, proved hard to establish. On average, a man's brain has a slightly larger size that goes along with his larger body; other than that, casual inspection does not reveal any obvious dissimilarity between the sexes. Even under a microscope, the architecture of men's and women's brains is very similar. Not surprisingly, the first significant observations of sexual dimorphism were made in laboratory animals.

Of particular importance is a study of rats conducted by Roger A. Gorski of the University of California at Los Angeles. In 1978 Gorski was inspecting the rat's hypothalamus, a region at the base of its brain that is involved in instinctive behaviors and the regulation of metabolism. He found that one group of cells near the front of the hypothalamus is several times larger in male than in female rats. Although this cell group is very small, less than a millimeter across even in males, the difference between the sexes is quite visible in appropriately stained slices of tissue, even without the aid of a microscope.

121

Gorski's finding was especially interesting because the general region of the hypothalamus in which this cell group occurs, known as the medial preoptic area, has been implicated in the generation of sexual behavior—in particular, behaviors typically displayed by males. For example, male monkeys with damaged medial preoptic areas are apparently indifferent to sex with female monkeys, and electrical stimulation of this region can make an inactive male monkey approach and mount a female. It should be said, however, that we have yet to find in monkeys a cell group analogous to the sexually dimorphic one occurring in rats.

Nor is the exact function of the rat's sexually dimorphic cell group known. What is known, from a study by Gorski and his co-workers, is that androgens—typical male hormones—play a key role in bringing about the dimorphism during development. Neurons within the cell group are rich in receptors for sex hormones, both for androgens—testosterone is the main representative—and for female hormones known as estrogens. Although male and female rats initially have about the same numbers of neurons in the medial preoptic area, a surge of testosterone secreted by the testes of male fetuses around the time of birth acts to stabilize their neuronal population. In females the lack of such a surge allows many neurons in this cell group to die, leading to the typically smaller structure. Interestingly, it is only for a few days before and after birth that the medial preoptic neurons are sensitive to androgen; removing androgens in an adult rat by castration does not cause the neurons to die.

Gorski and his colleagues at U.C.L.A., especially his student Laura S. Allen, have also found dimorphic structures in the human brain. A cell group named INAH3 (derived from "third interstitial nucleus of the anterior hypothalamus") in the medial preoptic region of the hypothalamus is about three times larger in men than in women. (Notably, however, size varies considerably even within one sex.)

In 1990 one of us (LeVay) decided to check whether INAH3 or some other cell group in the medial preoptic area varies in size with sexual orientation as well as with sex. This hypothesis was something of a long shot, given the prevailing notion that sexual orientation is a "high-level" aspect of personality molded by environment and culture. Information from such elevated sources is thought to be processed primarily by the cerebral cortex and not by "lower" centers such as the hypothalamus.

LeVay examined the hypothalamus in autopsy specimens from 19 homosexual men, all of whom had died of complications of AIDS, and 16 heterosexual men, six of whom had also died of AIDS. (The sexual orientation of those who had died of non-AIDS causes was not determined. But assuming a distribution similar to that of the general populace, no more than one or two of them were likely to have been gay.) LeVay also included specimens from six women whose sexual orientation was unknown.

After encoding the specimens to eliminate subjective bias, LeVay cut each hypothalamus into serial slices, stained these to mark the neuronal cell groups and measured their cross-sectional areas under a microscope. Armed with information about the areas, plus the thickness of the slices, he could readily calculate the volumes of each cell group. In addition to Allen and Gorski's sexually dimorphic nucleus INAH3, LeVay examined three other nearby groups—INAH1, INAH2 and INAH4.

Like Allen and Gorski, LeVay observed that INAH3 was more than twice as large in the men as in the women. But INAH3 was also between two and three times larger in the straight men than in the gay men. In some gay men, the cell group was altogether absent. Statistical analysis indicated that the probability of this result's being attributed to chance was about one in 1,000. In fact, there was no significant difference between volumes of INAH3 in the gay men and in the women. So the investigation suggested a dimorphism related to male sexual orientation about as great as that related to sex.

A primary concern in such a study is whether the observed structural differences are caused by some variable other than the one of interest. A major suspect here was AIDS. The AIDS virus itself, as well as other infectious agents that take advantage of a weakened immune system, can cause serious damage to brain cells. Was this the reason for the small size of INAH3 in the gay men, all of whom had died of AIDS?

Several lines of evidence indicate otherwise. First, the heterosexual men who died of AIDS had INAH3 volumes no different from those who died of other causes. Second, the AIDS victims with small INAH3s did not have case histories distinct from those with large INAH3s; for instance, they had not been ill longer before they died. Third, the other three cell groups in the medial preoptic area—INAH1, INAH2 and INAH4—turned out to be no smaller in the AIDS victims. If the disease were having a nonspecific destructive effect, one would have suspected otherwise. Finally, after completing the main study, LeVay obtained the hypothalamus of one gay man who had died of non-AIDS causes. This specimen, processed "blind" along with several specimens from heterosexual men of similar age, confirmed the main study: the volume of INAH3 in the gay man was less than half that of INAH3 in the heterosexual men.

One other feature in brains that is related to sexual orientation has been reported by Allen and Gorski. They found that the anterior commissure, a bundle of fibers running across the midline of the brain, is smallest in heterosexual men, larger in women and largest in gay men. After correcting for overall

123

brain size, the anterior commissure in women and in gay men were comparable in size.

What might lie behind these apparent correlations between sexual orientation and brain structure? Logically, three possibilities exist. One is that the structural differences were present early in life—perhaps even before birth—and helped to establish the men's sexual orientation. The second is that the differences arose in adult life as a result of the men's sexual feelings or behavior. The third possibility is that there is no causal connection, but both sexual orientation and the brain structures in question are linked to some third variable, such as a developmental event during uterine or early postnatal life.

We cannot decide among these possibilities with any certainty. On the basis of animal research, however, we find the second scenario, that the structural differences came about in adulthood, unlikely. In rats, for example, the sexually dimorphic cell group in the medial preoptic area appears plastic in its response to androgens during early brain development but later is largely resistant to change. We favor the first possibility, that the structural differences arose during the period of brain development and consequently contributed to sexual behavior. Because the medial preoptic region of the hypothalamus is implicated in sexual behavior in monkeys, the size of INAH3 in men may indeed influence sexual orientation. But such a causal connection is speculative at this point.

Assuming that some of the structural differences related to sexual orientation were present at birth in certain individuals, how did they arise? One candidate is the interaction between gonadal steroids and the developing brain; this interaction is responsible for differences in the structure of male and female brains. A number of scientists have speculated that atypical levels of circulating androgens in some fetuses cause them to grow into homosexual adults. Specifically, they suggest that androgen levels are unusually low in male fetuses that become gay and unusually high in female fetuses that become lesbian.

A more likely possibility is that there are intrinsic differences in the way individual brains respond to androgens during development, even when the hormone levels are themselves no different. This response requires a complex molecular machinery, starting with the androgen receptors but presumably including a variety of proteins and genes whose identity and roles are still unknown.

At first glance, the very notion of gay genes might seem absurd. How could genes that draw men or women to members of the same sex survive the Darwinian screening for reproductive fitness? Surely the parents of most gay men and lesbians are heterosexual? In view of such apparent incongruities, research focuses on genes that sway rather than determine sexual orientation. The two main approaches to seeking such genes are twin and family studies and DNA linkage analysis.

Twin and family tree studies are based on the principle that genetically influenced traits run in families. The first modern study on the patterns of homosexuality within families was published in 1985 by Richard C. Pillard and James D. Weinrich of Boston University. Since then, five other systematic studies on the twins and siblings of gay men and lesbians have been reported.

The pooled data for men show that about 57 percent of identical twins, 24 percent of fraternal twins and 13 percent of brothers of gay men are also gay. For women, approximately 50 percent of identical twins, 16 percent of fraternal twins and 13 percent of sisters of lesbians are also lesbian. When these data are compared with baseline rates of homosexuality, a good amount of family clustering of sexual orientation becomes evident for both sexes. In fact, J. Michael Bailey of Northwestern University and his co-workers estimate that the overall heritability of sexual orientation—that proportion of the variance in a trait that comes from genes—is about 53 percent for men and 52 percent for women. (The family clustering is most obvious for relatives of the same sex, less so for male-female pairs.)

To evaluate the genetic component of sexual orientation and to clarify its mode of inheritance, we need a systematic survey of the extended families of gay men and lesbians. One of us (Hamer), Stella Hu, Victoria L. Magnuson, Nan Hu and Angela M.L. Pattatucci of the National Institutes of Health have initiated such a study. It is part of a larger one by the National Cancer Institute to investigate risk factors for certain cancers that are more frequent in some segments of the gay population.

Hamer and his colleagues' initial survey of males confirmed the sibling results of Pillard and Weinrich. A brother of a gay man had a 14 percent likelihood of being gay as compared with 2 percent for the men without gay brothers. (The study used an unusually stringent definition of homosexuality, leading to the low average rate.) Among more distant relatives, an unexpected pattern showed up: maternal uncles had a 7 percent chance of being gay, whereas sons of maternal aunts had an 8 percent chance. Fathers, paternal uncles and the three other types of cousins showed no correlation at all.

Although this study pointed to a genetic component, homosexuality occurred much less frequently than a single gene inherited in simple Mendelian fashion would suggest. One interpretation, that genes are more important in some families than in others, is borne out by looking at families having two gay brothers. Compared with randomly chosen families, rates of homosexuality in maternal uncles increased from 7 to 10 percent and in maternal cousins from 8 to 13 percent. This familial clustering, even in relatives outside the nuclear family, presents an additional argument for a genetic root to sexual orientation.

Why are most gay male relatives of gay men on the mother's side of the family? One possibility—that the subjects somehow knew more about their maternal relatives—seems unlikely because opposite-sex gay relatives of gay males and lesbians were equally distributed between both sides of the family. Another explanation is that homosexuality, while being transmitted by both parents, is expressed only in one sex—in this case, males. When expressed, the trait reduces the reproductive rate and must therefore be disproportionately passed on by the mother. Such an effect may partially account for the concentration of gay men's gay relatives on the maternal side of the family. But proof of this hypothesis will require finding an appropriate gene on an autosomal chromosome, which is inherited from either parent.

A third possibility is X chromosome linkage. A man has two sex chromosomes: a Y, inherited from his father, and an X, cut and pasted from the two X chromosomes carried by his mother. Therefore, any trait that is influenced by a gene on the X chromosome will tend to be inherited through the mother's side and will be preferentially observed in brothers, maternal uncles and maternal cousins, which is exactly the observed pattern.

To test this hypothesis, Hamer and his colleagues embarked on a linkage study of the X chromosome in gay men. Linkage analysis is based on two principles of genetics. If a trait is genetically influenced, then relatives who share the trait will share the gene more often than is expected by chance—this is true even if the gene plays only a small part. Also, genes that are close together on a chromosome are almost always inherited together. Therefore, if there is a gene that influences sexual orientation, it should be "linked" to a nearby DNA marker that tends to travel along with it in families. For traits affected by only one gene, linkage can precisely locate the gene on a chromosome. But for complex traits such as sexual orientation, linkage also helps to determine whether a genetic component really exists.

To initiate a linkage analysis of male sexual orientation, the first requirement was to find informative markers, segments of DNA that flag locations on a chromosome. Fortunately, the Human Genome Project has already generated a large catalogue of markers spanning all of the X chromosomes. The most useful ones are short, repeated DNA sequences that have slightly different lengths in different persons. To detect the markers, the researchers used the polymerase chain reaction to make several billion copies of specific regions of the chromosome and then separated the different fragments by the method of gel electrophoresis.

The second step in the linkage analysis was to locate suitable families. When scientists study simple traits such as color blindness or sickle cell anemia—which involve a single gene—they tend to analyze large, multigenerational families in which each member clearly either has or does not have the trait. Such an approach was unsuited for studying sexual orientation. First, identifying someone as not homosexual is tricky; the person may be concealing his or her true orientation or may not be aware of it. Because homosexuality was even more stigmatized in the past, multigenerational families are especially problematic in this regard. Moreover, genetic modeling shows that for traits that involve several different genes expressed at varying levels, studying large families can actually decrease the chances of finding a linked gene: too many exceptions are included.

For these reasons, Hamer and his co-workers decided to focus on nuclear families with two gay sons. One advantage of this approach is that individuals who say they are homosexual are unlikely to be mistaken. Furthermore, the approach can detect a single linked gene even if other genes or noninherited factors are required for its expression. For instance, suppose that being gay requires an X chromosome gene together with another gene on an autosome, plus some set of environmental circumstances. Studying gay brothers would give a clear-cut result because both would have the X chromosome gene. In contrast, heterosexual brothers of gay men would sometimes share the X chromosome gene and sometimes not, leading to confusing results.

Genetic analysts now believe that studying siblings is the key to traits that are affected by many elements. Because Hamer and his colleagues were most interested in finding a gene that expresses itself only in men but is transmitted through women, they restricted their search to families with gay men but no gay father–gay son pairs.

Forty such families were recruited. DNA samples were prepared from the gay brothers and, where possible, from their mothers or sisters. The samples were typed for 22 markers that span the X chromosome from the tip of the short arm to the end of the long arm. At each marker, a pair of gay brothers was scored as concordant if they inherited identical markers from their mother or as discordant if they inherited different ones. Fifty percent of the markers were expected to be identical by chance. Corrections were also made for the possibility of the mother's having two copies of the same marker.

The results of this study were striking. Over most of the X chromosome the markers were randomly distributed between the gay brothers. But at the tip of the long arm of the X chromosome, in a region known as Xq28, there was a considerable excess of concordant brothers: 33 pairs shared the same marker, whereas only seven pairs did not. Although the sample size was not large, the result was statistically significant: the probability of such a skewed ratio occurring by chance alone is less than one in 200. In a control group of 314 randomly selected pairs of brothers, most of whom can be presumed to be heterosexual, Xq28 markers were randomly distributed.

The most straightforward interpretation of the finding is that chromosomal region Xq28 contains a gene that influences male sexual orientation. The study provides the strongest evidence to date that human sexuality is influenced by heredity because it directly examines the genetic information, the DNA. But as with all initial studies, there are some caveats.

First, the result needs to be replicated: several other claims of finding genes related to personality traits have proved controversial. Second, the gene itself has not yet been isolated. The study locates it within a region of the X chromosome that is about four million base pairs in length. This region represents less than 0.2 percent of the total human genome, but it is still large enough to contain several hundred genes. Finding the needle in this haystack will require either large numbers of families or more complete information about the DNA sequence to identify all possible coding regions. As it happens, Xq28 is extraordinarily rich in genetic loci and will probably be one of the first regions of the human genome to be sequenced in its entirety.

A third caveat is that researchers do not know quantitatively how important a role Xq28 plays in male sexual orientation. Within the population of gay brothers studied, seven of 40 brothers did not share markers. Assuming that 20 siblings should inherit identical markers by chance alone, 36 percent of the gay brothers show no link between homosexuality and Xq28. Perhaps these men inherited different genes or were influenced by nongenetic physiological factors or by the environment. Among all gay men—most of whom do not have gay brothers—the influence of Xq28 is even less clear. Also unknown is the role of Xq28, and other genetic loci, in female sexual orientation.

How might a genetic locus at Xq28 affect sexuality? One idea is that the hypothetical gene affects hormone synthesis or metabolism. A candidate for such a gene was the androgen receptor locus, which encodes a protein essential for masculinization of the human brain and is, moreover, located on the X chromosome. To test this idea, Jeremy Nathans, Jennifer P. Macke, Van L. King and Terry R. Brown of Johns Hopkins University teamed up with Bailey of Northwestern and Hamer, Hu and Hu of the NIH. They compared the molecular structure of the androgen receptor gene in 197 homosexual men and 213 predominantly heterosexual men. But no significant variations in the protein coding sequences were found. Also, linkage studies showed no correlation between homosexuality in brothers and inheritance of the androgen receptor locus. Most significant of all, the locus turned out to be at Xq11, far from the Xq28 region. This study excludes the androgen receptor from playing a significant role in male sexual orientation.

A second idea is that the hypothetical gene acts indirectly, through personality or temperament, rather than directly on sexual-object choice. For example, people who are genetically self-reliant might be more likely to acknowledge and act on same-sex feelings than are people who are dependent on the approval of others.

Finally, the intriguing possibility arises that the Xq28 gene product bears directly on the development of sexually dimorphic brain regions such as INAH3. At the simplest level, such an agent could act autonomously, perhaps in the womb, by stimulating the survival of specific neurons in preheterosexual males or by promoting their death in females and prehomosexual men. In a more complex model, the gene product could change the sensitivity of a neuronal circuit in the hypothalamus to stimulation by environmental cues—perhaps in the first few years of life. Here the genes serve to predispose rather than to predetermine. Whether this fanciful notion contains a grain of truth remains to be seen. It is in fact experimentally testable, using current tools of molecular genetics and neurobiology.

Our research has attracted an extraordinary degree of public attention, not so much because of any conceptual breakthrough— the idea that genes and the brain are involved in human behavior is hardly new—but because it touches on a deep conflict in contemporary American society. We believe scientific research can help dispel some of the myths about homosexuality that in the past have clouded the image of lesbians and gay men. We also recognize, however, that increasing knowledge of biology may eventually bring with it the power to infringe on the natural rights of individuals and to impoverish the world of its human diversity. It is important that our society expand discussions of how new scientific information should be used to benefit the human race in its entirety.

"It is impossible to prove that the behavior of homosexuality is a result of biological or genetic factors."

No Evidence for a Biological Cause of Homosexuality

Louis Sheldon and Chandler Burr

The following viewpoint, although separately written by Louis Sheldon and Chandler Burr, appeared as a single editorial in the *Washington Times*. Both authors refute the hypothesis that homosexuality is biologically determined. Sheldon accuses homosexual researchers of employing "faulty and unreliable methodology" in their studies. Burr argues that research on the subject of causality in homosexuality has produced no conclusive or irrefutable answers. Sheldon is a minister and chair of the Traditional Values Coalition. Burr is currently writing a book on the biological research on sexual orientation.

As you read, consider the following questions:

1. What arguments does Sheldon offer to refuge LeVay's contention that homosexuality is biologically determined?
2. According to Burr, what conclusions may we make after all the years of research on sexual orientation?

Louis Sheldon and Chandler Burr, "Homosexuality a Matter of Choice . . . or Genetics?" *The Washington Times*, October 16, 1994. Reprinted by permission of Scripps Howard News Service.

I

The myth that homosexuality is a genetic condition, rather than an environmentally influenced choice, has been spawned by the media's sensationalism and several less than accurate scientific pronouncements.

Recent research has come largely from homosexual scientists who seem anxious to explain complex aspects of human sexuality to bolster the homosexual political movement.

These researchers have been guilty of faulty and unreliable methodology in performing their studies (which have failed to be replicated) while their personal motivations have led to biased interpretation of the results.

Neurobiologist Simon LeVay, who is gay, released a study in 1991 asserting that a region of the brain's hypothalamus is smaller in some male homosexuals and women than in some male heterosexuals. Consequently, the media reported homosexuality was a biological condition, the proof of which was in the brain.

What wasn't widely reported was that Dr. LeVay studied the brains of 19 deceased homosexual men. He presumed they were homosexual based on their medical records. The 19 "homosexual" brains were compared against the brains of 16 men and 6 women whom Dr. LeVay presumed to be heterosexual because their medical records did not say otherwise.

Fallacious Conclusions

Although the results were reported in the press as though they were conclusive, the hypothalamus region for some of the heterosexuals was actually smaller, and in some homosexual subjects it was larger. Dr. LeVay blamed these "exceptions," which hurt his credibility, on "technical shortcomings" and insufficient information about the sexuality of the subjects.

Not long after, Drs. J. Michael Bailey and Richard Pillard released a research study on twins. After recruiting male homosexual subjects with brothers, they concluded that in 52 percent of identical twins and 22 percent of fraternal twins, both brothers were gay.

But identical twins have the exact same genetic makeup. Thus if one twin is homosexual, and homosexuality is genetic, the other twin must be homosexual 100 percent of the time. Drs. Bailey and Pillard have now conceded that environment must play some role in forming one's sexual orientation, since their own research shows identical twins having different sexual orientation 50 percent of the time.

Similarly information from this study was leaked to the press and subsequently reported as strong scientific evidence that homosexuality is genetic. Yet the studies were not "scientific" because they had yet to be published in a scientific journal and had not undergone the standard scrutiny of the peer review process.

Every study's accuracy and methodology must be validated by other scientists and the results replicated. Failure to allow peer review before publicizing one's work is unscholarly and undermines the integrity of the study.

The most recent "gay gene" report resulted from research led by Dr. Dean Hamer at the federally funded National Cancer Institute. While assigned to research cancer, which kills 540,000 Americans each year, Dr. Hamer and his team spent two years and $419,000 of taxpayers' money trying to find a gay gene.

What Dr. Hamer actually found was a DNA marker on the X chromosome in 64 percent of the homosexual brothers studied. Such a DNA marker would not conclusively make one homosexual; in fact the other 36 percent of the subjects who were homosexual did not share the gene marker.

Because most individuals are not exclusively homosexual throughout their lives, it is impossible to prove that the behavior of homosexuality is a result of biological or genetic factors.

In fact, many homosexuals, believing that theirs is the second sexual revolution, proudly proclaim that they have chosen their sexuality.

So far, no bisexuals have even tried to claim they are genetically inclined to have sex with both men and women. And what about ex-gays? Although the media scoffs at the possibility, there are a significant number of individuals who cease to engage in homosexual activity and instead lead their lives as heterosexuals.

Former homosexuals are subjected to great scorn and ridicule by homosexual activists, presumably because they are the largest proof that all sexual behavior is a matter of choice. What unsubstantiated studies will be next?

II

Those who say homosexuality is not genetic do not know what they are talking about. This statement as far as we know today is absolutely true. It is also absolutely meaningless.

When conservatives say homosexuality is not genetic, what they actually mean to say is homosexuality is chosen, changeable, and pathological.

But as every biologist and geneticist knows, whether a trait, like eye color, is chosen, changeable, or pathological is a completely separate question from what creates it—be it genes, hormones, or any other cause.

Take left-handedness. From decades of clinical observation, we know left-handers (A) don't choose to be left-handed, (B) cannot be made into natural right-handers, even when forced to use their right hands, and (C) suffer no mental pathology or physical illness from their left-handed orientation.

132

But we have no idea what causes left-handedness. Is it genetic? Some people think so; there is clearly a pattern of inheritance and evidence of what is called "genetic loading."

But identical twins, who have the same genes, are both left- or both right-handed only 50 percent of the time. It could be hormonal. Or maybe a combination. We don't know yet.

Is this interesting work scientifically? Very. Is it politically relevant? Not at all. We know from decades of observation what left-handedness is: a natural minority variant (around 8 percent of the population) of the human trait "handedness," a neurological motor orientation having not the slightest thing to do with one's fitness to do a job or vote in an election (although it is relevant to being a professional baseball player).

The fact is that after 50 years of clinical research with homosexuals and heterosexuals, we know virtually the same thing about sexual orientation. No one chooses either orientation, and the mountain of clinical evidence dating from the 1950s demonstrating that there is no more pathology involved in being gay than there is in being straight is universally accepted among serious scientists.

Ill-Conceived Experiments

Can science ever be immune from experiments conceived out of prejudices and stereotypes, conscious or not? (Which is not to suggest that it cannot in discrete areas identify and locate verifiable phenomena in nature.) I await the study that says lesbians have a region of the hypothalamus that resembles straight men and I would not be surprised if, at this very moment, some scientist somewhere is studying brains of deceased Asians to see if they have an enlarged "math region" of the brain.

Kay Diaz, Z, December 1992.

The claims of the reparative therapists are considered laughable, and virtually all reputable clinicians would say that as far as we know from the clinical record one's sexual orientation is as immutable as one's handedness; different behavior can be coerced but from everything we've observed, the interior orientation remains.

We have no idea what causes sexual orientation, heterosexual or homosexual. Is it genetic? Some people think so; pedigree analyses of homosexuality show a classic "genetic-looking" pattern of inheritance and "genetic loading."

But again, identical twins, who have the same genes, are only both gay—or both straight—about 50 percent of the time. Is it

133

hormonal? Could be. Researchers are looking into it.

Interesting science? Fascinating. Politically relevant? Not in the least, because although we don't know if homosexuality is caused by genes, we know what it is: a natural minority (around 5 percent of the population) variant of the human trait "sexual orientation" having nothing to do with one's fitness to do a job or vote in an election.

The position, usually Christian, that homosexuality is a chosen lifestyle and a disease is today absent from serious scientific and clinical debate.

Christian conservatives start with homosexuality from religious belief, by definition antithetical to science. But because this country has historically resolved its debates on the side of objective, empirical evidence—witness the standing Supreme Court opinion on creationism—and against religion when the religious position is held to be merely a reflection of baseless prejudice, Christians know viscerally they must bolster their opposition to homosexuality with science. It is a futile exercise.

In the long run, Christians will have to stand by science or stand by religion. Religion is a better bet. Homosexuality, measured by science, is as clearly not a disease as left-handedness or brown eyes.

But the theological belief that homosexuality is immoral, no one can argue with. The problem with this, we all know, is that while we can legislate against diseases, in this democracy we cannot legislate theology.

Periodical Bibliography

The following articles have been selected to supplement the diverse views presented in this chapter.

Sharon Begley "Does DNA Make Some Men Gay?" *Newsweek*, July 26, 1993.

Dorothee Benz "It's in the Jeans," *Democratic Left*, January/February 1994.

Katie Brown "Gender Outlaws," *Deneuve*, October 1994. Available from FRS Enterprises, 2336 Market St., #15, San Francisco, CA 94114.

Bonnie Bullough and Vern Bullough "The Causes of Homosexuality: A Scientific Update," *Free Inquiry*, Fall 1993.

Jared Diamond "Turning a Man," *Discover*, June 1992.

Kay Diaz "Are Gay Men Born That Way?" *Z Magazine*, December 1992.

Tere Frederickson "What Is Masculinity?/What Is Femininity?," *The Femme Mirror*, Winter 1993. Available from Society for the Second Self, PO Box 194, Tulare, CA 93275.

Richard C. Friedman and Jennifer I. Downey "Homosexuality," *The New England Journal of Medicine*, October 6, 1994.

David Gelman "Born or Bred?" *Newsweek*, February 24, 1992.

Richard M. Levine "Crossing the Line," *Mother Jones*, May/June 1994.

April Martin "Fruits, Nuts, and Chocolate: The Politics of Sexual Identity," *The Harvard Gay and Lesbian Review*, Winter 1994. Available from PO Box 1809, Cambridge, MA 02238.

Heather L. Moore "Preference vs. Orientation," *Off Our Backs*, June 1994.

David Nimmons "Sex and the Brain," *Discover*, March 1994.

Virginia Prince "Nature Made Females . . . Men Made Women," *Cross-Talk*, August 1994. Available from International Foundation for Gender Education, PO Box 367, Wayland, MA 01778.

Darrell Yates Rist "Are Homosexuals Born That Way?" *The Nation*, October 19, 1992.

Harriet Sergeant "Girls Will Be Boys," *The Spectator*, September 17, 1994.

Dick Teresi "How to Get a Man Pregnant," *The New York Times Magazine*, November 27, 1994.

Lindsy Van Gelder "The 'Born That Way' Trap," *Ms.*, May/June 1991.

What Constitutes Normal Sexual Behavior?

HUMAN
SEXUALITY

Chapter Preface

In the summer of 1994, at the nineteenth annual Michigan Womyn's Music Festival, dissension broke out between two groups of lesbians: those who endorse consensual sadomasochistic sex and those who oppose any type of sexual violence, including sadomasochism. Protesters demonstrated during the performance of an all-woman punk band that, they felt, overtly promoted violent sexual behavior; other concertgoers sneered at the protesters, expressing their disgust at what they believed was an attempt at censorship. The conflict at the music festival reflected an ongoing dispute between the sadomasochist faction, which argues that lesbians should support the exploration of all facets of lesbian sexuality, and their opponents, who characterize sadomasochistic sex as violent, abusive, and abnormal. This struggle to establish categories of acceptable and unacceptable sexual behavior within the lesbian community, however, appears utterly pointless to those people who regard *all* homosexual behavior as abnormal.

In many respects, the normality of sexual behavior is in the eye of the beholder. Some individuals enjoy sexual acts that others find disturbing or disgusting, and the assessment of these sexual acts as normal or abnormal may depend entirely on who is doing the assessing. Why then, one might wonder, do people even care about the sexual proclivities of others? Why not just live and let live, each according to his or her own preference?

One primary reason for these attempts to categorize normal and abnormal sexual behavior is that such behavior can greatly affect society. In the United States, for example, estimates of the number of active prostitutes range from 100,000 to 500,000. Prostitution is illegal in all states except Nevada, and the average cost of the arrest, court hearings, and incarceration of one prostitute is two thousand dollars. Should prostitution be recognized as normal sexual behavior and therefore legalized, advocates argue, the nation could save millions of dollars. In addition, they aver, legalizing prostitution would result in improved working conditions for prostitutes and the removal of the stigma surrounding prostitution.

However, those who believe prostitution is abnormal sexual behavior point to the high levels of drug abuse and violence among prostitutes. Opponents of legalized prostitution also argue that it would encourage the breakup of the family and would further the spread of AIDS and other sexually transmitted diseases. Although the two sides do not agree as to whether prostitution is normal or not, each is concerned with the ways in which this particular sexual behavior affects the structure of society and the welfare of individual citizens. The following chapter focuses on the debates surrounding the normality or abnormality of homosexuality, pornography, prostitution, and sexual addiction.

"Homosexuality . . . is nothing to be ashamed of, no vice, no degradation."

Homosexuality Is Normal Sexual Behavior

Carlton Cornett

Carlton Cornett is a psychotherapist and the author of *Affirmative Dynamic Psychotherapy with Gay Men*. In the following viewpoint, Cornett examines the history of the belief that homosexuality stems from a psychological disorder. Cornett maintains that this belief was based on prejudice and faulty research; therefore, he concludes, the 1973 decision by the American Psychiatric Association (APA) to remove homosexuality from its list of mental disorders was appropriate. Arguing that psychologists' efforts to change homosexual orientation have had little success, Cornett urges his colleagues instead to validate the sexuality of their gay clients.

As you read, consider the following questions:

1. What is the central premise of the reparative therapy movement, in Cornett's view?
2. According to Cornett, what are two popular ways in which homosexuality is defined?
3. According to Ronald Bayer, cited by the author, what are three possible reasons that some psychiatrists might have voted against homosexuality's removal from the APA's list of mental disorders?

The so-called reparative therapy movement focuses on a central premise: that homosexuals are psychologically sick and should be cured for the sake of both themselves and society. It is fascinating that psychotherapy, a process founded upon compassion and a desire to relieve human suffering, can be the vehicle by which much suffering is promulgated upon gay men and lesbians in America through attempts to change their sexual orientation.

An American Belief

The vehement belief that homosexuality is a form of emotional illness is predominantly an American phenomenon. Ronald Bayer, in *Homosexuality and American Psychiatry: The Politics of Diagnosis*, cites a letter written by Sigmund Freud in 1935 to an American mother who wanted her son "cured" of his homosexuality: "Homosexuality is assuredly no advantage, but it is nothing to be ashamed of, no vice, no degradation, it cannot be classified as an illness." Freud believed that psychological functioning could be understood in all its rich complexities but did not believe that all development outside the cultural norms of Europe constituted psychopathology. Freud strongly supported the decriminalization of homosexuality and encouraged psychoanalytic institutes to accept homosexual students.

In the United States, psychoanalysis developed differently than in Europe. Here it was almost exclusively a medical specialty. Only recently have psychoanalytic institutes been fully opened to mental health practitioners who are not medically trained. With the emphasis on psychoanalysts being medically trained came an emphasis on diagnosis. Psychoanalysts wanted the standing that other physicians were afforded. To gain that standing they needed to be seen as treating tangible diseases. Freud lamented, "America is a mistake, a giant mistake!"

This American emphasis on diagnosis led to the labeling of all development outside the white, middle-class, heterosexual norm as pathological. However, it also gave birth to at least one major problem of practicality: how to reach uniform agreement in understanding these psychological "diseases." A system was developed whereby psychiatric diagnoses gain legitimacy through a vote of the American Psychiatric Association, or APA. Reparative therapists complain that homosexuality was dropped from the official list of APA mental disorders in 1973 for political and not scientific reasons, but all psychiatric diagnoses essentially originate or end through the "scientific" process of the APA vote.

Little Success

Homosexuality was an easy target for diagnosis and became a concern of several American analysts. Their attempts to change sexual orientation, however, have been noteworthy mostly for their lack of success. In *The Psychoanalytic Theory of Male Homosexuality*, Kenneth Lewes reviews the literature regarding psychoanalytic attempts to change male homosexuals into heterosexuals. He notes that in 10 influential papers written on the topic, only five cases demonstrated a change in sexual orientation.

Psychoanalytic Bugaboos

Nobody knows what "causes" homosexuality any more than they know what "causes" heterosexuality. (Of course, there is far less interest in what causes the latter.) Overtly, the old psychoanalytic bugaboos are dead: there is no evidence, according to the Kinsey Institute, that male homosexuality is caused by dominant mothers and/or weak fathers, or that female homosexuality is caused by girls' having exclusively male role models. Furthermore, children who are raised by gay and lesbian couples are no more likely to be homosexual than children of heterosexual couples. Nor do people become adult homosexuals because they were seduced by older people or went to same-sex boarding schools. . . .

Though the causes of sexual orientation are unknown and the definitions fluid, the likelihood of converting a homosexual to a heterosexual orientation, or vice versa, is very slight. Some homosexual men and women voluntarily come for therapy to change from same-sex to opposite-sex partners, but it is not clear whether the limited "success" rate refers to a change in their feelings and the pattern of their desire, or just in their ability to consciously restrict their sexual contact to members of the opposite sex.

Patricia Hersch, *The Family Therapy Networker*, January/February 1991.

In 1962, Irving Bieber published *Homosexuality*, the results of a study conducted by the New York Society of Medical Psychoanalysts during the 1950s. The data showed that of 72 patients who were exclusively homosexual at the beginning of treatment, 57 percent remained unchanged, while 19 percent became bisexual and 19 percent exclusively heterosexual. When the results for those who began treatment as homosexuals were combined with the results among those who began as bisexuals, it was possible to state that 27 percent had shifted to exclusive heterosexuality. Bieber concluded that "a heterosexual shift is a possibility for all homosexuals who are strongly motivated to change."

By contrast, the success rate for psychotherapy involving other kinds of problems is much higher. In a recent study of psychotherapy outcome reported in *U.S. News & World Report*, Kenneth Howard of Northwestern University found that after six months of therapy, 75 percent of more than 2,000 patients undergoing treatment for a variety of psychological complaints showed improvement.

The dismal success rate in modifying sexual orientation may be related to the fact that one fundamental element traditionally has been absent from discussions of sexual orientation change: a lack of uniformity in defining what constitutes homosexuality. There are, of course, a variety of ways to define homosexuality. Two of the most popular focus on overt behavior or self-identification.

The difficulty of either measure is that many men whose behavior is clearly homosexual refuse to label themselves as such, while a number of self-described homosexuals occasionally have heterosexual relationships.

Richard Isay, a psychoanalyst and clinical professor of psychiatry at Cornell University, has proposed that the most important element in defining homosexuality is the orientation of the individual's fantasy life. The introduction of this element affords respect to the complex nature of human sexuality and also poses an important question regarding reparative therapy: Has there ever been even one true change in sexual orientation as a result of psychotherapy? We know that some individuals have changed their behavior, but has their fundamental yearning for members of their own sex, expressed through their fantasies, been changed? I have never seen this happen and doubt that sexual-orientation-change therapies would demonstrate any success if fantasy orientation change defined sexual orientation change.

The APA Controversy

Heated controversy about even the most basic issues involved in understanding homosexuality intensified in 1970, when the APA held its annual convention in San Francisco. The APA was met by gay rights activists who disrupted meetings and denounced participants such as Bieber and Charles Socarides, another strong voice for the view that homosexuality represents a profound psychopathology.

By 1972, however, at the APA convention in Dallas, the issues surrounding homosexuality were discussed more in convention meetings and less through demonstrations. Conference participants discussed the work of researchers such as Evelyn Hooker, a psychologist who had done rigorous research on homosexuality and concluded that it is not inherently pathological.

Many participants had the same experience that Judd Marmor, later president of the APA, had in 1956 when he first heard Hooker's results. Marmor relates in Eric Marcus's book *Making History* that initially he was unwilling to accept Hooker's contention that homosexuals are no more pathological than heterosexuals. However, as he continued to review her work, his perspective changed.

142

For the Dallas APA participants, there was, in addition to Hooker's research, a 1972 report on homosexuality by a National Institute of Mental Health task force declaring that the primary difficulty inherent in homosexuality is the injustice and rejection homosexuals suffer because "they live in a culture in which homosexuality is considered maladaptive and opprobrious." Like Marmor, many of the APA members concluded that the mental health professions were doing a disservice to homosexuals by attempting to change them.

In 1973, the APA's board of trustees voted to delete homosexuality from the official list of mental disorders. Socarides and Bieber maintained that gay political pressure had swayed the board, and they asked for an APA referendum on the issue. This was held in 1974, and 58 percent of the more than 10,000 psychiatrists responding voted to uphold the board's decision. Bieber and Socarides clearly were not in the majority in believing homosexuality to be inherently pathological.

While many, including Socarides, continue to claim that the board's decision and the membership's vote were influenced only by political considerations and the gay rights lobby, there is little evidence to support this.

Although gay lobbying may have affected the deliberations and ultimate vote of the board, it was probably not decisive in the national referendum. The gay rights movement, still in its infancy, had neither the financial resources nor the personnel to influence the outcome of this vote.

Reasons for Opposition

Bayer cites three possible reasons why some psychiatrists and psychoanalysts may have voted against the removal of homosexuality from the list of mental disorders. First, some members may have been unfamiliar with research literature on homosexuality, which is overwhelmingly supportive of the position that homosexuality is a healthy variant of human sexuality. Second, many who voiced opposition to depathologizing homosexuality may have been motivated by self-interest. Insurance reimbursement is dependent on a diagnosis. The more diagnoses available, the more reimbursement potential. Similarly, the higher the percentage of the population that can be considered to have a psychiatric disorder, the larger the potential pool of patients. Finally, the APA at that time was a largely conservative body, and the removal of homosexuality as a diagnosis was seen as a threatening liberal social action. Lewes proposes that for some, such as Socarides, the issue took on a very personal aspect that did not easily allow moving away from a conviction, even in the face of evidence contradicting it.

Twenty years later [1993], each of these reasons still has validity as one looks at opposition to viewing homosexuality as healthy and functional. (In *Making History*, Marmor estimates that perhaps one-third of American psychiatrists and one-half of American psychoanalysts still view homosexuality negatively.) However, there are a number of organizations that focus on changing sexual orientation, and many of them are staffed by individuals who have struggled with suppressing their own homosexuality. For some, the impetus for "repairing" other homosexual people may lie in an externalization of their own shame and self-hatred. . . .

The Cloak of Science

Socarides, writing in the *Journal of Psychohistory* in 1992, continued to oppose viewing homosexuals as healthy: "Some . . . say that homosexuals are healthy, society is sick and that science should cure society. Others raise false or outdated scientific issues in their war with traditional values." He employs the cloak of "science" and the language of psychoanalysis to argue for maintenance of the status quo. It is a position that seems founded on a fear of what might happen if traditional values (as he defines them) are replaced by values he does not understand.

Joseph Nicolosi and the National Association for the Research and Therapy of Homosexuality (the membership of which numbers about 150 in a field of more than 100,000 practitioners) propose that some homosexuals want to be heterosexual and should be allowed to change. When I hear this I am reminded of Freud's understated observation that "homosexuality is assuredly no advantage" in our culture. A gay person can be denied employment, housing, promotion, child custody, health insurance and a long list of other rights and privileges taken for granted by most other U.S. citizens.

Homosexuals are the only minority group in the country that cannot be assured even of family support. Most of us who are homosexual have been unhappy being "different" at some point or another. The facts are, however, that psychotherapy cannot change one's sexual orientation, and attempts to change sexual orientation increase the shame a homosexual feels and undermine his self-esteem. Such attempts alienate a person from the genuine feelings, wishes and desires that form the true self.

The Committee on Lesbian and Gay Issues of the National Association of Social Workers, or NASW, which represents the largest mental health profession in the country, protested in a 1992 position statement "efforts to 'convert' people through irresponsible therapies which can more accurately be called brainwashing, shaming, or coercion."

The committee further took the position that "the assumptions and directions of reparative therapies are theoretically and morally wrong" and that use of reparative therapies is a violation of the NASW Code of Ethics.

Dignity

Perhaps a better answer to the dilemmas society poses to homosexuals is to work toward ensuring that they are treated with the dignity and respect afforded all other citizens. . . . We must also work toward validating homosexual relationships; we must educate our children to be tolerant and to value all people.

Psychotherapists can empower their gay patients to discard their self-hatred and fear. By supporting them as they cast off their shame, the psychotherapists would then see them positively influence the world around them, making it safer and more accepting for the next homosexual.

If we as a culture truly embraced the idea that all people are equal and deserving of equal treatment and that psychotherapists should affirm their homosexual patients rather than try to prove an innate pathology, there would be no vulnerability to unrealistic promises of sexual orientation change. Indeed, there would be no interest in changing sexual orientation.

"Many [psychiatrists] still privately express the opinion that homosexual development is not normal."

Homosexuality Is Not Normal Sexual Behavior

Sy Rogers and Alan Medinger

In the following viewpoint, Sy Rogers and Alan Medinger contend that homosexual orientation is a sexual dysfunction that originates in early childhood difficulties and that can be cured by psychotherapy. The 1973 ruling of the American Psychiatric Association that removed homosexuality from its list of psychological disorders was forced by gay political organizations, the authors argue, and did not reflect the findings of psychiatric research. Rogers and Medinger conclude that reorientation from homosexuality to heterosexuality is highly successful among homosexuals who wish to change. Medinger is the director of Regeneration, a Christian ministry to persons struggling with homosexuality. Rogers is a worldwide lecturer on homosexuality and a Christian missionary based in Singapore.

As you read, consider the following questions:

1. What four claims for the normality of homosexuality do the authors contest?
2. What statistics do Rogers and Medinger quote to support their argument that homosexuality does not contribute to psychological well being?
3. According to Elizabeth Moberly, cited by the authors, what is the psychological cause of homosexual orientation?

Sy Rogers and Alan Medinger, *Homosexuality and the Truth*, a 1991 publication of Exodus International. (The original publication includes endnotes omitted in the present rendition.) Reprinted by permission.

For many years the politically-active segment of the gay community has effectively used the media as a means to change society's attitudes about homosexuality. In some ways, this has been helpful in curbing mistreatment of homosexuals.

However, for the purpose of social "legitimization" of homosexuality (attained through political and religious systems), the gay community has also disseminated much questionable information.

Is Homosexuality Normal?

They have attempted to convince society that homosexuality is innate, unchangeable, and a normal variable in the spectrum of human sexuality. If this is true, then homosexuals would be deserving of minority status, entitled to the rights and protection of other legitimate minority groups.

Rather than speculate on what that could mean, let's instead ask if the pro-homosexual message is based on truth.

Are their claims legitimate? The following is a compilation of responses to the most common pro-gay arguments.

#1. "Some people are meant to be gay—they're born gay."

Nothing has been published and gained wide acceptance in the scientific and medical communities to indicate that homosexuality is primarily genetic or otherwise prenatally determined.

One of the most widely recognized authorities on the subject is John W. Money, Ph.D., a professor at the Johns Hopkins School of Medicine, and Director of the Psychohormonal Research Institute.

In an article in *Perspectives in Human Sexuality*, he states: "Whatever may be the possible unlearned assistance from constitutional sources, the child's psychosexual identity is not written, unlearned, in the genetic code, the hormonal system or the nervous system at birth."

A psychiatrist who has written and spoken widely on the subject of homosexuality, Dr. Charles W. Socarides, of the Albert Einstein College of Medicine in New York, says this: "Homosexuality, the choice of a partner of the same sex for orgastic satisfaction, is not innate. There is no connection between sexual instinct and the choice of sexual object.

"Such an object choice is learned, acquired behavior; there is no inevitable genetically inborn propensity toward the choice of a partner of either the same or opposite sex."

Finally, we have the opinions of William H. Masters and Virginia E. Johnson, the most widely-known authorities in the field of human sexual behavior. In one of their books, they write: "The genetic theory of homosexuality has been generally discarded today. Despite the interest in possible hormone mechanisms in the origin of homosexuality, no serious scientist today suggests that a simple cause-effect relationship applies."

#2. "Homosexuals can't change—and to suggest they try is unrealistic, even harmful."

Again, some of the most prominent specialists in this field disagree.

Dr. Reuben Fine, director for the New York Center for Psychoanalytic Training, says in his 1987 publication, *Psychoanalytic Theory, Male and Female Homosexuality: Psychological Approaches*: "I have recently had occasion to review the result of psychotherapy with homosexuals, and been surprised by the finds.

"It is paradoxical that even though politically active homosexual groups deny the possibility of change, all studies from Schrenck-Notzing on have found positive effects, virtually regardless of the kind of treatment used . . . a considerable percentage of overt homosexuals became heterosexual. . . .

"If the patients were motivated, whatever procedure is adopted, a large percentage will give up their homosexuality.

"In this connection, public information is of the greatest importance. The misinformation spread by certain circles that homosexuality is untreatable by psychotherapy does incalculable harm to thousands of men and women."

Homosexuality Is Curable

Dr. Robert Kronemeyer in his 1980 book, *Overcoming Homosexuality:* "For those homosexuals who are unhappy with their life and find effective therapy, it is 'curable.'"

"The homosexual's real enemy is . . . his ignorance of the possibility that he can be helped," says Dr. Edmund Bergler in his book, *Homosexuality: Disease or Way of Life?*

"The major challenge in treating homosexuality from the point of view of the patient's resistance has, of course, been the misconception that the disorder is innate or inborn," writes Dr. Charles Socarides in his text, "Homosexuality," in the *American Handbook of Psychiatry*.

Here is what Dr. Irving Bieber and his colleagues conclude: "The therapeutic results of our study provide reason for an optimistic outlook. Many homosexuals became exclusively heterosexual in psychoanalytic treatment. Although this change may be more easily accomplished by some than others, in our judgment, a heterosexual shift is a possibility for all homosexuals who are strongly motivated to change."

Bieber states 17 years later, in 1979: "We have followed some patients for as long as ten years who have remained exclusively heterosexual."

Dr. Lawrence J. Hatterer says in *Changing Homosexuality in the Male*: "I've heard of hundreds of other men who went from a homosexual to a heterosexual adjustment on their own."

Even Masters and Johnson report in their 1979 book, *Homo-*

sexuality in Perspective, that the success rate in 81 gays desiring reorientation (after a six-year follow-up), is 71.6%.

"No longer should the qualified psychotherapist avoid the responsibility of either accepting the homosexual client treatment or referring him or her to an acceptable treatment source."

Injustices

The removal of homosexuality from the category of aberrancy by the American Psychiatric Association in 1973 . . . was naively perceived by many psychiatrists as the "simple" elimination of a scientific diagnosis in order to correct injustices. In reality, it created injustices for the homosexual and his family, as it belied the truth and prevented the homosexual from seeking and receiving help. . . .

It is the individual homosexual wishing to change who suffers the most.

Young men and women with relatively minor sexual fears are led with equanimity by some psychiatrists and nonmedical counselors into a self-despising pattern and lifestyle. Adolescents, nearly all of whom experience some degree of uncertainty as to sexual identity, are discouraged from assuming that one form of gender identity is preferable to another. Those persons who already have a homosexual problem are discouraged from finding their way out of self-destructive fantasy—discouraged from learning to accept themselves as male or female, discouraged from all those often painful but necessary courses that allow us to function as reasonable and participating individuals in a cooperating society.

Charles W. Socarides, *The Washington Times*, July 5, 1994.

#3. "Homosexuality is no longer considered a mental disorder."
The gay community claimed a great victory when they prevailed upon the American Psychiatric Association (APA) to remove homosexuality from the *Diagnostic and Statistical Manual of Mental Disorders*, its listing of psychological disorders.

This highly controversial action seems to fly in the face of the evidence of any commonsense definition of psychological well-being. Consider the following:

- Homosexual men are six times more likely to have attempted suicide than heterosexual men.
- Studies indicate that between 25% and 33% of homosexual men and women are alcoholics, compared to a 7% figure for the general population.
- Statistics give evidence of widespread sexual compulsion among homosexual men. A major Alfred C. Kinsey study revealed that 43% of the homosexual men surveyed estimated

that they had had sex with 500 or more partners; 28% with 1,000 or more partners. Either the APA is ignorant of what homosexuality entails for vast numbers of men, or their view of healthy sexuality indicates a serious disorder among members of the APA.

- The same Kinsey study revealed that homosexual men have to a great extent separated sexuality from relationship. The survey showed 79% of the respondents saying that over half of their sexual partners were strangers. Seventy percent said that over half of their sexual partners were people with whom they had sex only once. Surely this is an indication of either deep dissatisfaction, or else terribly destructive hedonism.

We *do* need to address the statement that the difficulties suffered by homosexuals are all a result of society's prejudice and unwillingness to support stable gay relationships. We can address this on several points:

- In areas where there is the greatest acceptance of homosexuality (San Francisco, West Hollywood, New York City), the detrimental effects don't decrease; they increase.
- Over the past 20 years, there has been a great increase in the acceptance of homosexuality, but during the same period, there has been a huge increase in homosexual suffering due to disease and other factors.
- For many years, society did not condone heterosexual sexual involvement outside of marriage. As far as we know, this did not force the people so inclined into greater sexual promiscuity, higher rates of alcoholism, suicide, and disease.

Disagreement

Additionally, *many* therapists disagree with the 1973 APA ruling that dropped homosexuality from its list of psychological disorders. Why?

Over 75 years of psychoanalytic knowledge underscoring homosexuality as a disorder was disregarded. Experts who viewed homosexuality as a disorder were pointedly left off the National Institute of Mental Health task force studying this issue. Others were silenced or disregarded.

Militant homosexual groups began disrupting numerous scientific programs and conferences in the early- to mid-1970s, including the APA and its meetings.

Gay political groups especially targeted and disrupted national and local meetings in which the psychopathology and treatment of homosexuality were being debated. . . .

Two hundred and forty-three practitioners and members of the APA petitioned for a referendum to vote on a reversal of the ruling. That vote occurred in April 1974 in which 40% of the voters disagreed with the ruling, asserting that there were no legitimate scientific reasons for the APA's change in fundamental psychiatric theory.

Late in 1977, 68% of the American Medical Association psychiatrists responding to a poll still viewed homosexuality as a pathological adaptation as opposed to a normal variation.

Dr. Joseph Nicolosi, in the February 1989 issue of *The California Psychologist*, said, "Many members of our profession still privately express the opinion that homosexual development is not normal. The 1973 APA ruling did not resolve the issue—it simply silenced 80 years of psychoanalytic observation."

#4. "I didn't choose to be gay."

"The homosexual has no choice as regards his or her sexual object," says Dr. Charles Socarides. "The condition is unconsciously determined, is differentiated from the behavior of a person who deliberately engages in same-sex sexual contact due to situational factors or a desire for variational experiences.

"These constitute non-clinical forms of homosexual behavior. The nuclear core of true homosexuality is never a conscious choice, an act of will; but rather it is determined from the earliest period of childhood, in terms of origin of course, not in practice."

Same-Sex Deficit

Dr. Elizabeth Moberly of Cambridge, England, author of two clinical books regarding origins and treatment of homosexuality, believes that it is important to see the homosexual condition as involving a same-sex developmental deficit, resulting in an insecure identity which cripples same-sex relationships.

Due to some early difficulty, especially with the same-sex parent—such as separation or emotional unavailability—there remains an unmet need for love and identification, together with a half-hidden sense of hurt or grievance, toward members of the same sex.

Dr. Moberly believes the path toward growth and change requires a same-sex therapist who will help the homosexual to build a more secure identity through fulfilling legitimate relational needs in healthy nonsexual ways and through resolving same-sex hurts and conflicts from the past.

Dr. Moberly concludes that realistic heterosexual relating becomes possible when same-sex issues have been addressed.

We recognize that many are content to pursue their homosexual orientation and the related lifestyle. However, many other homosexually-oriented persons do not wish to have their lives defined or determined by this inclination.

We live in a nation famous for our premise of self-determination. Those who are unhappy with their homosexuality have the right to explore their clinically-valid option of impulse control and orientational change.

"If one asks if porn is responsible for or causes any sex crimes, the answer is unequivocally in the affirmative."

Pornography Use Results in Abnormal Sexual Behavior

Victor B. Cline

Victor B. Cline is a psychotherapist specializing in sexual addictions and the author of numerous books, including *Where Do You Draw the Line? Explorations in Media Violence, Pornography, and Censorship.* In the following viewpoint, Cline maintains that the use of pornography leads to addictive behavior, unhealthy sexual relationships, and sexual deviation. Exposure to mild pornography eventually leads a person to search out more explicit and hard-core material and even to act out deviant behaviors seen in pornography, Cline argues. Furthermore, Cline writes, even if pornography users do not become involved in criminal sexual behavior, their intimate relationships will suffer as a result of their increasing addiction to porn.

As you read, consider the following questions:

1. What are the four factors of the pornography syndrome, in Cline's opinion?
2. According to the author, what are the adverse effects that pornography has on a marriage?
3. What types of sexual addictions can a pornography user become "locked into," according to Cline?

Excerpted from Victor B. Cline, *Pornography's Effects on Adults and Children*, a publication of Morality in Media. (The original publication includes endnotes omitted in the present rendition.) Reprinted with permission.

As a clinical psychologist, I have treated, over many years, approximately 300 sex addicts, sex offenders, or other individuals (96% male) with sexual illnesses. This includes many types of unwanted compulsive sexual acting-out, plus such things as child molestation, exhibitionism, voyeurism, sadomasochism, fetishism, and rape. With only several exceptions, pornography has been a major or minor contributor or facilitator in the acquisition of their deviation or sexual addiction.

However, where pornography was a contributor or facilitator, regardless of the nature of the sex deviation or addiction, I found a four-factor syndrome common to nearly all of my clients, with almost no exceptions, especially in their early involvement with pornography.

Addiction

The first change that happened was an addiction effect. The porn-consumers got hooked. Once involved in pornographic materials, they kept coming back for more and still more. The material seemed to provide a very powerful sexual stimulant or aphrodisiac effect, followed by sexual release, most often through masturbation. The pornography provided very exciting and powerful imagery which they frequently recalled to mind and elaborated on in their fantasies.

Once addicted, they could not throw off their dependence on the material by themselves, despite many negative consequences such as divorce, loss of family, and problems with the law (as with sexual assault, harassment or abuse of fellow employees).

I also found, anecdotally, that many of my most intelligent male patients appeared to be the most vulnerable — perhaps because they had a greater capacity to fantasize, which heightened the intensity of the experience and made them more susceptible to being conditioned into an addiction.

While any male is vulnerable, attorneys, accountants and media people seemed, in my experience, most vulnerable to these addictions. This is simply an anecdotal impression.

However, Sgt. Bob Navarro, a longtime investigator of the porno industry with the Los Angeles Police Department, has commented,

> Believe it or not, the higher their education, the more prone these people are to becoming addicted to this material, and, of course, the more money they have to spend on it. . . . Many people have testified as to their extreme addiction to the material in terms of having their whole lives consumed by it: sitting for hours masturbating to adult material and needing progressively stronger, heavier, harder material to give them a bigger kick. Like an alcoholic or a drug addict they are looking for that big kick and they need more just to keep them at that level of feeling "OK."

One of my patients was so deeply addicted that he could not stay away from pornography for 90 days, even for $1,000. It is difficult for non-addicts to comprehend the totally driven nature of a sex addict. When the "wave" hits them, nothing can stand in the way of getting what they want, whether that be pornography accompanied by masturbation, sex from a prostitute, molesting a child, or raping a woman.

Unable to Stop

An example might help illustrate this problem. Ralph was a sexual addict, married 12 years with three children. He was active in his church and held sincere, high moral principles. He believed in the Ten Commandments and opposed adultery. Yet his particular cycle involved pornography use, followed by paid sex with prostitutes. After each incident, he begged God for forgiveness and swore that it would never happen again. But it did, again and again.

Since the trigger of each adulterous act was pornography use, we decided to try to free him from his dependence on this material. I asked him to write me a check for $1,000, indicating that I would return it if he went 90 days without using pornography. Ralph loved to hang on to his money and was quite attracted to our strategy. "There's no way I'd look at dirty videos or magazines if I knew it would cost me a thousand dollars!" he said.

Porn's Devastating Effects

While we know that porn addicts are 40 percent more likely to commit a sex crime than nonaddicts, there are other effects that also have devastating effects on our society. Men who use porn lose faith in marriage and commitment; are more likely to have extramarital affairs and to visit prostitutes; would give lighter sentences to convicted rapists; and develop a belief that perversions are more common than they really are ("everyone's doing it"). Porn addicts' wives tell of feeling cheated on, and being led to engage in more deviant sex acts. Not surprisingly, such marriages often end in divorce.

Patty McEntee, *The Wanderer*, April 11, 1991.

He managed to resist temptation remarkably well for a while. But on the 87th day, he drove past an "adult" bookstore in an unfamiliar city while on a business trip. He slammed on the brakes, entered the store, and went virtually berserk for 90 minutes. When I saw him the following week, he tearfully confessed that he had lost his $1,000. Since he had gone 87 days "sober," I decided to give him another chance.

So we started another 90-day "sobriety" cycle. We both felt that if he could go 87 days, he could certainly make 90 if we tried again, especially if it meant recovering his $1,000.

This time he went only 14 days before he relapsed. He lost his money, which was given to a charity. He was extremely committed to quit in order to save his marriage and to live in harmony with his religious principles. But that was not the case. In my opinion, even if he had given me $10,000, he still would have relapsed. When the wave hits them, these men are consumed by their appetite, regardless of the costs or consequences. Their addiction virtually rules their lives.

Escalation

The second phase was an escalation effect. With the passage of time, the addicted required rougher, more explicit, more deviant, and "kinky" kinds of sexual material to get their "highs" and "sexual turn-ons." It was reminiscent of individuals afflicted with drug addictions. Over time there is nearly always an increasing need for more of the stimulant to get the same initial effect.

If their wives or girlfriends were involved with them, they eventually pushed their partners into doing increasingly bizarre and deviant sexual activities. In many cases, this resulted in a rupture in the relationship when the woman refused to go further—often leading to much conflict, separation or divorce.

Being married or being in a relationship with a willing sexual partner did not solve their problem. Their addiction and escalation were mainly due to the powerful sexual imagery in their minds, implanted there by the exposure to pornography. They often preferred this sexual imagery, accompanied by masturbation, to sexual intercourse itself. This nearly always diminished their capacity to love and express affection to their partner in their intimate relations. The fantasy was all-powerful, much to the chagrin and disappointment of their partner. Their sex drive had been diverted to a degree away from their spouse. And the spouse could easily sense this, and often felt very lonely and rejected.

I have had a number of couple-clients where the wife tearfully reported that her husband preferred to masturbate to pornography than to make love to her.

The third phase that happened was desensitization. Material (in books, magazines or film/videos) which was originally perceived as shocking, taboo-breaking, illegal, repulsive or immoral, though still sexually arousing, in time came to be seen as acceptable and commonplace. The sexual activity depicted in the pornography (no matter how antisocial or deviant) became legitimized. There was increasingly a sense that "everybody does it" and this gave them permission to also do it, even though the activity was possibly illegal and contrary to their previous moral beliefs and personal standards.

Acting Out

The fourth phase that occurred was an increasing tendency to act out sexually the behaviors viewed in the pornography that the porn consumers had been repeatedly exposed to, including compulsive promiscuity, exhibitionism, group sex, voyeurism, frequenting massage parlors, having sex with minor children, rape, and inflicting pain on themselves or a partner during sex. This behavior frequently grew into a sexual addiction which they found themselves locked into and unable to change or reverse— no matter what the negative consequences were in their life.

Many examples of negative effects from pornography use come from the private or clinical practice of psychotherapists, physicians, counselors, attorneys, and ministers. Here we come face to face with real people who are in some kind of significant trouble or pain. A few examples might illustrate this.

The 46-year-old Deputy Mayor of the City of Los Angeles attended a west L.A. porn theater one afternoon a few years ago. While watching the sex film, he became so aroused that he started to sexually assault a patron sitting next to him. The individual turned out to be an undercover city vice-squad officer. The Deputy Mayor was arrested, booked, and found guilty in a subsequent trial. This distinguished public servant left the office shamed and humiliated, his career in shambles.

A 36-year-old married male, college-educated, a professional and very successful financially, had an addiction to pornography, masturbation and frequenting massage parlors where he had paid sex. He had an excellent marriage, four children and was very active in his church, where he assumed important positions of responsibility. While he felt guilty about his engagement in illicit sex, which was contrary to his religious, ethic, and personal values and had the potential of seriously disturbing his marriage if found out, he compulsively continued to do that which, at a rational level, he did not want to do.

His problem came to light when he infected his wife with a venereal disease. This created many serious and disturbing consequences in his life and marriage. . . .

I was asked to consult on a case where a Phoenix-Tucson area professional person, president of his firm and head of his church's committee on helping troubled children, was found to be a serial rapist who had violently raped a number of women at gun or knife-point in the Arizona area. In doing the background study on him, I found him to come from an exemplary background and trouble-free childhood. He was an outstanding student in high school and college.

His wife, children, business, and church associates had not the slightest inkling of his double life or dark side. The only significant negative factor in his life was an early adolescent addiction to pornography which, for the most part, was kept secret from others. This gradually escalated over a period of years, eventually leading to spending many hours and incurring great expense in "adult" bookstores, looking at violent video-porn movies and masturbating to these.

His first rape was triggered by seeing a close resemblance in the woman he assaulted to the leading character in a porn movie he had seen earlier in the day. Reality and fantasy had become extremely blurred for him as he acted out his pathological sexual fantasies.

Consequences of Porn

However, in my clinical experience, the major consequence of being addicted to pornography is not the probability or possibility of committing a serious sex crime (though this can and does occur), but rather its disturbance of the fragile bonds of intimate family and marital relationships. This is where the most grievous pain, damage, and sorrow occurs. There is repeatedly an interference with or even destruction of healthy love and sexual relationships with long-term bonded partners. If one asks if porn is responsible for or causes any sex crimes, the answer is unequivocally in the affirmative, but that is only the "tip of the iceberg."

In some patients, I find that there is an almost instant addiction, while with others, it may take 5-10 years of erratic exposure to get hooked. But, like a latent cancer, it almost never disappears on its own or reverses its course unless there is some therapeutic intervention.

"Almost all men have used [pornography] . . . and a surprisingly large proportion of women too."

Pornography Use Does Not Result in Abnormal Sexual Behavior

Martyn Harris

Pornography use is normal and commonplace sexual behavior that does not necessarily lead to sexual deviation, Martyn Harris argues in the following viewpoint. Focusing on Great Britain, Harris contends that, although some hard-core and violent pornography exists, it is not readily available and is not used by the majority of pornography consumers. Harris insists that British mainstream soft-core pornography (similar to U.S. publications such as *Playboy*) is harmless, if not outright boring. Harris is a frequent contributor to the *Spectator*, a weekly British newsmagazine.

As you read, consider the following questions:

1. What was Harris's main conclusion about the pornography industry after his reporting work in Soho?
2. On what basis does the author consider mainstream pornography boring?
3. According to Harris, how do law enforcement agencies such as the Obscene Publications Squad benefit from public alarm over pornography?

Martyn Harris, "Porn Is a Yawn," *The Spectator*, December 10, 1994. Reprinted by permission.

Twenty years ago, when I was still a student, I was browsing in W.H. Smith when I noticed a man behaving oddly. He was standing in front of the angling papers, snatching furtive glances at the porn mags on the top shelf. Eventually he seized a *Hustler* or a *Rustler*; folded it with the booze ad outwards, paid the cashier with the exact change, and bolted, head down, from the shop. So far, so normal, except for me—because the man was my bank manager, the same tweedy and fatherly figure who scolded me every end of term for my £25 overdraft. It was one of the epiphanies of life: a flare of understanding which lit a dozen miserable, guilty corners. Everybody did it! If my bank manager bought *Hustler*, then so must the butcher and baker and Kwik-Kopy maker. I was ordinary after all.

Everyone Does It

Men become more honest with each other as they get older, and there has been plenty of confirmation of my belated adolescent insight over the years. One friend (a physics PhD and now a Treasury civil servant) kept an enormous stack of *Penthouses* under his bed. A liberal and feminist art lecturer preferred *Rustler* for its pioneering work with readers' wives. A financial journalist eschewed pictorial porn for the literary variety, with half a shelf filled with *A Man with a Maid, The Story of O, Emmanuelle*, and even, heaven help us, *The Adventures of a Window Cleaner*. I make these squalid revelations because they are an essential preamble to any honest discussion of pornography. Almost all men have used it, in times of loneliness or unrequited lust, and a surprisingly large proportion of women too. Nobody admits to it but everyone does it. Porn magazines sell 20 million copies a year in the United Kingdom: the curious thing is that nobody ever buys them.

I have written about the porn industry several times. When I worked for *New Society* in the early 1980s, I became that magazine's man in the dirty raincoat for a while, scouring Soho [an area of London] for prostitutes, rent boys, nude encounter parlours, rubber fetishists, swing clubs, hard porn merchants and the like. It was dirty work but somebody had to do it, and my reports from the front line of filth seemed to go down well in the senior common rooms and social work departments where *New Society* was read. My main conclusion from that experience was that, for all its fervid atmosphere and lurid reputation, there was practically no sex to be had in Soho, certainly not compared to the 'massage' parlours which operate in every town in England—never far from the local police station. Most of the pornography, too, was a con: pirated pages from Dutch and Swedish magazines with coloured blobs stuck over the interesting bits, and the whole swindle sealed up in clingfilm.

Quite early in the career of any aspiring dirty raincoat journalist, there comes an invitation to the offices of the Obscene Publications Squad in Scotland Yard. There, a nice [police officer] will show the reporter a row of filing cabinets full of magazines and a room full of videos that will mist his glasses, freeze his blood and turn his hair white. 'This is the sort of thing we have to deal with, you see,' says [the cop], patting our reporter's trembling shoulder as he comes tottering out of the viewing suite. 'Kiddies, grannies, gerbils. Now if only we had the proper resources . . . adequate budget . . . decent staffing levels . . . faster cars . . . nuclear assault rifles . . . unlimited powers . . . a change of government . . . *then* we might be able to do something about it.' And off the reporter goes to his office to write a piece which comes smoking off the typewriter, demanding a ban on everything from paedophile porn to the girl in the jogging bra on the back of the Kellogg's Cornflake box.

Plain Porn

There is evil porn—employing children, encouraging rape, wallowing in whips-and-chains humiliation—that belongs in the "violence" category. . . .

Then there is plain porn: people jumping on each other, brooding beauties manipulating themselves, soundtracks of grunted affirmations, and contorted positions. . . .

Edifying? No. Entertaining? Undeniably, judging by sales, though interest soon flags. Harmful? Not to adults who know the difference between sexual games, played mainly in the mind, and serious lovemaking.

Plain private porn is no big deal.

William Safire, *The New York Times*, November 25, 1993.

The *Guardian*, of all newspapers, ran a series of articles of this type last week [December 1994]—though I don't know why I should affect surprise at this, since it is the left-wing papers at the moment which vie to outdo each other in illiberal and repressive social attitudes. . . . But the author of this series was the normally level-headed Nick Davies, who specialises in sympathetic investigations of 'underclass' issues. His justification (and you *need* justification for dirty raincoat articles, which are always partly designed to titilate the readers) was that the porn debate had been caught in a 'sterile controversy' about the effect on consumers. British pornography is now 'bizarre, violent and very easy to obtain. Looking at the material it becomes easy to see . . . The real issue with pornography—the real reason why it might be outlawed is . . . the damage it obviously inflicts on those involved in its production.'

Child Pornography

One of these was 'Sally', who talked of being multiply raped and abused since the age of four as a player in her father's porn movies. Her last scene, at the age of eighteen, was with 'a little boy of five or six, a boy of about fifteen, a little girl of two or three; there was another girl the same age as me. My father was there with a friend of his and a couple of women, not my mother this time. . . .' The children were tied up, blindfolded and whipped. The little girl was penetrated anally and vaginally. 'The two older men and women were involved, sometimes several of them on one child, sometimes serial. . . .' There is a great deal of this kind of detail in the articles, particularly a series of vivid montages compiled, presumably, from videos Davies has been shown: 'Here are the women trussed and bound, while men fill them with dildos, telephone receivers, hair-dryers, knives, guns. . . . Here is sex with pigs, sex with eels, sex with midgets, sex with amputees. . . .'

The serious point is that Davies is using these images with intent to shock and disgust, and then managing to suggest that they are in some way typical of the pornography available on the high street. The corroboration for the story of 'Sally' above for instance, which has a distinctly suspect ring, is 'widely distributed, easily available, for sale to anyone who would like to look—the images of pornography in Britain in 1994. . . .'

Now this simply is not true, as the tide of technicolour filth presently spread out on my desk will testify: *Penthouse, Rustler, Knave, Men Only, Readers' Wives*—all the mainstream top-shelf soft porn—and what a yawn it is. Orange people with spotty bottoms, idiot grins, inane puns and feebly fictionalised photo captions. '"Both of my boyfriends are stationed on submarines," 20-year-old Lani from Hawaii states proudly. "They both say they miss my torpedo tits".' Har, har. There is, as Davies points out, a recent trend towards disgusting phone sex adverts along the lines of 'Piss on my tits' and 'Tied, bound and gagged for pleasure' etc., but I wonder if he bothered to phone any of them up, as I did. 'Hi, my name is Lola, and I'm gonna take you on a wet and wild sexual odyssey, but before I do, let me tell you about our other phone sex services . . . but before I do that, why don't I . . .' blah, blah, blah. They are as much as a con as the Soho near-beer bars, and as much to do with sex.

All the same, the phone ads are a vital link—really the only link—in Davies's attempt to conflate the criminal activities of

161

paedophiles and torturers with the top-shelf stroke mags, which, however shoddy and asinine they may be, cannot be convincingly damned as evil. And so

> the pornography industry in Britain has been riding on an escalator and, as Soho and the illegal dealers have moved upward towards more violent and bizarre material, so the legal top-shelf dealers have moved up behind to take their place . . . far from being different and distinct the two markets—the respectable and the hard core—have been intimately connected. And as time goes by the distinction is increasingly hard to spot.

Public Alarm

One interesting parallel is with the campaign against AIDS, where there has been the same attempt to create public alarm (awareness if you prefer) by insisting on the widespread and imminent nature of the threat even to heterosexuals with no intravenous habits. Another is with the antidrug campaign which always insists on the ratchet effect of soft drugs leading to hard drugs. 'The open supply of hard core pornography,' says Davies, 'has raised the threshold of frustration for consumers, so that they are moving up a kind of spiral of depravity, looking for more and more bizarre material.'

These large assertions deserve a correspondingly large dose of scepticism. Where does the material come from? Are the quotes attributed? Are the names real? Who are the pictures of? And above all, who benefits? The pictures of gagged and battered women which decorated the *Guardian* articles were from a book called *Against Pornography: the Evidence of Harm* by Diana Russell, published by Russell Publications in California, so this may indicate that images of porn are not as easily available as Davies asserts. The only attributed source of data is the Campaign Against Pornography (whose phone number is printed at the end—so we are hardly in non-partisan territory). The three female victims of porn-makers are not properly identified. In fact, the only fully identified source is a woman police officer. This is not necessarily to impugn Davies. It is hard to get witnesses in this kind of area to give their names and harder still to take their pictures, but on the other hand it is not impossible, and you have to weigh the almost complete lack of direct testimony and specific detail against the sweeping nature of the argument.

The key question, though, is *cui bono* [for whose advantage]? The answer lay in the third instalment of the series which consisted almost entirely of a sympathetic portrait of the Obscene Publications Squad, which has recently been threatened with severe cutbacks, and with good reason. The top shelf is nowadays effectively policed by the wholesale distributors themselves— such as W.H. Smith who recently pulled a perfectly inoffensive page from *Playboy*. The crimes against the person involved in

162

paedophile and sadomasochistic pornography, on the other hand, are arguably better dealt with by local, specialist squads, such as the Child Protection Teams, who can treat offences as straightforward matters of assault rather than obscenity, which has always been problematic in legal and civil liberties terms.

The American journalist, Heywood Broun, once wrote, 'Obscenity is such a tiny kingdom that a single tour covers it completely' and this is a fair description of pornography in Britain, for all the apocalyptic invocations of the new Left Puritanism. Of course there are mail order video companies selling horrible films; specialist clubs distributing disgusting books; vile people who exploit women and children. But it is fantasy to pretend they are typical of pornography in this country, which is already the most tightly controlled in Europe, and correspondingly the most vulgar, most silly and most tasteless.

There might be genuinely wicked pornography, based on real pain and exploitation for those who want it, but I don't believe it is the taste of more than a tiny minority, or easily available. For all the years it has been rumoured, for example, nobody has yet produced a single example of the 'snuff' video, and I doubt if they ever will, when common sense demands why any pornographer would bother to make something so risky and incriminating when it would be so much easier to fake it.

Pornography has always been around, and always will be, as a consolation to the lonely or as a harmless alternative to promiscuity for the married.

"*We chose sex work for money, independence, freedom and dignity.*"

Prostitution Can Benefit Women

Veronica Monet

Prostitution has existed, in one form or another, from the time of the earliest human civilization. However, in many modern cultures, prostitution is illegal and prostitutes are stigmatized as indecent, sinful women. Since the early 1970s, members of organizations such as COYOTE (Call Off Your Old Tired Ethics) have worked for the legalization of prostitution and for social acceptance of prostitutes. The author of the following viewpoint, Veronica Monet, is a member of COYOTE, an author, and a prostitute. Monet argues that prostitution is a normal sexual institution, one that can increase the self-esteem and well being of those women who choose it as their career.

As you read, consider the following questions:

1. In Monet's opinion, what are the benefits of prostitution as compared to office work?
2. What are the negative aspects of sex work, according to the author?
3. According to Monet, why do "bright, educated" women choose prostitution as their way of life?

Excerpted from Veronica Monet, "Sex Worker and Incest Survivor: A Healthy Choice?" *Gauntlet*, vol. 1, 1994. Reprinted with permission.

I've been a sex worker for over four years. I have worked as a whore and an X-rated actress. Before I became a sex worker, I graduated from college an honor student and spent the next seven years working as a dispatcher, office manager, secretary and marketing consultant. At the end of those seven years, I had my fill of corporate America and was on the verge of bankruptcy even though I was working long hard hours, and was always overtrained for whatever position I held since I was motivated to be upwardly mobile. I hated the idea that I had to sit at a desk all day even if I had completed all my work and half of someone else's by noon. I hated the fact that even though I often ran the office in my supervisor's absence, he was paid a lot of money and I was lucky to get an award or a rose for secretary's day. I guess the people I worked for just didn't think women needed money as much as men do. I did need money. And I wasn't going to go bankrupt. So I started working for my female lover who had been a prostitute for about ten years. She taught me everything she knew including how to set up a small business and pay my quarterly taxes. As a prostitute, I became a small business owner. I was my own boss after eight months when I went out on my own. I have never regretted that decision.

Perks

Well, there are parts of the job I don't like. I still have to deal with some men who are genuine jerks. But the upside is that I only have to deal with them for an hour and I get paid over $200 for that hour. I deal with far fewer jerks than I did as a secretary. A lot of my clients are very nice people. Because of the rates I charge they are mostly attorneys, doctors and company presidents. Some are also blue collar and they save their pennies to see me, and seem to feel that time with me is very special. My profession has many perks. My time is my own. I work my own hours. And I give myself vacations and raises whenever I feel like working for it. I am no longer at the mercy of office politics and gossip. My self-esteem and assertiveness have increased tenfold.

Last year I married the man who has been the love of my life for ten years. We met when I worked in telecommunications as his dispatcher. . . .

I'm complicated and defy the stereotypes about whores, as do most whores. We are a misunderstood and much maligned group of people (women, men and transgendered). Recent research has shown that many of us are extremely educated and experienced in the straight business world. We chose sex work after we did a lot of things we couldn't stand. Sex work is better. For me, sex work isn't my first choice of paying work. It just happens to be the best alternative available. It's better than being president of someone else's corporation. It's better than being a secretary. It is the most honest work I know of.

Unfortunately, most people would be shocked to find out how many women have left "good jobs" to become whores. "Good jobs" often require a lot of "kissing up" and taking orders and getting up early. You can almost never get a wage increase when you want one. As a whore, you can sleep in, and while it's true you have to suck cock, you don't have to do it for free, and you don't have to kiss the boss's butt (well, you might choose to do that for a client if he/she pays extra). If you want a raise it is often as easy as spending more time by the phone (or wherever it is you wait for business). Independence, self-motivation and skill are rewarded if you work as a whore.

Taken Out of Context

The first television show I did as a prostitute was Ed Bradley's *CBS Street Stories*. I was very nervous about coming out as a whore on national television. I also learned a valuable lesson about television that is filmed on location and edited later: You never know how the edits will slant the show. If something you say is edited out of context, it can appear that you said something you did not. And if the right pictures and/or soundtrack are superimposed on your piece, it can change the impact of your words, too. . . .

The segment of *CBS Street Stories* which I appeared on featured a female psychotherapist named Rita Belton who had just published a book "proving" that ALL prostitutes are survivors of incest and/or childhood sexual abuse. I was juxtaposed with a woman who had been a street prostitute and drug addict and had since gone back to school and stopped using drugs. This "changed" woman was presented as my counterpart. She was leaving a life of prostitution and drug addiction for an education and getting therapy for the incest she had suffered as a child. I was an incest survivor who still worked as a prostitute and was probably in denial about the severe adverse effects of prostitution on me and my sex worker sisters. Of course the fact that I had been clean and sober for six years (got sober four years before I became a prostitute) and had a bachelor's degree in Psychology (graduated with honors seven years before I became a prostitute) was completely edited out of the program. The fact that I have been in therapy for incest for over seven years and that that recovery process led me to prostitution was also edited out.

Instead, the case was made, absent any actual data or statistics, that all prostitutes are incest survivors. Rita Belton called prostitution the "re-victimization" of incest survivors and asserted that any prostitutes who say they enjoy their work are simply in "denial." She said incest survivors who enter prostitution do so to assert boundaries, have control and otherwise feel powerful in the sexual arena where they have for most of their lives experienced a lack of boundaries, control and power. She assured the viewers that instead of finding these solutions to their incestuous pasts, prostitutes merely "reenact trauma" and become "exploited" and "used."

An Adult Decision

[It] makes me angry when people try to associate some kind of childhood trauma with adult decisions. If I had gone into prostitution at the age of 14 after living in a very unstable home and a very abusive home, then you could draw the conclusion that I had gone from the frying pan into the fire, and that one had something to do with the other. But, by the time I was a 34-year-old adult female, I had put all those childhood traumas far behind me and I was basing my decision to become a prostitute on the fact that I no longer had hang-ups about sexuality and I viewed sex work as a very positive, a skilled profession, and it was something that I was doing because I wanted to rather than because there was any kind of internal pressure or external pressure or any other kind of negative input.

Norma Jean Almodavar, *Gauntlet*, vol. I, 1994.

Since I have not conducted any scientific research, I will refrain from asserting that my personal experiences and acquaintances are representative of all prostitutes. I can however speak for myself and share what I know as the friend of many prostitutes, leaving the reader with a personal account that may encourage at least an open mind on this subject. Maybe the prostitutes that Rita Belton has worked with aren't an accurate sample of all prostitutes. Maybe there are many different kinds of prostitutes with a variety of motivations just as there are secretaries. What a concept, huh?

My Life Has Improved

Well, this whore and incest survivor has found that sex work has been an arena where I could assert boundaries, control and power where I used to feel powerless, out of control and without boundaries as an incest and rape survivor. That's exactly what Rita Belton said on *CBS Street Stories*.

Where I disagree with Rita Belton, is, of course, that I do not feel that I am "merely reenacting trauma," being "exploited" or "used" as a prostitute. The reason I don't feel that sex work has been "merely" any of these negatives is that I am actively pursuing my recovery from incest, rape and an otherwise abusive childhood through therapy and 12-step programs. I have been doing this for over eight years. I started the recovery process years before I ever became a sex worker. My emotional well being and the general quality of my life have steadily improved over the last eight years in recovery and my last four years as a prostitute have been a part of that improvement. After becoming a prostitute, I was able to make enough money to pay my past due debts and pay for more therapy. I joined a gym and a tanning salon. I took a trip to England in search of goddess sites and a sacred past that was not so bent upon separating sexuality and spirituality. I became physically healthier. I smiled a lot. I looked forward to the beginning of each new day like I hadn't in at least two years.

For me, prostitution has been some of the negatives Rita Belton lists. I have at times experienced a "reenactment of trauma" as a sex worker although not nearly as often as I have in my personal relationships. Whenever I have experienced the perpetration of my past, whether in the sex industry or my personal sex life, I have promptly removed myself from those situations. I do not choose to avoid all sexual situations because I am an incest and rape survivor although I certainly have gone through periods of celibacy as part of my recovery from both. I also spent a great deal of time learning to date without "putting out" so much as a goodnight kiss. I learned the joy of relating with the opposite sex on a non-sexual basis and found unbelievable freedom and empowerment. And with that empowerment came the right and ability to choose. I found that after I learned to say no to sex I also knew how to say yes. I reclaimed my sexuality and my right to use it any way I choose as long as I don't harm anyone.

Sex work does cause me to feel some anger. I feel the sting of people's judgments. I have literally been dumped by friends, scorned by some, and certainly assaulted by a barrage of stereotypes and misconceptions and assumptions. That has hurt far more than the few lousy tricks I've had the misfortune to turn. . . .

Good Girl/Bad Girl

When I was a secretary, no one cared that I was a survivor of incest except my therapist. No one thought my status as a secretary was tied to my identity as an incest survivor. No, they chided me for not being a "good girl," for not "smiling enough" and for "thinking I was too good for my job."

Now that I'm a sex worker, people chide me for not "thinking more of myself" and for being "a bad girl." Now that I am a sex worker, my recovery as an incest survivor has become a grave concern to many people. They postulate about the connections between the incest and the sex work. They just can't figure out why a bright, educated woman like myself would wind up in "such a degrading way of life" unless it is connected to the sexual abuse. But while they are scratching their heads I just smile because the answers to their questions are so obvious, but they do not trust me to answer them and they do not want answers that will indict the prevailing societal system. After more than 6000 years of prostitution, the patriarchy still wants to know why? Are they really that stupid? I can only guess they are really that afraid of the truth.

The truth for me and many sex workers I know is that we chose sex work for money, independence, freedom and dignity. If you can't understand the last word, dignity, then you are mired in a viewpoint about sex in general, and sex and women in particular, that this patriarchal society wants you to buy.

There is another truth consequently about sex work. Yes, sex work can be dignified, honest and honorable. If you don't believe me, you may never have asked yourself why is the source of human life (of most life) considered a source of shame? Try to find the answer to that question for yourself and you will unlock a universe of hidden truths.

Recovery

Meanwhile, I am grateful for the beautiful progression of my recovery from incest and alcoholism and drug abuse and codependency . . . ad infinitum. And I celebrate the fact that I am finally free of a desk job that almost put me in the hospital because of the torture it was on me physically and emotionally. I celebrate the fact that I recovered enough from all the abuses this patriarchal society heaped upon me as a child and as an employee of its corporateness that I could extricate myself from its parasitic grip.

While I must still go to the system for my sustenance, I am glad that some semblance of freedom exists for those of us who do not flinch from being outcast, judged or in other ways punished for defying taboos. I am glad I can think for myself and reject a sex-negative, sex-obsessed, sex-phobic society as my basis for truth or lifestyle by choosing to be a sex-positive feminist, and a sexually-active, sexually-curious, sex-celebrating, and sexually-spiritual woman.

"Those who defend commercial sex seem to believe that women exploited and abused by not one but many men . . . are making a 'real choice.'"

Prostitution Harms Women

Jane Anthony

Jane Anthony is an activist, teacher, author, and former prostitute. In the following viewpoint, Anthony contends that prostitution inherently involves the exploitation and abuse of women. Taking issue with prostitution advocates who believe women can freely choose prostitution as a career, Anthony argues that women's economic inequality often forces them into sex work they might otherwise reject. Characterizing prostitution as a patriarchal and oppressive institution, Anthony calls on feminists to strive for the eradication—not the legalization—of prostitution.

As you read, consider the following questions:

1. According to Anthony, who are the casualties of the "victimless crime" of prostitution?
2. In what ways does pro-prostitution ideology focus on secondary victimization, in Anthony's opinion?
3. How does the pro-prostitution movement silence prostitutes, according to the author?

From Jane Anthony, "Choice," *Ms.*, January/February 1992. Reprint permission granted one time, by *Ms.* magazine, ©1992.

Prostitution remains today—as it has been for thousands of years—one of the most poorly understood, mythicized harms perpetrated against women. It is a cornerstone of patriarchy. The thirteenth-century philosopher Thomas Aquinas recognized this when he wrote that prostitution is like a sewer system—despicable *but necessary* (italics mine). Aquinas—along with many other "great thinkers," such as Augustine, the religious philosopher of the early Christian era, or Havelock Ellis, the twentieth-century sexologist—approached prostitution from this functional standpoint: as a victimless crime that helps preserve the institution of marriage by providing a readily available outlet for men's sexual desires.

Unfortunately, this viewpoint overlooks the casualties of such a system: one class of women is granted status as "wives" or "girlfriends" (each taking care of only one man), at the expense of another class, "whores" (who are reduced to sperm receptacles for numerous men).

Consequently, one might expect that feminism, which has dragged out of the closet such issues as rape, incest, and battering—all of which are frequently a part of the prostitution syndrome—would target commercial sex as the beginning and end of women's exploitation. But recent developments show that some individuals would like to see an "exclusive" place reserved in the feminist agenda for women in commercial sex. Some women who recognize rape and battering as violence (acts that could happen to them, regardless of their socioeconomic status) at the same time defend pornography and prostitution (acts that often involve rape and other violations, but are most likely not going to happen to them).

Prostitution's Advocates

Nowhere is this pro-prostitution stance clearer than in certain recent literature, written by women, which attempts to portray prostitution as a "career choice." In general, those who most adamantly promote this view, organizing various "whores' conferences" and positioning themselves as prostitutes' spokespersons with the male-dominated media, do not choose prostitution for themselves: some have abandoned it; some never worked as prostitutes; some work as "madams," selling other women's bodies but not routinely marketing their own; a few actually work as prostitutes. The numbers in the last group are much smaller than what the public is led to believe, especially given the millions of women worldwide who live as prostitutes in silence.

Pro-prostitution ideology, which has been linked to "sexual liberalism," is largely shaped by either/or dichotomies. It reflects a traditional masculinist mode of analysis, a dualism that easily lends itself to oversimplification. For example, in her introductory

171

chapter in the anthology *A Vindication of the Rights of Whores*, editor Gail Pheterson contrasts nineteenth-century views of prostitutes as victims with current views of prostitutes as women who make active decisions to become "whores." Unfortunately, this distinction places in opposition things that are, in reality, not mutually exclusive. Even though prostitution may be a choice for women, *among limited choices*, this doesn't mean it isn't simultaneously the epitome of gender-based exploitation.

Only if one completely decontextualizes commercial sex from the cultural constructs burdening women's "choices"—job discrimination, gender inequality in the courts, and, in general, sexism so pervasive it is often invisible—can prostitution be seen as a "choice." But this is what pro-prostitution ideology does: it marches in tune with traditional definitions of abstractions like "freedom" and "choice," definitions historically centered around the needs of Anglo-Saxon men and dependent on a curiously selective ignorance. However, if a woman faces poverty, hunger, sexual abuse, homelessness, inaccessible education, unobtainable medical treatment, or inadequate funds for child care, her possibilities of establishing herself in mainstream culture, or merely surviving, are well beyond the traditional concept of "choice."

As feminist attorney Catharine MacKinnon pointed out in her essay "Liberalism and the Death of Feminism," feminists have generally recognized that women who stay with a battering husband for the sake of economic survival are not making a real choice, despite the so-called consent implicit in a marriage contract. Yet those who defend commercial sex seem to believe that women exploited and abused by not one but many men for the sake of economic survival are making a "real choice."

Trivializing Prostitution

In decontextualizing women's choices, pro-prostitution ideology inadvertently trivializes prostitution. For example, in her introduction to the anthology *Sex Work*, coeditor Priscilla Alexander—who has never worked as a prostitute—compares her experiences as a coed at Bennington (a private college in Vermont) with prostitution. She notes that sometimes women in the dorms would wait for fraternity boys from nearby men's colleges to stop by and randomly pick up dates. Because of this, Alexander was, in her terms, "stigmatized" as a prostitute.

Indeed, a major premise of pro-prostitution thinking lies in the notion that the worst thing about prostitution is the stigmatization. Margo St. James, who organized COYOTE (Call Off Your Old Tired Ethics), a pro-prostitution group, has widely publicized this idea, noting that she herself was once "wildly promiscuous and was working as a prostitute." Thus pro-prostitution ideology stresses *secondary*, rather than *primary*, victimization: it views the name-calling as more harmful than the actual process of turning tricks, the very concrete risks of physical harm, and the psychic trauma that grows from having one's most private self routinely entered by one stranger after the next, day after day, week after week.

Prostitution Is Abusive

The liberal lies about prostitution: that it is a victimless crime, that it is a woman's free choice, that women enjoy sex while prostituted, that women become wealthy and are empowered in prostitution—all of these ignore the simple facts that prostitution is a terrible harm to women, that prostitution is abusive in its very nature, and that prostitution amounts to men paying for a woman for the right to rape her.

Melissa Farley, *Off Our Backs*, May 1994.

In general, those who view prostitution as a "career choice" see it as a form of empowerment, but this analysis is, again, shaped by decontextualization and logical inconsistency. For example, in *Sex Work*, Alexander notes a high incidence of previous sexual abuse (sometimes as high as 80 percent) among prostitutes. She also states that many prostitutes noted the first time they ever felt powerful was the first time they turned a trick; many even reported that prostitution was "a way of taking back control of a situation in which, as children, they had none." In spite of making this connection between abuse and "taking back control," Alexander does not acknowledge the "empowerment" as illusory or conditional. Instead she tells us that learning of this phenomenon began to change her ideas about the victimization of prostitutes.

Last, pro-prostitution ideology places itself in the tradition of "liberal reform." Its supporters generally see themselves as nonconformists working on behalf of their sisters in prostitution. They place themselves in opposition to "abolitionists," women who dare to envision the end of prostitution. Generally, they depict the abolitionists as conservative purists on moral crusades.

Abolitionists vs. Reformers

In reality, both liberal defenders of prostitution and abolitionists want prostitutes to be treated as "persons" under the law, that is, to have recognized civil rights so that they have legal recourse against crimes like rape or robbery. Abolitionists, however, see prostitution as a *crime against women* and therefore generally advocate the enforcement of laws against clients and pimps, as well as the eradication of laws punishing prostitutes. Reformers, on the other hand, would like to see prostitution decriminalized altogether. Abolitionists believe this would merely increase the number of women vulnerable to commercial sexual exploitation. It is the *abolitionists* who harbor the most radical stance insofar as they are challenging the patriarchal institution of commercial sex itself.

Perhaps the most disturbing aspect of the pro-prostitution movement is that while it parades as a forum for prostitutes' voices and claims to represent diversity among those voices, it may instead contribute to their silencing. For example, *Sex Work* appears to have been structured to reinforce the opinions of its nonprostitute editors. The first part, "In the Life," begins and ends with the pro-prostitution writings of a woman who works as a part-time hooker. Of the 45 pieces in this section, her writing appears nine more times, composing nearly one fourth of the selections.

Another example of questionable accuracy regarding claims of diverse representation can be seen in Amber Hollibaugh's review of *A Vindication*. Hollibaugh, whose work aligns her with the sexual liberal philosophy, states that this book represents the voices of "hundreds" of prostitutes. However, the book itself lists a total of 57 contributors, including prostitutes and *nonprostitutes* alike.

No doubt it is easier to view prostitution as a "choice" than to address its implications. This institution has been with us for millenia, has no prospects of disappearing anytime soon, and is often, even as we approach the twenty-first century, a source of cruel and insensitive jokes about women's condition. It is no wonder that women would prefer not to ask themselves what this means about their own lives, their own relationships, and their own struggles for freedom. In "Confronting the Liberal Lies About Prostitution," Evelina Giobbe of WHISPER (Women Hurt In Systems of Prostitution Engaged in Revolt), in Minneapolis, has noted, "Dismantling the institution of prostitution is the most formidable task facing contemporary feminism."

Feeling Nonhuman

Feminist theory derives from concrete personal experience. So does the above analysis. My experience would fit the paradigm of "career choice" in pro-prostitution ideology: I made a decision *as an adult* to work as a prostitute and felt "empowered" when I turned my first trick. Shortly thereafter, I became aware of the disillusion. I lived as a full-time prostitute for a year and a half, and then continued prostitution on an occasional, part-time basis for three more years. Despite the relatively short period I was a prostitute, years later I find myself still, in my most vulnerable moments, living with the ghost of prostitution—the sense of being nonhuman.

It may be comforting for some women to see prostitution as a "career choice." But when they promote this message to an all-too-eager male-dominated media, they may be sentencing other women to years of dehumanization and numbness. Or, in some cases, death. *Real* death, unlike some "choices."

"Sexual addiction . . . typically occurs in families where other addictions are present and where sexuality is inappropriately addressed."

Sexual Addiction Is a Serious Problem

Mark Matousek

A relatively recent concept, sexual addiction is the focus of a controversy between those who believe people can form harmful addictions to sex similar to alcoholism and those who disagree. In the following viewpoint, Mark Matousek writes of his own struggle with sexual addiction and examines various facets of the problem. Matousek argues that sexual addiction is common among persons who were sexually abused as children and who therefore formed unhealthy associations and obsessions around sexual behavior. Therapy and 12-step programs that emphasize stopping destructive behavior and gaining spiritual strength can help sexual addicts to lead a normal life, Matousek contends. Matousek is the coauthor of the book *Dialogues with a Modern Mystic* and a contributing editor for *Common Boundary*, a bimonthly magazine focusing on psychotherapy and spirituality.

As you read, consider the following questions:

1. According to Patrick Carnes, cited by the author, how does sexual excitement produce a neurological high?
2. How is sexual addiction defined by the 12-step programs, according to Matousek?
3. What is the goal of sexual recovery, in Matousek's opinion?

From Mark Matousek, "Addicted to Sex." Reprinted from the March/April 1993 issue of *Common Boundary*, 5275 River Rd., Bethesda, MD 20816. Used with permission.

When I was 10, I raped my baby sister. We were in the bathtub and I did something to her that I have never done to anyone since. Belle screamed. I laughed. And we made up quickly.

I forgot about this incident, or rather, came to believe that I'd made it up. When fragments of the episode surfaced unexpectedly over the years—the horrified look on her seven-year-old face, my hand over her screaming mouth—it seemed too offensive to be true, an outrageous contradiction of the protective love I felt for this little girl.

Then reason cracked. During a recent family dinner, surrounded by her own three boys, Belle turned to me out of the blue and said, "Remember when you did that to me in the tub?" This time, it was she who laughed. I stopped eating. The table fell silent. My mother, the amnesiac, ordered us to shut up and forget it. It was never discussed again.

Sex Was a Game

Thirty-year silences are common in families where incest happens, where rape in its many forms is taken for granted and imitated by children. In the house where I grew up, sex was the game of choice. While friends in the neighborhood played with Lincoln Logs and Raggedy Anns, my sisters and I entertained ourselves with genitals, vibrators, and porn. The absence of generational boundaries, the confusion between innocence and profanity, love and penetration, turned us into precocious hybrids, grown-ups trapped in the bodies of dwarfs.

"I was never a child," Belle says today. As for myself, I'm unable to recall a time since birth when I was not a sexual being, not molesting other children, not exposing myself, not thinking of myself as a pleasure toy or a seducer. I took this distortion to be normal: In my child's eyes, the world was an enterprise founded on lust. Sex was the grease that spun the wheel, the bottom line, the prime mover. It gave rise to everything crucial for happiness: power, identity, love, and spirit. Strengthened by a promiscuous society, this worldview was camouflaged as I grew older. No one seemed to notice that my conversation, wardrobe, hobbies, humor, writing, choice of friends—my entire personality, in fact—were driven by sexual obsession. Instead, I was viewed as a cocky guy, a garden-variety narcissist with a bawdy mouth and athletic appetites.

It wasn't until I began to explore a spiritual path that I became aware of something desperate, callous, and exploitive in my sexual nature, a split between my penis and my heart. Despite an unceasing parade of lovers, the pain of this rupture steadily grew as I learned about intimacy. The profligate voice I'd taken for wisdom ("more is better, love is free, the body's for pleasure, grab what you can") began to acquire a tinny sound.

177

The habit with which I'd been raised at home, of reducing myself and others to objects, of using my body for profit and power, showed itself to be corrupt. . . .

It became clear that sexual compulsion was a bitter fact needing to be swallowed, not only by myself but by thousands who were raped as children, then tossed into a world where multiform violence masquerades, too often, as love.

Out of Control

Sex addiction can involve a wide variety of practices. . . .

The essence of all addiction is the addicts' experience of powerlessness over compulsive sexual behavior, resulting in their lives becoming unmanageable. The addict is out of control and experiences tremendous shame, pain and self-loathing. The addict may wish to stop acting out—making promises and many attempts to stop—yet repeatedly fails to do so. The unmanageability of addicts' lives can be seen in the consequences they suffer: low self-esteem, loss of interest in things not sexual, difficulties with work, financial troubles, loss of relationships, arrest, imprisonment, despair, disease, and death.

Pamphlet, Sex Addicts Anonymous, 1990.

In Spring 1993 I spoke for the first time in a meeting for sex addicts. Surrendering my resistance, joining the ranks of the wounded, my heart slowly opened and I acknowledged what I shared with the people in the room. Their voices emerged with a new and urgent poignancy. This is what I heard.

The field of sexual addiction is loosely divided into two camps: those who believe that there is such a disease and those who do not. There is more than a semantic difference that separates them, for in denying that sexual behavior can become an addiction, skeptics are also, if indirectly, denying the spiritual source of the condition and the need for a spiritual recovery. If alcoholism is indeed the "prayer gone awry" that Gregory Bateson says it is, one wonders whether the dependency on sexual behavior must not be an equally desperate, addictive plea?

Skepticism

"Absolutely not," says Dr. Robert Francoeur, a Catholic priest and professor of human sexuality and embryology at Fairleigh Dickinson University. "Addiction is caused in the brain by a chemical dependency. Sex is not a chemical you can become neurologically dependent on. You may be compulsive and use sex to reduce anxiety, but you can't become addicted to behaviors," says Francoeur, whose textbooks are read in college sexuality courses across the country. Speaking for the mainstream majority in his field, Francoeur attributes the addiction misnomer to an "American compulsion to find and label diseases."

"All this 12-Step stuff is misguided," he claims. "People seem to need something to feel bad about so they can go to a therapist and get cured." Echoing a common caveat, Francoeur wonders how sex can be called an addiction when abstinence is not the goal of recovery. "You don't tell an alcoholic he can have just one drink, do you? The notion is absurd."

Francoeur also sides with traditional sexologists in the belief that the sexual addiction movement is fundamentally moralistic. "The founding fathers themselves were not monogamous!" he argues. "Our attitudes toward sex are hypocritical, puritanical, and unshared by other civilized nations."

"That's what they all say," laughs Gina Ogden, Ph.D., a sex therapist and author of *Sexual Recovery: Everywoman's Guide Through Sexual Co-Dependency*. "The Francoeurs in this field always maintain that sexual addiction is a term invented by right-wing people to put down sex. They depict us as saying that sex is bad, that sex will kill you and so on. They totally miss the point."

Two points, in fact. To begin with, physiological data support the claim that sexual excitement does produce a neurological high which may be said to create chemical addiction. As Dr. Patrick Carnes, a leading authority on sexual addiction in this country, explains, drugs are involved in sex in the form of "naturally occurring peptides such as endorphins which govern the electrochemical interactions within the brain. These peptides parallel the molecular construction of opiates like morphine, but they are many times more powerful. . . . When the pleasure centers of the brain are stimulated, releasing endorphins, rats will go through even more suffering [for sex] than they will for morphine or heroin."

The Matrix of Addiction

The second missed point concerns the matrix of addiction itself. Parting ways with the conservatives, recovery professionals such as Anne Wilson Schaef maintain that *processes*, as well as *substances*, can be addictive. Characterized by powerlessness, loss of control, and escalating compulsion leading to death, substance and process addictions function similarly in Schaef's model. Endorphin dependency notwithstanding, sexual addiction tends to be more deeply linked to process, the "specific series of actions or interactions" associated with the individual's sexual obsession. This process frequently involves other addictive behaviors, including the abuse of drugs and alcohol, which is why sex addicts are often described as "multiply addicted."

For example, a bourgeois gentleman who frequents prostitutes may habitually drink himself silly beforehand. A woman who uncontrollably cheats on her husband may be as hooked on the intrigue and deceit of her addiction as she is on the sexual gratification itself.

Finally, it is fascinating to note that many alcoholics and drug addicts have discovered in recovery that their primary addiction is to sex, which stemmed from childhood abuse. Their sexual abuse preceded substance abuse, which they claim they have used to medicate the early sexual trauma. . . .

Addictive Behavior

Because sexual addiction has more to do with process than with substance, its profile and means of diagnosis are particularly complex. Often the circumstances (internal and external) surrounding the behavior are the source of obsession; that is, the force of attachment and its consequences, as much as the details of the activity, determine whether or not addiction is at play. Unlike substance addiction, which may be simplistically termed "objective," process addiction is a "subjective" condition, meaning that the form it takes is essentially personal, even eccentric, in nature. The spectrum of behaviors that justify a diagnosis of sexual addiction is as diverse as eros itself. Beneath this addictive umbrella, one finds the Connecticut spinster hooked on the erotic fantasies of romance novels and the nightcrawler tying up children in leather harnesses. There are those who "act out" with hundreds of partners and those who "act in," never touching anyone at all, limiting themselves to obsessive imagining. Variable as sexually addictive behavior is, however, Patrick Carnes asserts that it can be broken up into 11 general types.

1. Fantasy sex (thinking/obsessing about sexual adventures)
2. Seductive role sex
3. Anonymous sex
4. Paying for sex
5. Trading sex (pimping, making explicit videotapes and photographs, hustling, posing for hire)
6. Voyeuristic sex
7. Exhibitionist sex
8. Intrusive sex (making inappropriate sexual advances or gestures)
9. Pain exchange
10. Object sex (masturbating with objects, cross-dressing, fetishes, animals)
11. Sex with children.

Of course, none of these behaviors offers proof positive of sexual addiction. But as Anne Wilson Schaef implies, it's not always *what* the addict does but *why* he or she does it that determines the nature of the disease. "Getting enough sex translates into avoiding tensions and feelings," Schaef writes. "[Addicts] use sex [and each other] to keep from having to deal with themselves. When a sex addict gets a fix, it serves the same purpose as a drink or a drug, and the personality dynamics that develop are essentially the same." These dynamics include feelings of shame, numbness, and alienation—the antithesis, it might be said, of what sexual union is intended to provide. . . .

Childhood Roots of Sexual Addiction

Experts agree that this pattern of emotional dissociation among sex addicts emerges in the climate of early childhood. In fact, sexual addiction itself typically occurs in families where other addictions are present and where sexuality is inappropriately addressed. This impropriety takes many forms, from overt demonstration—verbal or physical abuse—to intense repression. In this latter regard, Veronica Vera, prostitute, porn star, and author of *Memoirs of a Sexual Evolutionary*, goes so far as to say that it was her strict Catholic upbringing that inspired her career in the sex business. "Guilt is a tremendous aphrodisiac," says the uninhibited Vera. "So is revenge."

Furthermore, because sexual abuse may be physically pleasurable, Ogden notes, it is likely to create an ambiguous response in the child, a confusion between pleasure and pain, love and violence, which characterizes sexual addiction. Far from being self-destructive in its inception, Ogden emphasizes that sexual addiction begins with a desire for love. "Unfortunately, in crazy families, the child isn't taught about appropriateness, when desire can get him into trouble and when to stop. He learns that bad feels good and vice versa."

Steven, a 31-year-old man dying of AIDS, tells the story of being forced to perform fellatio on his father as a child. The resulting sexual fixation compelled him to service thousands of men during the next two decades, and to swallow their ejaculate, even after the advent of AIDS and down to the present day. So dependent is Steven on this particular sexual practice that he is forced to keep a baby's bottle by his bed and to suck on it when anxiety threatens to consume him. "It's like scratching a terrible itch," says Steven. "I just can't stop myself." . . .

Treatments

The primary benefit of naming sexual addiction arises in the process of recovery. While a variety of therapeutic methods are available for treating obsessive-compulsive disorders—psychotherapy, behavior modification, neurological procedures—addiction as defined by the 12-Step programs is primarily a spirituality malady. Viewed as such, the condition—long attributed to moral weakness or rank perversion—can be understood for what it actually is; namely, a replacement behavior, a reenactment of childhood abuse, a compensation for love, and a grasping for divine connection. . . .

The Signs of Sexual Addiction

1. A pattern of out-of-control behavior
2. Severe consequences due to sexual behavior
3. Inability to stop despite adverse consequences
4. Persistent pursuit of self-destructive or high-risk behavior
5. Ongoing desire or effort to limit sexual behavior
6. Sexual obsession and fantasy as a primary coping strategy
7. Increasing amounts of sexual experience because the current level of activity is no longer sufficient
8. Severe mood changes around sexual activity
9. Inordinate amounts of time spent in obtaining sex, being sexual, or recovering from sexual experience
10. Neglect of important social, occupational, or recreational activities because of sexual behavior

Mark Matousek, *Common Boundary*, March/April 1993.

Because the nature of sexual addiction is to veil authentic desire with fantasy and confusion, the creation of an explicit plan helps addicts break through their delusion and out-of-control behavior, freeing themselves from having to make anxiety-provoking choices in the contusion of sexual excitement. Establishing a bottom line of activities harmful to themselves and others, addicts are able to step back from the shadow that hitherto overwhelmed them, to confront their sexual fears, and to replace their destructive behaviors with healthy ones. The plan's details are discussed only with one's sponsor; in group meetings, it matters only whether members have been off their program or on. Criticism is forbidden, slips are not judged, and everyone is encouraged to keep coming back.

Since idealism is the nemesis of all addicts, beginners in the program are warned against putting too many restrictions on themselves, creating a recovery plan whose standards they cannot possibly meet. Sexual sobriety is a more complex issue than abstinence from alcohol or drugs; like other process addictions (food, in particular), its solution is never clear-cut. Although a period of celibacy may be useful at the outset of sexual recovery, it is not generally recommended as a permanent life style. Integration, not abstinence, is the goal.

Recovering addicts are called upon not to extinguish their desires nor to retreat from sexuality but to learn slowly and with renewed care, like a child taking its first steps, how to participate honorably in this potentially dangerous arena. As psychologists from Sigmund Freud to Abraham Maslow have warned, the recovery of sexual health is vital for self-actualization. Expression, not repression, is the objective. "The cure of sexual addiction is not to quit having sex," Gina Ogden says, adding that abstinence can actually exacerbate the "split of body, mind, heart, and world" central to the addictive dilemma. "An individual might have to quit for a while in order to get back in harmony with what feels right for himself, but eventually he will be called upon to incorporate that knowledge into his relationships." Without such integration, Ogden says, complete recovery is impossible. "Frustration of our natural impulses only leads into the old addictive pattern of never being satisfied."

The road to satisfaction, however, is paved with distress, and begins with a scrupulous examination of the pain that the addict has habitually medicated with sex. Among themselves, sex addicts reveal personal stories of heartbreaking emptiness, of the twisted search for tenderness through sexual activities of the most lascivious kind. One learns in these meetings that in a world outwardly stripped of the sacred, God-hungry lovers look to romance as a plaster-footed theology; they seek salvation in an amorous union, whose ultimate guarantor and sealer is sex. This search for some magical quality in others that will complete oneself and alleviate suffering is among the most common characteristics of sexual addiction. (Unfortunately, this quality nearly always disappears after sex.) This tendency toward mysticizing sex and misplacing spiritual hunger helps to give sexual addiction its supernatural force.

"Obsessive-compulsiveness . . . seems almost ubiquitous among humans and has its distinct advantages . . . particularly [in] sexual activity."

Sexual Addiction Is Normal Human Behavior

Albert Ellis

Albert Ellis is a psychotherapist and the president of New York City's Institute for Rational-Emotive Therapy, an organization that provides information about a psychological therapy based on the premise that people can stop negative behavior through consciously changing their thoughts. In the following viewpoint, Ellis maintains that the designation of certain sexual behaviors as abnormal is often based on puritanical beliefs rather than scientific fact. Obsessive-compulsive behaviors and addictions—including sexual ones—are part of the general human condition, Ellis argues, and only cause significant problems in a small percent of the population. Ellis contends that our conception of what constitutes sexual disturbance and sexual normalcy is flexible, changing as society grows more accepting of activities that were once condemned.

As you read, consider the following questions:

1. What are the three major kinds of "absolutist demandingness," according to Ellis?
2. In Ellis's view, sexual disturbance mainly includes what sex acts?
3. How can obsessive-compulsive behavior enhance sexual satisfaction, according to the author?

Albert Ellis, "What Is Sexual Disturbance?" *The Humanist*, July/August 1992. Reprinted by permission of the American Humanist Association.

I recommend that we stop speaking about sex "deviations" and "perversions"—with all the nasty, pejorative, puritanical connotations that almost invariably accompany the use of such terms—and that we instead merely try to distinguish between sexual (and nonsexual) behaviors that are disturbed or healthy. I shall try to define psychosexual disturbance and apply this definition equally—and I hope nonprejudicially—to both gay and straight sexuality.

Sexual Disturbance

What *is* sexual disturbance? No one can say with absolute certainty; however, on the basis of almost 50 years of clinical experience, and on the basis of my theory of rational emotive therapy (RET), I define it the same way I define any form of emotional disturbance, even when it has no sexual underpinnings or overtones.

As RET theorizes, sexual (and nonsexual) disturbance largely stems from three major kinds of *absolutist demandingness*.

Self-demandingness. Sexually disturbed or neurotic individuals frequently make inordinate demands on themselves. They take their *preferences* for "good" and enjoyable sex and raise them to dysfunctional insistences: "I *absolutely must* perform well sexually at practically all times and I *have to* thereby win others' approval—or else I am an *inadequate, worthless person!*" Horribly fearing failure and rejection because of these *musts*, they severely castigate themselves when they don't fulfill their expectations and frequently are unassertive, withdrawing to "safe" acts like abstinence, masturbation, or peeping; or they compulsively resort to behaviors (for example, promiscuity) that "prove" how "good" they really are; or they compulsively resort to behaviors (such as sex with children) in which they are likely to achieve little failure and rejection. They also often make themselves anxious, depressed, and self-hating about their sexual (and nonsexual) activities.

Self-demandingness about sex—or what William H. Masters and Virginia E. Johnson, following some of my own leads, called "performance anxiety"—is very common among Western females and, especially, males. There is no reliable evidence that it is more prevalent among straight or gay people. There is some clinical evidence that some people become gay because of their fear of sexual rejection and failure in a heterosexual world, but there is also evidence that some people with gay inclinations avoid gay encounters and turn to heterosexual ones because of their fear of rejection and failure in the gay world. It is unlikely that performance anxiety is a main cause of people becoming straight or gay, though it may be an important factor in some cases.

Demandingness in others. In addition to, or instead of, demand-

185

ing great sexual performances of themselves, many men and women disturb themselves sexually by making unrealistic demands of others. Thus, they insist: "People *absolutely must* treat me kindly and help me fulfill myself sexually or else they are *rotten individuals* and deserve to be thoroughly avoided or sexually (and otherwise) punished."

Sexual Commanding

This kind of sexual commanding often results in strong feelings of rage, unlovingness, and self-pity. It may lead to sexual withdrawal or to obsessive-compulsive hostile sexual behavior (such as rape). It is reasonably frequent in both straight and gay people, but we have no conclusive evidence that it is more frequent in either group. Psychoanalysts often claim that a male's hostility toward his mother, combined with his incestuous obsession with her, drives him to become gay, but this is largely an unproven hypothesis. We could also guess that a male's jealousy and hostility toward his father drives him into heterosexuality, but this, too, seems unlikely. Hostility toward others may be a cause of some gay or straight behavior, but it is seldom a prime cause.

Demandingness of world conditions. Like most disturbed individuals, the sexually disturbed person tends to demand that the world treat him or her kindly and make sexual fulfillment (or other pleasures) easy to obtain. Sexual disturbances often include low frustration tolerance, short-range hedonism, and lack of discipline, stemming from the basic irrational or dysfunctional belief: "I *absolutely must* obtain easy and quick sexual enjoyment—and it's *awful* and *I can't stand it* when I am frustrated or deprived!" As a result of this underlying outlook, millions of men and women foolishly engage in unsafe promiscuity, fail to take contraceptive precautions, and compulsively practice immoral and illegal acts (such as rape, sexual assault, and seduction of children).

Both gay and straight individuals are sexually (and generally) disturbed because of their low frustration tolerance; no one knows which of these groups has more addicted members. Ian Campbell, a gay psychologist, and Edward Sagarin (pseudonym: Donald Webster Cory), a gay sociologist, have pointed out that some males and females who are predominantly heterosexual but who find it "too hard" to get what they want "cop out" and turn to the gay life. I have talked with a number of predominantly gay men who found it "too difficult" to go to bed with men and who therefore "copped out" by mating monogamously with women. But low frustration tolerance, once again, seems to be at most a minor "cause" of people turning to either a gay or straight life-style.

186

Sexual disturbance, then, doesn't mean what some person or group finds peculiar, unnatural, immoral, illegal, animalistic, ungodly, or even antisocial. It truly means *disturbance*, or needless self-defeating thoughts, feelings, and behaviors. Thus, we'd better not call it by pejorative, denigrating terms like *deviation* or *perversion*. When more accurately described and defined, sexual disturbance mainly includes sex acts performed in a compulsive, overrigid, panic-stricken, hostile, disorganized, or overimpulsive manner. They almost always come under the heading of general disturbances and rarely exist without some kind of general demandingness.

A constant difficulty in defining sexual disturbances arises from our inability to tell exactly when a sex act is the result of dysfunctional, self-defeating behavior. The same difficulty arises in connection with love. If you fall madly in love with a rather stupid person and utterly dedicate yourself to him or her for many years, even though this person gives you a very hard time and exploits you in many ways, we might easily label your behavior obsessive-compulsive or neurotic, and we might think it best for you to go for some sort of psychological treatment to help you overcome this kind of "mad" love. But suppose you genuinely love this person, achieve immense joy from staying with and having great sex with him or her mainly because of the intensity of your feelings for this person, and always consider your relationship eminently worthwhile. Suppose, also, that you have many opportunities with other partners—virtually all of them brighter, more attractive, kinder, sexier, and less exploitative. You may still decide to stay with this person and ignore all the others.

Obsession

How, then, shall we diagnose you? As utterly crazy? As at least moderately neurotic? As self-defeating? Who, exactly, can say? Certainly, from an "objective" point of view, you seem to do yourself in. But subjectively—ah, that's another story! Similarly with sex; for many years you may remain, say, a fetishist who "madly" dotes on women wearing high-heeled shoes. You may follow them on the street, try to have affairs with them, persuade all your wives and lovers to wear very high heels, spend a great deal of time and money seeking out and reading fetishistic magazines that feature pictures of women in high heels, acquire a closetful of women's high-heeled shoes, and spend much time looking at them and masturbating while you observe them. This all would seem pretty crazy to the rest of us who have little or no similar interest.

But would such a very consuming interest in high heels—and the great degrees of arousal and satisfaction accompanying such an interest—prove you crazy? Yes—if you ruined your entire life because of this obsession. Yes—if you trained yourself to suffer complete impotence when you temporarily had no access to high-heeled shoes. Yes—if you kept getting yourself arrested for molesting women who happened to wear very high heels.

But suppose you kept yourself only moderately obsessed with women's high heels and never got into any serious trouble because of your obsession? What then? Would we still call you disturbed or neurotic? Would we recommend treatment for you?

Healthy and Harmless

In sex therapy it is not unusual to hear people report being sexually aroused by art, music, particular foods or drink, a particular setting such as the seashore, a stream, a mountain lake, vacations, or strenuous activities like sports. Particular clothes, parts of the body, certain smells, and good communication are also often listed as important to a person's ability to experience erotic feelings. I consider these healthy and positive aspects of a person's sexual orientation. There are also unusual, but harmless, objects or activities, such as rubber artifacts, dressing in clothes of the opposite sex, or particular articles of clothing which are needed for erotic arousal.

William R. Stayton, *SIECUS Report*, April/May 1992.

Let us not forget, in this connection, that innumerable people—perhaps, if we really knew the score, the great majority—have some kind of obsession or other. Jane Smith, for example, spends more money than she can really afford on collecting china. John Jones obsesses, for literally hours every week, about baseball batting averages. Jim and Dora Thompson devote practically all their time to building their liquor business and neglect their children and friends in the process. All these individuals thoroughly enjoy themselves and, in fact, feel miserable when something (such as an illness) interferes with their obsessive pursuits. None of them, moreover, gets into any serious trouble, regularly feels anxious or depressed, or considers him- or herself deprived. Disturbed? Yes—according to *some* standards. But how much so? And how many psychiatrists or psychologists would think that they really need help or that getting intensive psychotherapy (assuming that it would really serve any purpose) would be worthwhile for people like these?

Obsessive-compulsiveness, in other words, seems almost ubiquitous among humans and has its distinct advantages. It is particularly a natural concomitant of much sexual activity—perhaps the majority of young males in our society more or less obsess about sex and the great majority of females of practically all ages about loving. To some degree, moreover, sexual obsessiveness and compulsivity help arousal and orgasm, since people who have real difficulty in getting themselves to the heights of sexual excitement or achieving orgasm after they get there frequently resort to all kinds of sex fetishes, obsessions, and extreme fantasies to get themselves over the top. Millions of otherwise "normal" males and females, for example, frequently resort to intense sadomasochistic fantasies to make themselves more effective in their masturbational and interpersonal sex encounters.

Frequent Behavior

The question remains: shall we view all, some, or a few of these individuals as sexual neurotics? In one sense, I would say few. For if practically all of us act neurotically and do so a good portion of the time, then the terms *neurotic* or *disturbed* tend to seem unrealistic, and perhaps we'd better avoid using them for any kind of behavior that appears so frequent. On the other hand, as I have shown in *Reason and Emotion in Psychotherapy*, if some form of disturbance exists as the human condition, perhaps we had better acknowledge this fact, stop putting ourselves down for having emotional disturbances, and devote a good deal of our time and energy toward various techniques of making ourselves less disturbed.

In regard to sex, I tend to take a middle-of-the-road position. On the one hand, I believe that the *tendency* toward disturbance is high among humans. For if we investigate the number of people who turn up with fairly serious sexual disturbances—including such behaviors as compulsive exhibitionism, peeping, and sexual assault that actually lead to their getting into overt trouble, like arrest or institutionalization—we find that perhaps 5 percent of our citizens have distinct problems for a large part of their lives. But we could well add to this list perhaps three or four (maybe five or six) times that number of people who rigidly and self-defeatingly abstain from various kinds of sex for highly arbitrary reasons.

Take, for example, the large number of people who engage in regular petting and intercourse but who rigidly abstain from ever trying oral or anal sex. If these individuals practiced *only* orality or anality, we might designate them as having a sexual problem or disturbance. We would tend to say that they've fixated themselves upon this monolithic form of sex and have rigidly refrained from all other modes. But what if they rigidly, fixatedly *abstain* from oral or anal sex—and do so without ever trying it to see if they would or wouldn't like it? Doesn't their rigidity *then* constitute a problem?

If we consider all the various sex acts that humans never try, that they studiously avoid trying, and that they feel disgusted by, it would appear that perhaps the majority of us have some kind of hangup. Does this mean that you have to try *everything* in the sex books to prove your normalcy? Not at all! The fact remains, however, that most of us seem to avoid many kinds of sexual activity—not a few of which we feel revolted by even though we have had no experience of them.

All of which means—what? That sex bigotry and prejudice exert a mighty influence on most of us much of the time. And since emotional health in virtually any area—from food to sex to politics—largely consists of open-mindedness, of the ability to at least *consider* viewpoints other than our usual ones, my conclusion tends to remain. A vast amount of sexual disturbance still exists—though much less than existed decades ago. Much has changed for the better in this respect. Whereas, in the old days, practically every member of our society seemed to abjure the possibility of appearing nude in public places, attending "pornographic" movies and shows, living in a nonmarital union with a member of the other sex, coming out of the closet if he or she led a gay life, openly engaging in adulterous affairs, and participating in various other forms of unconventional sex, a sizable minority (and sometimes the majority) of us participate in some of these kinds of activities today.

So our sex life has significantly changed, has become much more open, in some of these ways. Good! But sexual closedness, prejudice, and anxiety still remain the rule rather than the exception. The sexual revolution marches on—but slowly, with many regressions. Therefore, I repeat: sexual disturbance in one form or another still exists pandemically. Less, I think, than ever before in our culture—but still very widely.

Periodical Bibliography

The following articles have been selected to supplement the diverse views presented in this chapter.

Bob Davies
"What Homosexuals Need Most," *Focus on the Family*, March 1991.

John Finnis and
Martha Nussbaum
"Is Homosexual Conduct Wrong? A Philosophical Exchange," *The New Republic*, November 15, 1993.

Focus on the Family
"Once Gay, Always Gay?" March 1994.

Laura Fraser
"Nasty Girls," *Mother Jones*, February/March 1990.

Laura Fraser
"Posing Questions: A Critic Looks at Pornography from the Inside," *EXTRA!*, July/August 1993.

C.K. Gandee
"Portrait of a Lady of the Night," *Vogue*, February 1993.

Stephanie Gutmann
"Waging War on Sex Crimes and Videotape," *Insight on the News*, May 3, 1993. Available from 3600 New York Ave. NE, Washington, DC 20002.

Margot Hornblower
"The Skin Trade," *Time*, June 21, 1993.

Sandra Antoinette Jaska
"The Pornographers Are Winning," *Off Our Backs*, April 1994.

Robert Knight
"Sexual Disorientation: Faulty Research in the Homosexual Debate," *Family Policy*, June 1992. Available from the Family Research Council, 700 13th St. NW, Suite 500, Washington, DC 20005.

Yaakov Levado
"Gayness and God: Wrestlings of an Orthodox Rabbi," *Tikkun*, September/October 1993.

Wendy McElroy
"Talking Sex, Not Gender," *Liberty*, November 1994. Available from PO Box 1181, Port Townsend, WA 98368.

Ms.
"Where Do We Stand on Pornography?" January/February 1994.

The New Internationalist
Special issue on prostitution, February 1994.

Joseph Nicolosi
"Let's Be Straight: A Cure Is Possible," *Insight on the News*, December 6, 1993.

Off Our Backs	"My Life Will Not Be Negated! A Pornography Survivor Speaks," April 1993.
Donald E. Olson	"The Value of Erotica," *The Humanist*, September/October 1989.
Robert Pela	"The Ex-Ex-Gay," *The Advocate*, June 30, 1992.
The Ramsey Colloquium	"The Homosexual Movement," *Human Events*, March 25, 1994. Available from 422 First St. SE, Washington, DC 20003.
Mark Satin	"Some of Our Daughters, Some of Our Loves," *New Options*, Oct. 29/Nov. 26,1990. Available from PO Box 19324, Washington, DC 20036.
Laurie Shrage	"Should Feminists Oppose Prostitution?" *Ethics*, January 1989.
Sallie Tisdale	"Talk Dirty to Me," *Harper's Magazine*, February 1992.

How Is Society's View of Human Sexuality Changing?

HUMAN
SEXUALITY

Chapter Preface

Since the 1950s various surveys of human sexual behavior have reflected and shaped America's interest and views on sexuality. Early studies, reinforced by reader polls in such magazines as *Redbook* and *Playboy*, generally reported that Americans were promiscuous, unfaithful, and sexually adventurous. However, a more recent study released in October 1994 by the National Opinion Research Center at the University of Chicago, entitled *Sex in America: A Definitive Survey*, presents evidence suggesting that Americans' sex lives may be much more conservative than in past decades. Eighty-three percent of the 3,400 18- to 59-year-olds surveyed reported having one or zero sexual partners a year.

This surprising result indicates that many Americans may have changed their sexual attitudes and behaviors since the earlier surveys were conducted. According to the 1994 study, during the sexual revolution of the 1960s and 1970s, more people had casual, promiscuous sex. The percentage of adults who have had 21 or more sex partners, according to the study, is significantly higher among the baby-boom generation than among any other age group. According to *Los Angeles Times* reporter Andrea Heiman, "In the '60s and '70s, sex was used so freely and casually that many people never really got intimate, psychologists say—people substituted sex for intimacy."

If Americans' sexual behaviors and attitudes have indeed changed so drastically, it may be due in part to an increased desire for intimacy. Another survey conducted in 1994 showed that 79 percent of men questioned said they found sex without any emotional involvement difficult, up from 59 percent in 1984. Many believe the threat of AIDS has also made people rethink their attitudes towards casual sex. According to the University of Chicago study, 76 percent of those who had five or more partners during the previous year had changed their sexual behavior, in part by reducing the number of partners they had, because of the possibility of contracting HIV.

Given the prevalence of sex on television and in the movies, many people continue to argue that Americans' sexual behavior is promiscuous and shows little sign of the changes the University of Chicago study has indicated. The viewpoints in the following chapter debate whether and how Americans' views on sexuality are changing.

"Although America may not be a hotbed of eroticism, it is a nation of people who are largely satisfied with the sexual lives that they've chosen."

Americans Are Satisfied with Their Sex Lives

Robert T. Michael et al.

In 1992, a group of researchers interviewed 3,500 Americans about their sexual behaviors. In the following viewpoint, adapted from their book *Sex in America: A Definitive Study*, the researchers summarize their findings and conclude that although Americans are less sexually active than is popularly believed, they are for the most part comfortable with their sex lives. The researchers were Robert T. Michael, a professor at the Irving B. Harris Graduate School of Public Policy Studies at the University of Chicago; John H. Gagnon, a professor of sociology at the State University of New York at Stony Brook; Edward O. Laumann, a professor of sociology at the University of Chicago; and Gina Kolata, science reporter for the *New York Times*.

As you read, consider the following questions:

1. According to the authors, why do people choose the sexual partners they do?
2. What conclusions do the researchers draw about the effect of marriage on Americans' sex lives?
3. What are some of the sexual practices that Americans find most appealing, according to the authors?

Americans have a sexy image of themselves. There's a widespread impression that people are having more and more sex with more and more partners; even those who would describe their own sex lives as boringly everyday believe that everyone *else* is having endless, fascinating, varied, possibly even kinky sex.

But what are the facts? How many sexual partners do Americans really have? Where do they find their partners? How common is infidelity? Until now, there were no answers to these and dozens of other questions, because there were no recent studies that were sizable enough, responsible enough, and well-executed enough to provide solid information. . . .

The Sex Survey

Conducted in 1992 [this] study is the most comprehensive and scientifically sound sex survey ever conducted in the United States: We surveyed nearly 3,500 adults—aged 18 to 59, chosen randomly from across the country to get a representative sample of the population—and interviewed each of them extensively. Our findings reveal a society that behaves very differently in real life than in the tales we tell ourselves.

Why We Choose Whom We Choose

Many researchers have explained sexuality as an inborn drive that follows the whims of our hormonal surges and even genetic predispositions. But according to our data, the choices people make about their sex lives are dramatically influenced by social circumstances. Sexual behavior is very much like other sorts of social behavior. We play by the rules—those set up by our own social groups—when we choose someone to take to bed. Our sexual partners are expected to be part of our crowd, so they have to be appropriate to fit in—which means that they are expected to be much like ourselves, our friends and our families.

Though a weekend sex partner may go unnoticed by one's social group, once two people are falling in love, they must gain the approval of an array of "stakeholders"—parents, friends, coworkers, employers, church and political associates. The more serious a relationship gets, the more the stakeholders try to have their way. The pressure to choose someone of the same race, for example, can begin as soon as teenagers start to date and becomes greater the closer a couple comes to marrying. Race is not the only issue; what's striking is the extent to which stakeholders discourage—either subtly or directly—other sorts of mismatched relationships: those that include differences of class, for instance, or education.

Our research found that *whether or not marriage is the object*, people usually have sex with people who are remarkably like themselves—in age, race or ethnicity, and education. More than

90 percent of couples—married or dating—are from the same race or ethnic group; more than 80 percent have the same level of education. (For instance, not one woman in our study with a graduate degree had had a sexual relationship with a man who had not finished high school.) More than three quarters of married couples are around the same age, and the same is true of more than 80 percent of short-term dating couples. In fact, on every measure except religion, people who are in *any* stage of a sexual relationship are remarkably similar to each other. The reason: The social world is organized so that you will meet people like yourself. It's not that you'll never see a stranger across a crowded room and fall in love—it's that the stranger in that room will likely be of your race, educational status, social class, and probably religion, too.

Another reason we choose sexual partners who resemble ourselves: Similarity eases the high-stakes game of initiating and maintaining sexual intimacy. Nearly everyone is nervous as sex enters a relationship. The price of a mistake is high. But the more characteristics that our sexual partners share with us, the fewer uncertainties there are. We are more confident if our partners had the same sort of upbringing that we had or share the same religious scruples. Any advantage that sharing a social background brings to a relationship is magnified by the lens of sexual intimacy.

Love and Sex: Where Americans Find Them

Most couples in the study met in conventional ways. They were introduced by family members or friends. They met at work. They met at a party. They met at church.

Despite the mushrooming business in personal ads and singles bars—despite even the emergence of erotic E-mail, where people sit at their computer terminals and type messages to strangers—social networks reign supreme in bringing couples together. And the more stable the relationship, the more likely the couple had met through social networks: Two thirds of married couples were introduced by a family member, friend, coworker, classmate or neighbor. Those who ventured outside their networks were more likely to have had short sexual relationships that never blossomed into anything more.

People who ended up marrying, we found, knew their partners longer before having sex with them than couples in short-term sexual relationships did. This was true whether they met their partners at a bar, a party, school or work.

For relationships that didn't develop into something serious, though, where the couples met seemed to have an effect on how quickly they slept together. Almost *half* of those who met a partner in a bar and ended up having only a short-term liaison had sex within a month of meeting. Apparently, there is also some love at first sight on the job—or more accurately, *sex* at first sight; 41 percent of those who ended up in a brief relationship with someone from work had sex within a month of first meeting. Students who met their partners in college, though, were unlikely to have sex within the first month of meeting each other, suggesting that college students are not, as was thought, hopping from partner to partner.

The Marriage Effect

The common perception that Americans have more sexual partners today than they did a decade or two ago is true. Still, when we asked people how many partners they had in the past year, the usual reply was zero or one. The explanation is linked to one of our most potent social institutions and how it has changed.

About 90 percent of Americans have married by the time they are 30. And marriage regulates sexual behavior with remarkable precision. No matter what they did before they wed, no matter how many partners they had, married people in the study had similar sexual drives: The vast majority were faithful while their marriages were intact.

The reason that people now have more sexual partners over their lifetimes is that they are spending longer periods of time unmarried and sexually active. Few Americans wait until they marry to have sex. The average age at which people first have sexual intercourse has crept down and the average age at which people marry for the first time has edged up. And people are more likely to divorce now, which means they have time between marriages for relationships with new partners.

The average age at which people first move in with a romantic partner has remained nearly constant throughout the years— around age 22 for men and 20 for women. The difference is that a person's first union is now much more likely to be cohabitation. And since many couples who live together break up within a short time, the result has been an increase in the average number of monogamous partners that people have before they marry.

Despite all this, our research shows that nearly all Americans have had sex with a modest number of partners, both over their adult lifetimes and in the previous year. Even men and women in their late teens and early twenties don't have very large numbers of partners—more than half had just one sex partner during the year of the study, and another 11 percent had none in the previous year. The number of partners that people reported having in the previous year varied little with education, race or religion—instead, it was determined by marital status.

The marriage effect is so dramatic that it swamps all other aspects of our data. *More than 80 percent of adult Americans aged 18* to 59 *had no or just one sexual partner in the previous year*—which might sound ludicrous to anyone who knows that she and her friends have had more than one partner in a year. But the figure reflects the fact that most Americans in that broad age range are married and are faithful. And many of the others are living with someone, and they are almost as faithful as married couples.

We found that the more educated people were, the more partners they had had over their lifetimes. One important reason for this is that people who have been educated longer are more likely to postpone marriage while they finish their schooling. The longer they wait, the more time they have to meet, have sex with, and often live with a succession of partners.

Only 3 percent of Americans—most of them young and male—had five or more partners in 1992. But considering that the population of the United States is more than 260 million, this translates into a large number of people—which underlines the need for education about safer-sex practices. These people are the most likely to have been infected with a sexually transmitted disease because of the sheer number of partners that they've had.

Single, Footloose—and Frustrated?

Some single people feel there is something wrong with them if they do not have frequent and passionate sex. They should take heart: Only one third of Americans aged 18 to 59 have sex with a partner as often as twice a week.

The rates of sexual activity are so modest that they confounded our expectations. After all, most adult Americans are married or living with someone. And sex really does not take that long—most people told us that they spend less than an hour making love. So if people really wanted more sex, they could probably manage to fit it in.

Three things made a difference in how often people had sex: age, marital status and how long they've been in a relationship. No matter what a person's race, ethnic group, religion, political leaning, education level or region of the country, sexual frequency is determined by these three factors. A conservative Southerner who has been married for a decade will probably have sexual intercourse about as often as a West Coast libertarian of the same age who has been married as long.

Here's the surprise: The people that have the *most* sex—no matter what the gender or race or ethnicity—are not the young and the footloose, but those who are married or living together. Having more partners, in other words, does not translate into having more frequent sex. People who have extramarital partners, or those who are unmarried and who have several partners in a year, actually end up having sex less often than people who have only one partner.

199

Given all this, it's not surprising that married people reported being the most physically pleased and emotionally satisfied. The lowest rates of satisfaction were among men and women who were neither married nor living with someone—the very group portrayed in our culture as having the hottest sex.

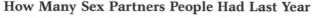

How Many Sex Partners People Had Last Year

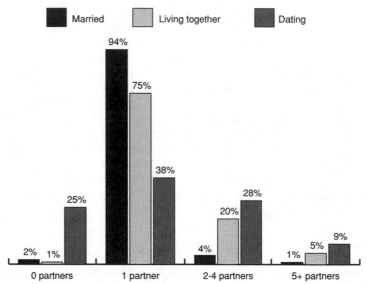

Because of rounding, totals may not equal 100%.

Source: Robert T. Michael et al., *Glamour*, November 1994.

Married women are much more likely to usually or always have orgasms (75 percent) than women who have never been married and aren't living with someone (62 percent). Most telling, however, is the fact that these single women have much higher rates of *never* climaxing—11 percent—than married or cohabitating women—2 percent.

The most educated women were a little less likely to always have orgasms (25 percent) than high-school graduates (35 percent) or women who have not completed high school (30 percent). Those with no religious affiliation are somewhat less likely to always have orgasms, while conservative Protestant women have the highest rates. The racial differences are also striking: Only 26 percent of white women always have orgasms, while 38 percent of black women and 34 percent of Hispanic women reported that they always do. And men aren't always clued in to whether or not their partners climax: Although just 29 percent of women said that they always have an orgasm, 44 percent of men said that *their* female partners always do.

What Americans Do in Bed

One surprise in our findings was that what people do in bed, and what they'd like to do, depends upon their race, social class, income, religion, even their geographical location. Another surprise was how few sexual activities are seen as appealing.

Only one practice—vaginal intercourse—stood out as having nearly universal appeal. It is, of course, the only sexual activity that can result in the birth of a baby, and it is the only practice that is sanctioned by all religions. It is the sexual activity that defines the loss of virginity, the one that teenagers dream of when they think of "going all the way."

No other genital sexual activity even approaches the status of vaginal sex. Ninety-five percent of our respondents told us that they had vaginal sex the last time they made love. Eighty percent said that every time they had sex in the past year they had vaginal sex.

What about other practices? Are people interested in trying group sex or using a dildo or having sex with a stranger? When we asked people what activities sounded appealing to them, we found that besides vaginal intercourse, only two practices have a strong attraction for many people.

One of these was watching a partner undress. Younger men and women were more attracted to this than older people, and more men than women said they like it—though 81 percent of women between the ages of 18 and 44 said that they find it very or somewhat appealing.

The other practice that garnered a large response is oral sex, but the reaction to it ranged from strongly enthusiastic to extremely unenthusiastic. Both men and women were more interested in receiving it than giving it. When we asked who had actually performed this act, we found that oral sex is most popular among young, higher-educated whites. Almost *twice as many* women who went to college have given or received oral sex than those who did not finish high school, and twice as many of these college-educated women had given or received oral sex the last time they had sex. A similar pattern was seen among men.

Another popular sexual practice: masturbation. About one quarter of men and 10 percent of women said that they masturbate at least once a week. The youngest people in our study masturbate slightly less than any other group except people over age 50. And our study showed that women begin to masturbate at older ages than men do; in fact, many women probably start

201

to masturbate *after* they begin having sexual intercourse rather than before.

The most sexually active people in America are also the most likely to masturbate. Nearly 85 percent of men and 45 percent of women who were living with a sexual partner said they had masturbated in the past year. Married people are significantly more likely to masturbate than people who are living alone. And the same groups that are most likely to have oral sex—white, educated liberals—are also the most likely to masturbate. Masturbation, we concluded, is not a substitute for those who are sexually deprived, but rather is an activity that stimulates and is stimulated by other sexual behavior.

Exploding the Myths

At every turn, our research has shown that social forces are powerful and persistent in determining sexual behavior. We have found that our society constrains us, nudging us toward partners who are like ourselves. But at the same time, it frees us: It puts us together with people who have the same general understandings about sex as ours, and so, eases our way into sexual intimacies and revelations.

By seeing where and how social pressures are brought to bear, we can break away from the myths and magical thinking that have captured us in the past. Although America may not be a hotbed of eroticism, it is a nation of people who are largely satisfied with the sexual lives that they've chosen or that society has led them to.

"When Americans are less imprisoned by public expectations and a private sense of sexual shame, perhaps more couples will earn their full satisfaction."

Many Americans Are Unsatisfied with Their Sex Lives

Lynn Rosellini

In the following viewpoint, Lynn Rosellini explores two types of sexual desire disorders: hypoactive sexual desire (HSD) and compulsive sexual behavior (CSB). People experiencing HSD have little or no interest in sex, while those exhibiting CSB have an abnormally high interest in it. According to the author, an estimated one in four Americans suffers from one of these disorders, the roots of which lie predominantly in the human psyche. She adds that the sexual partners of those afflicted often suffer, as well. Because a large number of Americans may experience these disorders, Rosellini concludes, the sex lives of many Americans are less than satisfactory. Rosellini is a senior writer for *U.S. News & World Report*, a weekly newsjournal of world affairs.

As you read, consider the following questions:

1. According to Rosellini, what are some symptoms of the two kinds of desire disorders?
2. How do the partners of those who suffer from one of these disorders feel, according to Rosellini?
3. What are the causes of HSD and CSB, according to the author?

She won't look at him. Keeps staring out the window, even though there's nothing to see but the black Minnesota night and a car speeding past, headlights sliding along the glass. "I thought it would just go away," the petite woman says finally, in a small, tired voice. "That it was just a phase I was going through. I would make excuses."

The muffled thuds and shouts of playing children drift from the basement. Her wiry husband, seated on the Early American sofa, is a machinist in his late 30s. She is a homemaker. And all that matters now is that they haven't had sex in eight months. "He'd start a little foreplay. I'd say 'No. Just leave me alone!'"

"Boy, would that put me away," says her husband, his bearded face stony above a red T-shirt. "I was already feeling hurt. I'd roll over and go to sleep."

"Sometimes, every three to four months, I'd force myself," she confesses. "Grit my teeth and get through it."

A Common Situation

Neither partner looks at the other, and a hesitant hush hovers over the room. Finally, the husband turns to psychologist Eli Coleman, who runs a sex-therapy clinic in nearby Minneapolis. "There's just one thing I want to know," he says, frowning. "Is this a common situation?"

Common? Try epidemic. The problem under discussion is sexual desire, an instinct that should flow as freely and unselfconsciously between two loving humans as the urge for a fine meal or a good night's sleep. This is a story about what happens when desire goes askew. It is a tale of people who typically are articulate, competent and to all appearances quite ordinary, yet they cannot enjoy one of humankind's most basic pleasures. Madonna may be falling out of her bustier on MTV, Prince may be singing the joys of masturbation on FM and the latest sex-and-gore thriller may be packing them in at the Cineplex, but in the bedroom, an estimated 1 in 5 Americans—some 38 million adults—don't want sex at all. As many as 9 million more, meanwhile, suffer almost uncontrollable sexual desire, compulsively masturbating or prowling a surreal landscape of massage parlors and rumpled beds in a frenzied quest for loveless sex.

Sexual-Desire Disorders

To be sure, sexual-desire disorders date back a lot further than "The Devil and Miss Jones," or even Don Juan. What's new is that such complaints now constitute the No. 1 problem bringing clients to sex therapists. Women without orgasms and men who ejaculated prematurely once dominated the practice; now—because of the pioneering research of Dr. William Masters and Virginia Johnson in the 1960s—people with such common conditions seek do-it-yourself solutions. "The simpler cases can go out and get self-help books," says Dr. Constance Moore, head of the Human Sexuality Program at Houston's Baylor College of Medicine. "Today, sex therapists are seeing the more complicated problems."

Fostering Healthy Sexuality

Amid the 1990s scourges of AIDS and child molestation, parents now have one more reason to worry about what they tell their kids about sex. Therapists confirm that children who learn that sex is dirty or evil are especially prone to sexual desire disorders later in life.

U.S. News & World Report, July 6, 1992.

No one is sure whether the onslaught of Americans seeking help reflects a real rise in desire disorders or whether such problems are simply more visible. In the 1960s, public expectations of sex began to shift in profound ways. Thanks to the birth-control pill, women could for the first time in history separate sex from the fear of pregnancy. Suddenly, it was not only OK for women to enjoy sex—it was *de rigueur.* The 1953 Kinsey report that as many as 29 percent of single women were sexually unresponsive now seemed as old-fashioned as stiff petticoats and white gloves.

At the same time, new cultural messages glorified casual sex. More than 80 percent of women and 90 percent of men now engage in premarital intercourse, compared with 50 percent of women and 80 percent of men in the 1920s. And from seductive Calvin Klein–jeans ads to the estimated 176 monthly sex scenes on prime-time TV, free sex has emerged as the presumptive symbol of the good life. Sexual health has become a right.

Fear and Sex

And so they come for help: A man who, after pursuing his bride-to-be for months, shuts down sexually on his wedding night in their $200-a-day bridal suite. A school administrator with five boyfriends who sandwiches frenzied appointments for sex between dashes to office and supermarket. They are farmers and salesmen, consultants and lawyers, homemakers and clerks. In the sanitized confines of therapists' offices, they haltingly reveal their secrets—it's hard, after all, to confess even to a best friend that one masturbates five times a day or hasn't slept with one's spouse in a year. Eyes downcast, voices leaden, they evoke the anguish of abusive fathers, of religiously suffocating mothers, of families where sex, if discussed at all, was shameful and dirty and where dad sometimes slipped into bed with the kids.

What unites them is fear. As children, they learned that caring too much for others was risky. As adults, they found they could control their fear by controlling sex. Instead of an intimate and loving act, sex became a tool to manipulate those who might get too close. And while no one can properly distinguish why some people channel childhood anxieties into food or booze while others fasten on sex, it may be that what eating disorders were to the '80s, desire disorders will be in the '90s: the designer disease of the decade, the newest symptom of American loneliness and alienation. "Sex isn't just sex," explains Raul C. Schiavi, head of the Human Sexuality Program at Mount Sinai Medical Center. "It's an avenue to express many more needs: intimacy, support, self-esteem or whatever.". . .

What Is Normal?

At first it was fun: feverish kisses in his red Chevy, giggly nights of passion in the apartment. But then came marriage, two kids, and suddenly her husband's hands on her flesh felt like tentacles, and the sight of him approaching made her body stiffen with revulsion. Then the disagreements began, hurtful scenes ending with each of them lying wedged against opposite sides of the bed, praying for sleep. "I didn't know what to do—look in the yellow pages?" recalls Karen, 35, a clerk-cashier in suburban Minneapolis. Her husband didn't know, either. "We finally got a phone number from our family doctor," he says. "It was three more months before we called."

It wasn't so long ago that low sexual desire was considered a good thing—at least in women. Madame Bovary scandalized 19th-century France with her extramarital fling in Gustave Flaubert's novel. And no one ever said that the remote Estella of Dickens's *Great Expectations* had a low-desire problem. Indeed, from Eve's seduction of Adam, women's sexuality outside of procreation was often considered evil, and early Christian thinkers were just as unsparing toward men—a philosophy that found particularly fertile ground in the New World. As recently as 1907, Dr. John Harvey Kellogg developed his popular corn flakes in an unsuccessful effort to curb desire.

Nor were men and women always physically able to enjoy sex. In late 17th-century England, for instance, people suffered from long bouts of crippling illness, not to mention bad breath from poor dentistry, running sores, ulcers and skin diseases. Without antibiotics, women endured repeated vaginal and urinary tract infections that made sex painful.

In fact, the idea of "normal" sexual appetite is such a 20th-century artifice that few experts are comfortable defining it. Clinically, hypoactive sexual desire [HSD] means having sexual urges, fantasies and/or activity less than twice a month. But even that is the loosest of definitions, since if both partners are happy, once a month may be as "proper" as once a day. "I make the diagnosis [of HSD] if there's been a definite change in desire," says sexologist Moore, "and if it's causing the patient some distress." In Karen's case, the distress was acute: Each night she huddled on her side of the bed, tormenting herself with guilt and dread that her marriage was slipping away.

The Partner's Distress

More typically, though, it's the patient's *partner* who is in distress. Consider Tom, 35, a Midwestern advertising executive whose wife has HSD. "I would try to ignore it as long as I could," he says. "Then she'd give in [and have sex]. But she'd lie limp, waiting for me to get it over with. She could have been downtown. I felt terrible afterward, very guilty."

Prodded by their mates, victims of desire disorders often show up for therapy complaining of impotence or lack of orgasm. But in the mid-1970s, therapists began to notice that the real problem was often that, as in Karen's case, they didn't truly *want* to have sex. In her groundbreaking 1979 work, *Disorders of Sexual Desire*, Dr. Helen Singer Kaplan found that unlike sexual arousal, desire exists primarily in the mind. As a result, Kaplan concluded, HSD stems not from a lack of ability to perform but from a lack of motivation. Even so, the fact that HSD may be "all in your mind" doesn't make living with it any easier. "The most important part of sex," Kaplan says, "is the emotional, subjective part. Without that, mechanical function is not gratifying."

Therapists have found that HSD appears to be about twice as prevalent in women as in men. While no national samples are available, one 1978 study of 100 nonclinical American couples found that 35 percent of the women reported lack of sexual interest, compared with 16 percent of the men. But despite this gap, the causes of HSD for both men and women are the same, and the problem usually begins with the emotions.

Causes of Low Desire

The memories started coming after two years in therapy: gauzy, not quite distinct, yet so haunting that tears slowly squeezed from her eyes right in front of the therapist. Jeanine was 8 years old, lying in bed in her Wisconsin home, watching the door creak open. Suddenly, her father was silently over her, breathing heavily. She never told anybody. How could she? There were crucifixes in every room of the house, and her father led the family in the rosary nightly during Lent. Her mother once lectured her on how little girls who "touched themselves" must confess to the priest. Years later, after she got married, Jeanine never had an orgasm with her husband, Tom. Later, she shut down altogether. She and Tom last had sex 4½ years ago.

The roots of desire disorders often lie between the *Sesame Street* years and junior high. Some adults, like Jeanine, report having been sexually abused as children; for others, the abuse was more emotional. John Money, who has pioneered treatments for deviate sexuality at Johns Hopkins University, says children raised in homes where sex is viewed as evil and harmless activities like "playing doctor" are cruelly punished are likely to grow up with warped sexual identities. "In girls, often you extinguish the lust completely, so that they can never have an orgasm, and marriage becomes a dreary business where you put up with sex to serve the maternal instinct," says Money. "In boys, sex gets redirected into abnormal channels."

Not surprisingly, women like Jeanine, who learn as children not to trust those closest to them, often have trouble melding passion and intimacy. Although victims of low desire may be drawn to hit-and-run encounters with strangers, when they get close to a partner, it's too dangerous to let themselves go sexually. Many men suffer from Freud's famous "Madonna-whore complex," whereby a man endows his partner with the "Madonna-like" qualities of his mother. "You find a sudden cessation of interest in sex right after the wedding, even on the night the engagement was announced," says Harold Lief, professor emeritus of psychiatry at the University of Pennsylvania. "These men can't lust after someone they love, or vice versa."

Then there are the tangled cases, where the core problem is not so much historical as personal: The husband and wife detest each other. Marital difficulties, say Lief and other therapists, underlie as many as half of desire disorder cases. Often the problem stems from suppressed anger. "If a couple comes into my office," says Kaplan, "and they fight about where they're gonna sit, and the only question is who's gonna complain about the other more, I know why they're not having sex."

Childbirth, stress and depression can also precipitate low sexual desire. But only in a minority of cases—roughly 15 percent—are the causes medical, such as hormone deficiencies or diseases like diabetes. Some antidepressants and antihypertensives can also squelch desire. The good news is that such problems usually have a medical solution, sparing patients lengthy hours on an analyst's couch. But the story is not so simple for most HSD sufferers. . . .

When Sex Becomes Compulsive

Gary's pattern was always the same: first, the unbearable anxiety, never feeling good enough to handle the latest stress at his architect's job. Then, the familiar response—a furtive scanning of newspaper ads, a drive to a strip show, two straight Scotches to catch a buzz,

and finally a massage parlor. He would park about a block away,
slip off his wedding ring and dart through the door, where $100
bought a massage, sex and momentary relief. Afterward, he'd sit
naked on the edge of the bed, his thoughts roiling in disgust: "I must
be sick . . . I can't change." But a few days later, the anxiety would
begin again and he'd pore over the ads.

Too *much* sex? For many Americans, especially young men, the
notion sounds like an oxymoron. In fact, the downside of sexual
compulsiveness has been largely overshadowed throughout
history by a romanticized view of the rake, from Casanova to
basketball legend Wilt Chamberlain, with his claims of 20,000 affairs. Compulsive sexual behavior [CSB] is perhaps easiest to define by what it is not: It does not include someone who mastur-
bates occasionally, periodically rents an X-rated video or engages
in a limited period of promiscuity following the breakup of a relationship. As best therapists can tell, those prey to CSB alternate
between profound anxiety and all-embracing self-loathing.

But these are not perverts in raincoats. Gary, the architect described above, wears a well-cut tweed sports jacket and speaks
in measured tones. "I was two different people," he says quietly,
seated in a psychologist's office in Minneapolis. "Most people
who knew my wife and me would say we were a good couple.
But when I was home, I wasn't really there. I felt like a dirty
person, rotten." Indeed, one hallmark of compulsive sexual behavior is secrecy: Gary's wife didn't find out about his clandes-
tine visits to porn shops and prostitutes until she discovered a
phone bill listing multiple calls to a "900" sex line.

Treating Stress with Sex

So secret are their escapades that CSB victims have never
even been counted, and experts' figures—they estimate roughly
5 percent of the adult American population—are the merest
guess. But if the figures are flimsy, the portrait is precise. To the
sexual compulsive, sex is not about love or intimacy or even
pleasure. It is mainly about relief. "These are highly anxious
people who respond to stress by attempting to 'medicate' their
pain through sex," says Eli Coleman, director of the University
of Minnesota's Program in Human Sexuality, and a pioneer in
treating CSB. Just as the obsessive compulsive washes his hands
100 times in a row, the sexual compulsive turns to a vast erotic
menu that might include compulsive masturbation, feverish
cruising and anonymous sex, frenzied multiple affairs or insa-
tiable demands within a relationship.

A small proportion of CSB victims cross the criminal divide
into hard-core deviations: voyeurism, obscene phone calls, pedophilia, exhibitionism and others. But the majority prefer ordinary sex—taken to an extreme. What they share is an over-

whelming sense of powerlessness. Like the alcoholic, the sexual compulsive is so intent on diverting his pain that he often doesn't even *see* a choice. "If I saw a prostitute on the street, that was it," says Jeff, 36, a public-relations executive from St. Paul, Minnesota. "It was impossible to not do it."

The Causes of CSB

His parents were strict Catholics who said the rosary every night and sent their 11 kids to parochial school. The messages about sex began early. Once, at age 12, Jeff overheard his 19-year-old sister tell his father: "Sex is fun." His father shouted: "Don't you ever say that!" Jeff's mother didn't even like hugging and protested loudly on the rare occasions that her husband kissed her in front of the children. As for the nuns, Sister Frances told Jeff's third-grade class: "One should never be naked for longer than necessary." The little boy worried that he had condemned his soul to hell by dawdling in the bathroom. "The message was: 'Lord I am not worthy,'" says Jeff, who became hooked as an adult on compulsive phone sex, masturbation and prostitutes. "I took all of it to heart."

Certainly most people survive strict religious upbringing without becoming "Fantasy Hotline" junkies. Yet over and over, as CSB victims have recounted their stories, therapists have seen a disturbing pattern: As children, these men and women learned that sex was anything but a loving, natural experience. Their parents were rarely able to nurture them or allow them to express feelings in healthy ways. In some cases, they simply neglected the kids: Jeff remembers going weeks without a bath and wearing his clothes to bed. Other parents expected their kids to toe some unattainable line of perfection. "My dad yelled at me, taunted me," says Kevin, 32, a professional from the Midwest who started cruising for anonymous sex in public bathrooms at 16. "Sometimes, he would shake me or choke me. He called me Sissie, told me I was worthless, a mess."

In recent years, family therapist Patrick Carnes—author of the 1983 book *Out of the Shadows*—has gained thousands of followers for his claim that CSB is not an anxiety-based disorder but an addiction, much like alcoholism. It is a spiritual disease, he believes, as well as an emotional and physical one, and his plan for recovery involves belief in a higher power. But while the addiction model has spawned four popular nationwide AA-style support groups, many researchers are skeptical, maintaining that it's impossible to be "addicted" to sex since there is no addictive substance involved. Both the chemical and spiritual explanations, they maintain, grossly oversimplify a complex phenomenon. "It's also sex-negative and moralistic," argues Howard Ruppel of the Society for the Scientific Study of Sex. "They confuse normal activity like masturbating with addiction.". . .

Ultimately, the problem with treating both extremes of sexual desire is that researchers still struggle with their own ignorance. . . . Key research—studying the areas of the brain that control sexual behavior or the effects of drugs on desire—awaits funding. "We have almost no information about how people form their sexual habits," says psychologist Elizabeth Allgeier, co-author of *Sexual Interactions*, a widely used college text. "If we don't know how it develops, we can't change it."

Still, for millions of Americans it is reassuring to know that no one is doomed to a life of torment by sex. At the very least, educating and encouraging adults to have more enlightened sexual attitudes might enable children to grow up with healthier feelings toward sex. Psychologist John Money says that sexually repressive attitudes now force "at least 50 percent of the nation to get 57 cents to the dollar on their sex lives." When Americans are less imprisoned by public expectations and a private sense of sexual shame, perhaps more couples will earn their full satisfaction.

"In America, men and women are moving away from casual sex and placing more importance on intimate relationships."

Sex Is Becoming More Intimate and Less Casual

Mark Clements

In February 1994, Mark Clements conducted a survey of Americans' sexual behavior and attitudes, an updated version of a study done in 1984. In the following viewpoint, Clements discusses the findings of his survey and concludes that after more than two decades, the effects of the sexual revolution—frequent and casual sex—have diminished. More men and women, he argues, are finding sexual and emotional satisfaction in long-term, monogamous relationships. Clements runs Mark Clements Research, Inc., a firm that does research and conducts surveys.

As you read, consider the following questions:

1. What changes have men made in their attitudes toward sexuality, according to Clements?
2. What are some of the changes in sexual behavior and attitudes since the 1984 survey, according to the author?

In America, men and women are moving away from casual sex and placing more importance on intimate relationships. In an exclusive new survey—covering 1049 men and women aged 18 to 65 and representative of the population as a whole—conducted by Mark Clements Research for *Parade* magazine, nearly eight out of ten respondents say it's difficult for them to have sex without emotional involvement. Married people (this survey defines "married" as any long-term, monogamous relationship) report higher levels of sexual activity and satisfaction than singles. Singles report significant changes in sexual habits because of fear of AIDS.

Survey Results

"The findings are phenomenal," says Beverly Whipple of Medford, New Jersey, an associate professor at Rutgers University's College of Nursing and a member of the boards of the American Association of Sex Educators, Counselors and Therapists (AASECT) and the Society for the Scientific Study of Sex. She notes a higher percentage of people using condoms and a lower rate of extramarital affairs than in other studies. "This survey may be more valid than many others," she adds, "because it is based on a cross-section of the population, rather than just college students."

Are Americans becoming more sexually conservative? Perhaps, says the psychologist Sallie Schumacher of Winston-Salem, North Carolina, a past president of AASECT. "But what struck me is that men and women seem more committed and caring."

Men in particular are paying more attention to the emotional side of sex. The percentage of men who say it is difficult for them to have sex without emotional involvement rose from 59% in 1984 to 71% in 1994. The proportion of women feeling this way remained the same: 86%. And 74% of men today say it is easy to talk about sex with their partners, compared with 59% in 1984. Today, 70% of women find conversations about sex with a partner easy—up from 63% in 1984. Overall, men show more changes in sexual attitudes than women.

"The survey shows a trend toward men and women becoming more similar in their sexuality," says Karla Baur, a sex therapist in private practice in Portland, Oregon, and co-author of the college text *Our Sexuality*. "With the shift from recreational sex, both genders are seeking more emotional meaning in sex. There's more interest in quality rather than quantity."

Many more Americans now say they are happy with life in general than those surveyed in 1984 (82%, compared with 54%). "In this age of cynicism and anxiety, I would not have expected this," observes Shirley Zussman, a sex and marital therapist in New York City. "Perhaps as the outer world has become more dangerous and fraught with problems, people are putting more emphasis on their private lives."

Among other key findings in our survey:

- 3% of male respondents identify themselves as homosexual. "This is much lower than the 10% estimate that has been used in the past," says Beverly Whipple of Rutgers. "But it confirms recent research showing that 1% to 3% of the male population is gay." Among the women surveyed, 1% say they are homosexual; 3% of the men and 0.4% of the women say they're bisexual.

- The average age for first heterosexual intercourse among both men and women responding to the survey is 18.

- Men report that they've had sex with an average of 15 women; women have had sex with an average of 8 men. Among those who report having a partner of the same sex at some time in their lives, the average number of same-sex partners is 18 for men and 3 for women.

- 67% of respondents say the actual sex act is better than foreplay. Men (73%) are more likely to feel this way than women (58%).

- 83% of the survey respondents describe themselves as, at least, "knowledgeable" about sex; 29% say they are "very knowledgeable.". . .

A Changing Perspective

When *Parade* conducted its first sex survey in 1984, the sexual revolution had been in full swing for more than a decade, and there was not yet widespread awareness of AIDS. "Back then, the feeling was 'anything goes,'" says Brenda Sellars, 32, a sales and customer service representative in Cincinnati. "But people have realized that you can't separate sex from emotion. A lot of women have always felt this way, but now men are catching on too."

Anna Maria Rodriguez, 31, of Norman, Oklahoma, a car rental reservations agent, agrees: "Maybe the reason is that today's men were raised by women coming of age in the '60s; maybe they read more; maybe they're more sensitive. But they're definitely figuring out what matters."

In 1994, 80% of the men participating in our survey, compared with 77% in 1984, say that sexual activity is important; the proportion of women who agree has stayed about the same: 65%. More men and women also say that orgasm is important: 88% of men, up from 81% in 1984, and 74% of women, up from 60%. In addition, 91% of all men and women surveyed say that it's important that their partner has an orgasm; 82% say it's important that they achieve orgasm themselves.

In assessing their own sexual skills, survey respondents may have become more modest. In 1984, 74% said they were excellent lovers. In 1994, only 51% rate their ability as "excellent" or "very good." Furthermore, in 1984, 73% of men and 57% of women agreed with the statement "I have a strong sex drive." In 1994, only 52% of men and 32% of women describe their sex drive as somewhat or very high.

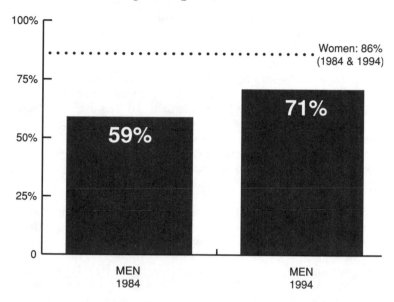

The Emotional Side of Sex: Growing in Importance for Men

Percentage of men who say they find it difficult to have sex without emotional involvement, 1984 and 1994. In both years, 86% of women said they felt this way.

Mark Clements, *Parade*, August 7, 1994.

"The population has gotten older, and people have gotten busier," notes Shirley Zussman. "Men and women today work harder than any other generation I've known. They're tired all the time. They've got kids, jobs, worries. They may have less energy and time for sex."

In 1994, 16% of respondents report sexual problems, compared with 14% in 1984. Among today's men, just as in 1984, impotence is the most frequent difficulty, affecting 46% of those who report sexual problems. Among women, "low sex drive" has replaced "sexual incompatibility" as the most common problem—mentioned by 60% of the women reporting sexual difficulties (as well as by 38% of the men).

Sex in the '90s

Respondents to this survey report an average of seven acts of sexual intercourse a month, a small increase from six a decade ago. There has been no change in the average number of orgasms that respondents report among their last ten sex acts: nine for men, seven for women. Men and women aged 25 to 34 have sex most often—nine times a month, compared with eight for those aged 18 to 24, eight for those 35 to 44 and seven for those 45 to 54. Survey participants of all ages say they would like to make love more frequently—ideally, an average of thirteen times a month.

Respondents devote an average of 39 minutes, including foreplay, to making love; 11% spend an hour or more. The average time reported for achieving orgasm is 16 minutes for men, 17 for women. Respondents aged 35 to 65 reach orgasm more quickly than younger ones: 16 minutes, compared with an average of 19 minutes for those under 35. Of those surveyed, 38% of women and 16% of men report that they usually have multiple orgasms, while 15% of women and 2% of men say they usually do not reach orgasm.

Men report initiating sex more often than women, with 60% of men saying they "always" or "almost always" make the first move, compared with 22% of women.

Both men and women love kissing, which 93% of respondents find pleasurable. Genital touching is enjoyed by 93% of men and 88% of women; 93% of women and 87% of men say they like hugging. Other top-ranked pleasures include mouth on breasts (enjoyed by 90% of respondents), hands on breasts (91%) and body-kissing (80%). The sexual repertoire of the survey participants includes cunnilingus (mentioned by 45% of respondents), mutual masturbation (35%), fellatio (32%), anal sex (8%) and bondage (5%). Frequent use of pornographic material during sexual activity is reported by 18% of respondents, while 11% say they often employ sexual devices to enhance their enjoyment.

Wedded Bliss

According to the survey, 78% of those who are married are happy with their marital status, compared with 53% of singles. "This is a very important finding," says the psychologist Sallie Schumacher. "People may be working harder to make their lives better and happier." Men generally are the most content, with 40% of those surveyed describing themselves as "extremely happy" with their marital status; 33% of the women surveyed and 18% of the singles say the same.

"I know I'm happier than I would be as a single man," says Vernon Davis, 40, who works for the streets department in Cincinnati and who has been married for 20 years. "It's more difficult to be single these days. I think that's why men have gotten more interested in establishing a good relationship."

Husbands and wives report greater sexual satisfaction than singles, with 67% vs. 45% saying they are happy with their sex lives. Sexual activity is considered "important" by 77% of married people, compared with 57% of singles. Married folks also have sex more often—eight times a month, compared with five for singles (who masturbate twice as often). More husbands and wives (73%) find it easy to talk with their partners about sex than singles (67%). More than half of married people (56%) report having orgasms each of the last ten times they had sex, compared with 48% of singles. And more married respondents (65%) than singles (57%) say it is "very important" that their partners have orgasms.

One out of six married respondents—19% of men and 15% of women—say they have had an extramarital relationship. The percentage reporting such liaisons rises with age, from 7% of those under 25 to 23% of those 55 to 65. "These rates are lower than we've seen in the past," notes the psychologist Beverly Whipple.

The Impact of AIDS

Two-thirds of married people say fear of AIDS has not affected their sexual behavior; more than half of all respondents aged 25 to 65 say the same. Among singles, 8 out of 10 say they have made changes in their sexual behavior because of fear of AIDS; 6 out of 10 say the changes are "drastic." In general, single women (77%) are more aware of and concerned about AIDS than single men (54%).

"Fear of AIDS certainly makes you think twice about getting into a relationship," says Roberta Osuna, 39, a divorced secretary with five children in Temecula, California. "I think women are more cautious because they're concerned about the possibility of infecting a child in the future or of not being able to care for the children they already have."

Among those who have altered their sexual practices, the most frequent change has been the use of condoms for intercourse—reported by 48% of men and 32% of women. About a third of the respondents say they have become monogamous (32%) or have fewer sex partners (35%) than in the past; 18% abstain from sex. In addition, 35% discuss sexual histories with partners; 37% wait until knowing a partner well before having unprotected sex.

Among singles, 61% say they would insist that a potential partner be tested for HIV before entering a new sexual relationship;

38% of both men and women would insist that a partner be tested for HIV if they found out that he or she had had sex with someone else. More than a quarter of all respondents—26%—say they know someone who is HIV-positive and/or has AIDS.

About 60% of the women surveyed say they would be tested for HIV if they were contemplating pregnancy. This figure rises to 76% among single women. Almost 50% of the men surveyed—and 68% of those aged 18 to 24—say they would insist that their partners be tested if they were anticipating a pregnancy.

Sex and Aging

According to our survey, men and women aged 55 to 65 make love an average of five times per month. "This group of aging Americans is the first one in history to have been exposed to so much information about sex," observes the sex therapist Shirley Zussman. "They're far more interested and informed than their parents and grandparents." An almost equal percentage of respondents aged 55 to 65 (62%) and those aged 18 to 24 (63%) say sexual activity is important to them, while 77% of those aged 25 to 54 find it important.

Older partners may be sensual as well as sexual. As with younger respondents, men and women aged 55 to 65 rank hugging and kissing as top sexual pleasures. "Hugging and kissing have always been a big thing in our relationship, and they still are," says Kathryn Sena, 59, a retired mother of four and grandmother of 10 in South San Francisco. "But there's also more openness about the fact that older people are still doing it. In the past, it wasn't something people talked about. That's changed, and it has become acceptable."

While older respondents remain just as satisfied with life in general, the percentage of those who say they're happy with their sex lives drops from 66% for those aged 18 to 44 to 55% for those 55 to 65. And a higher percentage report sexual problems—22%, compared with 14% of those under 55. Among those reporting sexual difficulties, the most common are low sex drive (52%), impotence (42%) and difficulty achieving orgasm (40%). Other sexual complaints, such as self-consciousness during sex and problems with a partner, become less frequent with age. "Personally, I don't see why sex shouldn't be just as good as it ever was," says Kathryn Sena. "Sex is a pleasure that people can enjoy at every stage of life."

"Sex and love have been granted a divorce."

Sex Is Becoming More Casual and Less Intimate

B.K. Eakman

B.K. Eakman is the author of *Educating for the "New World Order"* and its sequel *Microchipped: How the Education Establishment Took Us Beyond Big Brother* and a contributor to *Chronicles,* a monthly journal of cultural commentary. In the following viewpoint, originally a speech entitled "What They Did to Love," Eakman argues that the American education system and media communicate the idea that frequent, casual, and loveless sex is the most desirable kind of sexual interaction. The author contends that these messages are perpetuating a distorted view that hormones and violence, not respect and love, are the true basis for sexuality.

As you read, consider the following questions:

1. According to Eakman, what is the strongest animal drive after hunger? What is the strongest human drive?
2. Why do orthodox religious people resist "government-mandated sex training," according to the author?
3. According to Eakman, how is sex now defined?

Excerpted from B.K. Eakman, "When Sex Conquers Love," *Chronicles,* June 1994. Reprinted by permission of *Chronicles: A Magazine of American Culture,* a publication of the Rockford Institute, Rockford, Illinois.

Much as I hate to admit it, former AIDS czarina Kristine Gebbie got it right [Gebbie was the National AIDS Policy Coordinator]. The message to youngsters these days does indeed give the impression that sex is ugly, dirty, and a more perverse than pleasurable experience. Ms. Gebbie bungled only when she took on the role of anti-Victorian-morality crusader.

In the space of a few months, I read about public school teachers who "have sex with" (not merely "seduce") their students; priests who sexually abuse little boys; naval officers who apparently make orgies an annual, celebrated event; and movie stars who take on the names of solemn religious figures to promote videos and books portraying kinky sex. Then there was the ongoing debate over gays in the military, which meant that newspaper and magazine readers were treated to ever more graphic descriptions concerning the sexual gymnastics performed by homosexuals. Rap music lyricists got accolades for their latest achievement in moving the term 'hos into the mainstream of American lexicon. The Whitney Museum of American Art launched its exhibit "Abject Art: Repulsion and Desire," which managed to outdo even Robert Mapplethorpe, Annie Sprinkle, and Madonna. And South Florida installed a "public service" hotline for teenagers (377-TEEN) called "The Link," which promotes sex as a means of getting rid of tension, abortion on demand without parental consent, and homosexuality as a lifestyle as opposed to a handicap.

All this doesn't begin to include the multifarious accounts of rape-torture murders; the endless articles exploring the DNA analysis of semen found on some poor, dead girl's panties; the demands of the Man-Boy Love Association; the aborted fetuses in our faces; and the new horrors on the sexually transmitted diseases front, such as cytomegalovirus (CMV), which is causing birth defects in pregnant women. At a subway station entrance, my husband and I were shocked by a billboard as stunningly tasteless as the sexual message it sought to rebut. The billboard was designed to appear spattered with blood. The caption read: "'Virgin' is not a dirty word."

Sex Education

By summer's end, I was glad I wasn't a kid anymore. Somehow such an introduction to the world of sexuality would have failed to inspire passion, raging hormones or no. Indeed, if we observe the admonitions of former Surgeon General Joycelyn Elders and deposed New York School Chancellor Joseph Fernandez, we shouldn't wait until youngsters' hormones are raging. We should assault their sensibilities in kindergarten with a panoply of condoms, sex toys (no kidding), and legitimized pornography. The National Guidelines for Comprehensive Sexual Education, produced in 1992 by the Sex Information and Education Council of the United States, recommend teaching kindergartners to feel comfortable with their genitals by having them shout "penis" and "vulva." By fourth grade, the sex education curriculum has youngsters performing the now-familiar ritual of unrolling condoms on bananas and discussing the benefits of "mutual masturbation." In seventh grade, children advance to discussing oral and anal sex, role-playing sexual situations, and learning the street names for a variety of sexual acts. In high school, young students are awash in bisexuality, transvestitism, sadomasochism, and bestiality. Teachers are supposed to pass around "finger cots," which are condoms for the fingers, and "dental dams," a kind of condom for oral sex, and discuss "brachiopractic penetration," which the curious can look up. The idea, supposedly, is to make youngsters hygiene-conscious at dating time. This is sold in catchy phrases like "safe sex" and "no glove, no love!"

Love, indeed. What happened to it?

"Love" and "Sex"

The word "love" now applies to almost everything except the overwhelming attraction of one individual for another. And sex is a timid pseudoscientific word which tells us only that individuals have certain bodily needs. There is an appalling matter-of-factness in public speech about sex today. On television, schoolchildren tell us about how they will now use condoms in their contacts—I was about to say adventures, but that would be overstating their significance. On talk shows, young collegians tell us about how they decide whether they have been raped in their various encounters. There is nothing in these tales of the now-impossible complaint about outraged virginity. Sex is spoken of coolly and without any remains of the old puritanical shame, as an incidental aspect of the important questions of disease and power. The sexual talk of our times is about how to get greater bodily satisfaction or how to protect ourselves from one another. The old view was that delicacy of language was part of the nature, the sacred nature, of eros, and that to speak about it in any other way would be to misunderstand it. What has disappeared is the risk and the hope of human connectedness embedded in eros. Ours is a language that reduces the longing for another to the need for individual, private satisfaction and safety.

Allan Bloom, *The New York Times Magazine*, May 23, 1993.

Somewhere between the bluegrass-country ballads that the Everly Brothers and the Kingston Trio interpreted for their teenage audiences—songs that expressed an amorous sentimentality,

incorporated complex harmonies, evoked an entreating innocence, and connected sex with affection—and the heavy metal-
rap era, music moved from seduction to sadism, from beautiful
to brutal, from romantic to repulsive. Today it is difficult to find
a station to wake up to in the morning that isn't filled with
squealing and shrieking and a what's-love-got-to-do-with-it men-
tality. Talented new instrumental composers like John Nilsen,
Danny Wright, Tom Barabas, Karunesh, Gary Sills, and Clifford
White are ignored by disc jockeys and can be located only
through independent music distributors and heard about only
by word of mouth, as increasing numbers of individuals seek to
escape the cacophony of pulsating commercials and sexploitive
song lyrics for more uplifting and romantic fields.

Meanwhile, television languishes in the language of abuse—
nonstop sexual innuendos, putdowns, and lascivious catcalls
from the audience. Youngsters cut their teeth on the putrid
squalor of *Beavis and Butt-head*. Media moguls say these and
other shows are successful because they attract a large share of
the viewing audience.

But what about the nonviewing, nonlistening audience? How
about those who rarely turn on the tube or radio anymore?
Where are the statistics on us? More to the point, when did sex
become a mere animalistic instinct? When did "flirting" and
"courtship" become synonyms for "sexual harassment"?

Sex and Love

As a final indignity, Ann Landers, after 38 years of preaching
commitment and caring, offered her commentary on a piece she
reprinted from the *Los Angeles Times* by a Dr. Steven Sainsbury
of San Luis Obispo, California. He had written to comment on a
15-year-old girl he was treating for "a rip-roaring case of gonorrhea"—a typical occurrence in his practice, apparently. It was
bad enough that he criticized experts who equate condoms with
"safe sex," saying the high breakage rate during normal, vaginal
intercourse did not support such a claim. But Dr. Sainsbury
committed the ultimate blasphemy when he maintained that the
only safe sex is no sex, until one is ready "to commit to a monogamous relationship." The key words, he reiterated, were "*abstinence* and *monogamy*."

The good doctor didn't mention marriage, but no matter. Ann
Landers took on the heretic, declaring that she was going to
"stick her neck out" and "suggest a more realistic solution than
abstinence." Her recommendation? "Self-gratification or mutual
masturbation, whatever it takes to release sexual energy." "This
is a sane and safe alternative to intercourse," she wrote, "not
only for teenagers, but for older men and women who have lost
their partners." Her rationale was that "the sex drive is the

222

strongest human drive after hunger."

It was this sanctimonious diatribe that brought me to the word processor. I'm going to stick *my* neck out and say: No. The sex drive is *not* the strongest human drive after hunger. It may be the strongest *animal* drive after hunger, but it is not the strongest *human* drive. Love is. Love is what separates animals from humans. Animals may exhibit loyalty, trust, and affection, but these are not the equivalents of compassion and commitment, which comprise the key elements of what we know as romantic love. Certainly there's physical attraction, or "chemistry." But having celebrated my 25th wedding anniversary, I can tell you it's commitment and compassion that keep the "chemistry" intact 25 years after the wedding march is over. Conversely, as any separated or divorced couple will tell you, when there is no love left in a relationship, sex is the first thing to go.

Down through the centuries, music from popular to opera has revolved around love. Love lost. Love gained. Endless love. Falling in love. Unrequited love. Sometimes naive, corny, and sentimental. Occasionally erotic in an amorous, lighthearted way. But love, nevertheless. Until recently, song lyrics were never mean, grotesque, or disrespectful. The music did not remind you of *a grand* mal seizure. Certainly love was not reduced to crotch-grabbing, cruel images of caged, raped, or battered women and of ripped genitalia (à la 2 Live Crew).

Teenagers and Sex

How ironic that the 60's generation—*my* generation—which once proselytized "Make love, not war" now admonishes its young to "have sex, not love" and to equate love with a glove, sex toys, and condoms; these, Ms. Gebbie, are the "negative" images; these, Ms. Elders, are the "criminal" messages. Too many psychologists, too many grownups in general, have forgotten what it was like to be a child. Never mind whether it was the 1950's, 60's, or 30's. Just a child. We all had hormones, you know. Today's kids didn't invent them. But that first exposure to sexual topics, if I remember correctly, was not about our hormones.

Before I knew where babies come from, before I knew about menstruation, before I knew about the sex act, before I needed a bra, my little friends and I fantasized about love. Paul Newman was handsome; we weren't interested in his groin. And from the teenage years on into young adulthood, flirting was fun; conversation was the means of exploring the first exhilarating feelings of attraction; and those initial fleeting moments of physical intimacy were exciting. We were in love with being in love. An off-color joke, if it was clever, drew a smile. The details of people's sex lives did not. They were private. A person's virginity intensely so. . . .

I think I understand why those sneeringly referred to as "religious" these days get bent out of shape when the topic of teaching evolution comes up. It's not merely that they are offended that humankind may technically at some point have had some close relatives among the simian family, although no direct proof of that theory has ever been confirmed. What really gets under the skin of orthodox religious parents is the suggestion, frequently passed along *with* this theory, that humans are really just advanced animals. . . .

At the heart of the resistance by orthodox religious people to today's government-mandated sex training is that children are being encouraged to consider themselves as animals, with slightly more complex brain functions, of course—i.e., animals cannot be trained to use a condom. But the fact is, animals don't need condoms. Nature did not construct animals in such a way that "promiscuous" or indiscriminate sex is going to hurt them. The purpose of sex in the animal kingdom is reproduction. Period. To animals, procreation is of serious interest only when the female is *in heat*. In humans, procreation is of serious interest mainly when two people are *in love*.

A Private Matter

Love is most fulfilling when it involves loss of self to another person. For that reason, sex tends to fall short of expectations if its sole purpose is self- (much less group-) gratification, when it becomes, in effect, a sporting event. It is this point that is at the core of what is called the "sanctity of the family." Sex, the most intimate way possible to express love on a physical level, is an intensely private matter.

Which brings up the other source of objection among orthodox religious parents to the currently voguish sexual teachings: the rejection of a "privacy ethic" by sex educators. Look at the surveys and the distribution of sexual paraphernalia to young, impressionable children. What is the message? It is that you won't have any problem with this "unless you have something to hide." And also that nothing is private. Not even "what you think about when you think of sex." Not your bowel habits, either, if you read the sex surveys. And when you move on to some of the drug and alcohol surveys, and even to some so-called academic tests, like the Metropolitan Achievement Test put out by Psychological Corporation, it is clear that the details of your family life are not private—and shouldn't be. Do your parents do such-and-such? Do your parents have this or that in their homes? If you believe the literature, the purpose of this information-gathering is to construct a curriculum that will instill ethical values.

Isn't it ironic that we once had social sanctions that worked in this country. That kept behavior within tolerable limits and the libido in check. When adults, not adolescents, held cultural authority, young men were actually taught that certain behaviors are unacceptable around women. They were taught attentiveness and courtesy and to avoid foul language. They weren't given lame excuses about their sexuality peaking at the age of 17.

Codes of Conduct

Similar codes of conduct were taught young girls. You didn't go alone to a man's room, much less at all hours of the night, and expect no consequences. You were taught what it meant to conduct yourself in a dignified fashion. You didn't even consider going to bed with a fellow on a first, second, or third date. You didn't go braless in tank-tops, wear skin-tight skirts, fishnet hose, and spike heels, get your legs shaved by a bunch of drunken sailors, and then turn around and complain about being sexually harassed. Bearing a child out of wedlock was disgraceful and showed a lack of self-discipline and character.

Then the mental "health" experts and the courts came along and in just 30 years managed to remove the stigma from behaviors that, today, are completely out of control. No law against "sexual harassment," no sex ed course, no "deadbeat dads" legislation is going to bring back the morality and sense of privacy-in-intimacy that was once passed down from generation to generation—values like modesty and chastity, which parents are no longer *permitted* to pass along, because the schools and the media—backed up unwittingly, perhaps, by the courts—continually undermine the efforts of responsible parents trying to do their job.

Thus has sexuality become the stuff of billboards and bumper stickers, each vying for attention, each more shocking than the last. Oh, yes. Today's teachings about sex are negative, all right, just as AIDS czarina Kristine Gebbie says. But no more so than allusions to and discussions about the subject in entertainment and the nightly news. As a result, the allure of physical attraction and the rituals of courtship are no longer cute, fun, flirtatious, titillating, or even risqué; they're just plain gross. Sex and love have been granted a divorce.

Sex is now defined as "release of tension." Art, music, and much of literature focus not on romance, but on genitals, multiple orgasms, and little-understood chromosomal mix-ups that result in unfortunate genetic mistakes like homosexuality and the penchant for pedophilia.

What have we done to love? We have debased it. Defiled it. Desensitized it. Depersonalized it. Disparaged it. We've even urinated on it. And, judging from our drug and crime statistics, society is paying the heaviest possible price.

"A large number of American men and women are at risk of acquiring a sexually transmitted disease (STD)."

Many Americans Still Practice High-Risk Sexual Behavior

Dore Hollander

In the following viewpoint, Dore Hollander reviews the 1988–1990 results of an annual survey by the National Opinion Research Center at the University of Chicago in Illinois. Based on this data, Hollander concludes that many Americans continue to have multiple sexual partners and to have sex with strangers, putting them at risk for a variety of sexually transmitted diseases (STDs), including the human immunodeficiency virus (HIV), the virus that causes AIDS. Hollander is the editor of *SIECUS Report*, published bimonthly by the Sexuality Information and Education Council of the United States, located in New York City.

As you read, consider the following questions:

1. What specific groups are most likely to practice high-risk sexual behavior, according to the author?
2. According to Hollander, what age group is most likely to engage in high-risk behavior?

Reprinted by permission of The Alan Guttmacher Institute from Dore Hollander, "Young Americans, the Unmarried and Blacks Are Most Likely to Have Had Multiple Partners in the Past Year," *Family Planning Perspectives*, vol. 25, no. 2, March/April 1993.

A large number of American men and women are at risk of acquiring a sexually transmitted disease (STD) because they have multiple sexual partners or have sex with strangers. Young people, men, single people and blacks are more likely than others to engage in these high-risk activities, according to an analysis of 1988–1990 data from the General Social Survey (GSS).

A Survey of High-Risk Behavior

The GSS, based on a nationally representative sample of U.S. adults aged 18 and older, is conducted annually by the National Opinion Research Center, at the University of Chicago. The GSS includes adult men and women of all ages, and asks several questions concerning sexual behavior. For this analysis, investigators examining data for a subsample of 2,896 respondents sought to identify factors associated with three behaviors that can increase an individual's risk of acquiring an STD: having two or more sexual partners, having five or more partners and having sex with a stranger.

Overall, 13% of respondents had had two or more partners during the year preceding the survey; 3% had had five or more; and 4% had had intercourse with a casual date or pickup or had paid for sex (see Table 1; figures in text are rounded off). About 1% had had at least five partners and had also had sex with a stranger (not shown).

Bivariate analysis showed that age, gender, race and marital status were strongly related to all three outcome measures. For example, respondents aged 18–24 were the most likely to have had multiple partners and to have had sex with a stranger (37% and 13%, respectively); these proportions declined steadily with age (to 21% and 8%, respectively, of those in their late 20s, and to 9% and 2%, respectively, of those aged 40–49). Men were twice as likely as women to have had multiple partners (18% vs. 9%), and were considerably more likely to have had sex with a stranger (7% vs. 1%). Relatively few currently married respondents (3%), but sizable proportions of previously married and never-married respondents, (17% and 35%, respectively), had had more than one partner. Blacks were more likely than members of other racial and ethnic groups to have had multiple partners (25% vs. 11%), particularly black males, regardless of marital status; racial and ethnic differences with respect to having had sex with a stranger were not statistically significant.

Life-Style Affects Behavior

Education and income were not associated with the outcome variables (not shown), but certain life-style characteristics were: Respondents who never attend church were more likely than those who attend occasionally or regularly to have had more than one partner (21% vs. 6%) and to have had sex with a stranger (7% vs. 1%). Those who occasionally drink heavily were more likely than those who do not to have had multiple partners (26% vs. 8%) or to have had sex with a stranger (9% vs. 2%). Smoking also had a positive association with risky behavior.

Table 1. Percentage of U.S. men and women by number of sexual partners during preceding year and percentage who had had sex with a stranger during preceding year, according to various characteristics, General Social Survey, 1988–1990 (N = 2,590)

Characteristic	No. of partners		Sex with
	≥2	≥5	stranger
Total	**12.7**	**2.7**	**3.6**
Age			
18–24	37.2	9.4	13.2
25–29	21.0	3.8	7.5
30–39	10.8	2.0	2.1
40–49	8.5	1.1	1.8
50–59	5.6	1.7	1.4
60–89	1.6	0.3	0.2
Sex			
Male	17.7	5.0	6.7
Female	8.5	0.8	1.1
Marital status			
Currently married	3.3	0.5	0.6
Separated, widowed or divorced	17.3	2.2	3.5
Never married	35.4	9.2	13.3
Race			
White	11.3	2.1	3.4
Black	25.0	7.7	6.4
Other	10.5	3.0	2.2
Church attendance			
Never	20.8	6.5	7.2
Monthly or less	15.0	2.9	4.5
Nearly weekly	5.7	0.6	0.9
Ever drink alcohol			
Yes	15.7	3.2	4.4
No	6.0	1.5	1.8
Sometimes drink heavily			
Yes	25.7	6.5	8.8
No	8.2	1.4	1.9
Currently smoke			
Yes	18.3	4.2	5.1
No	10.1	1.9	2.9

Dore Hollander, *Family Planning Perspectives*, March/April 1993.

Results of a multivariate analysis revealed four factors to be significant predictors of having had at least two partners, having had at least five partners and having had sex with a stranger: age, gender, marital status and alcohol consumption. As respondents' age increased by one year, their likelihood of engaging in any of the three behaviors decreased by 5%. Likewise, men were close to three times as likely as women to have had at least two partners, more than seven times as likely to have had five or more partners and nearly six times as likely to have had sex with a stranger.

Those who were currently married had a significantly reduced risk of engaging in these three behaviors compared with other respondents, and those who drank heavily on occasion were somewhat more likely than others to have engaged in these types of behavior. Race had no effect on the likelihood of having had sex with a stranger, but blacks were more likely than other respondents to have had two or more and five or more partners. Independent of the effect of heavy drinking, alcohol consumption was associated with respondents' having had multiple partners. The effects of smoking and church attendance were not significant at this level of analysis.

Multiple Partners and HIV

The investigators estimated that 4.8 million U.S. adults have five or more sexual partners in a year and that 6.6 million have sex with a stranger. Thus, a substantial number of men and women each year increase their risk of acquiring STDs, including the human immunodeficiency virus (HIV), through such behavior.

However, although the GSS is useful for estimating the number of Americans who may be at risk of acquiring an STD, the investigators note that it has certain limitations. Because the survey does not include questions on condom use, it cannot indicate whether individuals engaging in high-risk behaviors are taking measures to reduce their risk of acquiring an STD. The survey also does not ask about illegal drug use, which may interfere with condom use. Because the section of the GSS regarding high-risk behavior is self-administered, judging the validity of responses is difficult, and a certain amount of misreporting may account for some of the observed differences.

More information about high-risk sexual behavior among American adults is clearly needed, the investigators conclude. Future research covering STD history, condom use, drug use and partner selection will provide critical guidance for STD interventions and treatment programs.

"Both sexes are definitely more cautious about having sex."

Many Americans Are Trying to Abandon High-Risk Behavior

Andrea Heiman

Andrea Heiman, the author of the following viewpoint, writes that the threat of AIDS and other sexually transmitted diseases (STDs) has led many Americans to rethink their sexual attitudes and behaviors. While a large number of Americans continue to engage in risky sex, says Heiman, a contributing writer for the *Los Angeles Times*, many are consciously trying to change their sexual habits. Heiman reports that the gay community has been extremely successful in reducing high-risk behavior, and that the heterosexual community has made progress as well.

As you read, consider the following questions:

1. How have attitudes toward sex and sexual behavior changed, according to Heiman?
2. According to Heiman, what attitudes did Americans have toward sex before the threat of HIV?
3. How did the gay community change its behavior with the advent of AIDS, and how can others learn from the changes, according to the author?

Andrea Heiman, "New Rules, New Attitudes?" *Los Angeles Times*, August 8, 1994. Reprinted with permission.

Sex in the '90s is certainly not simple. Not that sex has ever been simple. But combine the fear of AIDS with the epidemic of sexually transmitted diseases (STDs) and the changing cultural roles of men and women, and you end up with a confused and weary society of singles.

The Effects of AIDS

What, exactly, are contemporary attitudes about sex and dating? One study reports that the AIDS epidemic has had a chilling effect on the sex lives of singles. But companion surveys report that promiscuity is as popular as ever.

One thing is certain, based on interviews with singles and relationship experts: Attitudes toward sex and relationships have become more conservative. Equally certain is that this change in mores doesn't always translate into a change in behavior.

"I was in my early 20s in the late '70s," said Rebecca, a 36-year-old single attorney in Ventura. "That was the time of disco and the Village People and one-night stands. That's what everyone did and they didn't think twice about it."

Rebecca said that since 1989, she has thought much harder before getting involved with a man. "The last three years, the warnings about getting AIDS have been deafening," she said. "My friends and I all talk about needing to be careful."

Still, Rebecca admitted that within the last six months she had unprotected sex with someone she didn't know well and hasn't dated since. "I did it because I guess I just wanted an attachment, and I had sex, because that's what he wanted. Passion or need or loneliness motivate us to do stupid things in the face of all the facts."

More Concerned

Andy, a 38-year-old screenwriter, said he is more concerned about protecting himself against AIDS and STDs than he was in the past, but he also said that he has had unprotected sex within the last six months outside a monogamous relationship. "I didn't see her as a promiscuous woman, so I didn't really worry about it," he said. But Andy, who lives in Los Angeles, said dating has changed a lot since the days of the "three-date rule."

"In the past, I would have expected to sleep with a woman by the third date, if not before," he said. "Now, I wouldn't expect it, and in fact, I would worry if she did sleep with me on the first date."

Andy said that although he's looking toward marriage, he would have sex with a woman he didn't know or like much, if he was attracted to her. But he would wear a condom. "Men are still men," he said. "They basically want to sleep with every woman they see."

231

Sound crass? Psychologists say that despite the conservative trend in sexual activity and warnings about the dangers of unprotected sex, people continue to operate emotionally in the same way they always have.

Some Success

If education alone could affect people's behavior, sexually transmitted diseases would be a thing of the past—but then, so would drugs. The one group that has unquestionably changed its behavior is middle-class homosexual men, who had the most incentive, and the example of countless friends who died of AIDS. It would be almost inconceivable now for a man to lead the kind of life described by songwriter and author Michael Callen, who estimates he had more than 3,000 different sexual partners between 1973 and 1982—contracting in the process "hepatitis A, hepatitis B, hepatitis non-A/non-B, herpes, syphilis, gonorrhea, chlamydia, cytomegalovirus . . ." and eventually AIDS. Few heterosexuals ever lived like that in the first place, and the changes in their lifestyles have been less pronounced. More typical is someone like Sharon Taylor, 34, a Denver lawyer who hit a rocky patch with her husband when she questioned his fidelity. "We decided to work on our relationship and see a counselor," she says, "but when I insisted we start using a condom he balked. I think I surprised myself by sticking to my guns. He kept saying 'don't you trust me?' and I kept saying, 'no'." They separated for a while, reconciled, and recently have begun sleeping with each other again. Now that she's not so mad at him anymore, she has relented on the question of condoms. "I figure I'm taking a risk no matter what I do," she says. "Safe sex is an option, but at some point you have to draw the line and leave it in the hands of providence."

Jerry Adler, *Newsweek*, December 9, 1991.

Which is why, psychologists say, many heterosexuals who are well-educated about AIDS still think they are immune to it. "In some ways, the heterosexual community doesn't believe it is affected by AIDS," said Wanda von Kleist, a Chicago psychologist who counsels many singles. "There is a lot of denial, because they have not had as many deaths as the gay men's community. In the heterosexual community, the majority of people do not use condoms or safer sex because they do not believe they will get it."

Women Say No

What has changed in the past few years, thanks to the AIDS epidemic, is women's ability to say no, von Kleist said. "It's more socially acceptable for a woman to say upfront that she doesn't want to have sex," she said. "For a long time, women felt like if they said no, something was wrong with them. I think now women have an opportunity to say what they want."

Debra, a 33-year-old actress who lives in Hollywood, said she insists that a man wear a condom and get not one but two AIDS tests. She said she has sex less often now, partly out of fear and partly out of her own changing attitude.

"I do feel freer to say no now, and I'm more likely to than I would have in the past," she said. "And when it comes to AIDS, I take it very seriously—I've had a good friend die from it. Men tend to think I'm accusing them when I tell them to get an AIDS test—but most men are more careful with pregnancy than they are with AIDS. Because they're at less risk to getting AIDS."

The more conservative swing in sexual behavior has also affected the way men and women relate to one another. In the '60s and '70s, sex was used so freely and casually that many people never really got intimate, psychologists say—people substituted sex for intimacy. Men and women are now forced to deal with each other in a different way.

"Both sexes are definitely more cautious about having sex," said Stanley Teitelbaum, a New York psychologist who specializes in sex and relationships. "For a long time, many people used sex as a way to relate, instead of relating and then having sex. So people who had problems relating used sex to cover up those difficulties. They can't do that so freely and readily anymore."

The Gay Community

But the most blatant changes in attitudes about sex and dating can be seen in the gay men's community. Michael Koth, a 38-year-old professional trainer, remembers the days when everyone in the gay community was "footloose and fancy free" when it came to sex.

"You could go in any alley in certain neighborhoods and cruise certain areas and see all kinds of sex," said Koth, who has delivered 172 eulogies for friends who have died of AIDS. "Everyone went to sex clubs and bath houses every night. It was just so much a part of how everyone lived."

Koth, who lives in West Hollywood, said he and his friends practice safe sex and are now much more aware of their sexual behavior.

Still, he said, there are people who don't take AIDS seriously. "There is a whole new phase of young people who seemingly don't care, who think that they're invincible," said Koth.

There is also a new wave of sex clubs popping up around L.A. and New York, he said. Although management supplies condoms and posts safe-sex rules on the walls, there is no way of really monitoring and enforcing people's behavior.

One of the high-risk groups for contracting HIV are teenagers, who, psychologists say, are scared but also maintain a high level of denial.

"The more they find out about STDs and AIDS, the more their heads are saying that they need to be more conservative," said Lorraine Sterman, a Los Angeles psychologist who counsels adolescents. "But their bodies are no different than teens' bodies have always been—raging with hormones. It's a very, very ambivalent situation."

Susan, a 17-year-old high school senior at a Catholic school in Orange County, said many of her friends are sexually active, but that they are more afraid of pregnancy than of AIDS and STDs.

"A lot of my girlfriends are on the pill. But people are not concerned about AIDS—it's not a part of our lives here," said Susan, who added that although her friends know they need to use protection, they often don't.

Despite the problems and the very real fears facing this generation, there are many valuable lessons available for those who choose to learn them, psychologist Teitelbaum said.

Good Judgment

"It's more important in the '90s than ever before to develop those qualities in yourself that give you good judgment, to use your perception, to know what the other person is about," he said. "You need to know who you are getting involved with, to tune in rather than tune out. If people are more forthright, and put their needs and concerns on the table, that can be a positive step toward building healthy relationships."

Periodical Bibliography

The following articles have been selected to supplement the diverse views presented in this chapter.

Jerry Adler	"Sex in the Snoring '90s," *Newsweek*, April 26, 1993.
Allan Bloom	"The Death of Eros," *The New York Times Magazine*, May 23, 1993.
Caryn Brooks	"Hand Jive," *Utne Reader*, March/April 1993.
Michael Callen	"Come Together," *Utne Reader*, July/August 1993.
Philip Elmer-Dewitt	"Now for the Truth About Americans and Sex," *Time*, October 17, 1994.
Suzanne Fields	"Dirty Little Secrets in Sex Survey," *Conservative Chronicle*, October 26, 1994. Available from Box 11297, Des Moines, IA 50340-1297.
Ellen Goodman	"Sex in America Somewhat Staid," *Liberal Opinion Week*, October 10, 1994. Available from PO Box 468, Vinton, IA 52349.
Michael Hirschorn	"The PC Porn Queen's Virtual Realities," *Esquire*, June 1993.
Marjorie Ingall	"S-E-X in the U.S.A.: Wake Us When It's Over," *Ms.*, January/February 1993.
Michele Ingrassia	"Virgin Cool," *Newsweek*, October 17, 1994.
Issues & Views	"On the Abstinence Front," Summer 1994. Available from PO Box 467, New York, NY 10025.
Garrison Keillor	"It's Good Old Monogamy That's Really Sexy," *Time*, October 17, 1994.
Tamar Lewin	"Sex in America: Faithfulness in Marriage Thrives After All," *The New York Times*, October 7, 1994.
Tamar Lewin	"So, Now We Know What Americans Do in Bed. So?" *The New York Times*, October 9, 1994.
Amy Pagnozzi	"*Two Thousand* Virgins: They're Not Who You Think," *Glamour*, April 1992.
Joannie M. Schrof with Betsy Wagner	"Sex in America," *U.S. News & World Report*, October 17, 1994.

Jeffery L. Sheler with Joannie M. Schrof and Gary Cohen	"The Gospel on Sex," *U.S. News & World Report*, June 10, 1991.
Tim Stafford	"The Next Sexual Revolution," *Christianity Today*, March 9, 1992.
R. Turner	"AIDS Threat Leads Some U.S. Women to Change Their Sexual Behavior," *Family Planning Perspectives*, March/April 1994. Available from 120 Wall Street, New York, NY 10005.

For Further Discussion

Chapter 1

1. In his viewpoint, Paul Murray maintains that not using contraception increases the love and concern a husband shows to his wife. Do you think that Anthony Walsh would agree with this statement? Why or why not?

2. Both Sallie Tisdale and Mark Gramunt focus on the significance of sexual orgasm. On what points do they agree or disagree? How do their beliefs about the basic purpose of orgasm affect their views of the nature of sex? Explain.

3. This chapter provides a variety of opinions on the primary purpose of sexual intercourse. Are there any reasons that you feel were not, but should have been, included in the chapter? Explain.

Chapter 2

1. Sidney Callahan states that, although she does not support polygamy, she does believe homosexual couples should be allowed to marry. How does this statement affect your assessment of her views on polygamy, if at all? Do you believe that the issue of homosexual marriage and the issue of polygamy are comparable in any way? Explain.

2. According to Callahan, monogamy benefits individuals, families, and societies in various ways. In her viewpoint, Deborah M. Anapol gives several reasons why she believes committed nonmonogamy is preferable for these same groups. Which of these arguments do you find more convincing? Why?

3. In her viewpoint, Amy C. Gregg maintains that the Christian church has fostered certain beliefs that have contributed to unhealthy marriages and divorce. Do you believe that change within the church would promote healthier relationships? Why or why not?

4. William Norman Grigg uses historical examples in his argument that there is little practical distinction between homosexuality and pedophilia. In your opinion, does Grigg successfully prove that this link between homosexuality and pedophilia exists in modern society? Explain.

5. Terry Tafoya's contention that homosexuality has an important place within society is specifically based on a Native American worldview. In what ways, if any, do you think this

argument can be applied to non-Native cultures? What aspects, if any, cannot be applied?

Chapter 3

1. Jo Durden-Smith and Diane deSimone believe that the case of the descendants of Amaranta Ternera is sufficient documentation for their claim that gender identity is determined by prenatal hormones. Do you agree with their argument? Why or why not?

2. Judith Lorber contends that culture and social practices, not biology, determine gender. Susan Golombok and Robyn Fivush, while acknowledging the importance of social practices, still attribute a role to biology in gender determination and development. Whose argument is more persuasive? Why? Does the Golombok/Fivush viewpoint more closely agree with the Durden-Smith/deSimone viewpoint or the Lorber viewpoint? Explain.

3. Simon LeVay and Dean H. Hamer are scientists who argue that homosexuality is biologically determined. Louis Sheldon and Chandler Burr are not scientists yet argue that it is impossible to discover the causes of homosexuality. What aspects of the discoveries of LeVay and Hamer do Sheldon and Burr challenge? Do you believe that only scientists should be challenging the conclusions of other scientists? On what do you base your answer?

Chapter 4

1. Carlton Cornett asserts that one significant problem regarding reparative therapy is the lack of a uniform definition of homosexuality. What do you think he means by this? What would you consider an accurate definition of homosexuality?

2. The atmosphere that surrounded the APA's 1973 ruling that removed homosexuality from its list of psychological illnesses is described in the viewpoints by Cornett and by Sy Rogers and Alan Medinger. How do these accounts differ? Who do you believe offers the more convincing account? Explain.

3. Victor B. Cline is a psychologist who works with sex addicts. Martyn Harris is a journalist who has reported on the pornography industry. How does knowing their respective careers affect your assessment of their viewpoints, if at all? How might their professions influence their opinions?

4. Both Jane Anthony and Veronica Monet have worked as prostitutes. Monet focuses on her life experiences to support her contention that prostitution can benefit women. Anthony

bases her argument against prostitution on feminist theory and only refers briefly to her personal background. What are the strengths and weaknesses of their techniques in supporting their respective arguments? Explain.

5. Albert Ellis characterizes sexual addiction as resulting from a psychological disturbance called absolutist demandingness. Mark Matousek asserts that sex addicts become addicted because of a neurochemical high produced by sex and, often, because of childhood sexual abuse. In what ways do their definitions of sexual addiction differ? On what points do they agree?

Chapter 5

1. Robert T. Michael, John H. Gagnon, Edward O. Laumann, and Gina Kolata conclude, based on their survey *Sex in America: A Definitive Study*, that Americans are mostly monogamous and content with their sex lives, and that married people have more (and more satisfying) sex than those who are single. How does this jibe with conventional wisdom about sex in America, in your opinion? How does the viewpoint by Lynn Rosellini contrast with this view?

2. A 1994 study of Americans' sexual attitudes, discussed in the viewpoint by Mark Clements, suggests that the emotional side of sex is becoming more important to men and that married people are happier with their sex lives than singles are. B.K. Eakman, however, argues in her viewpoint that the opposite is true—the emotional side is less important. She maintains that the American educational system and the media are training young people to believe that frequent, casual sex is better. Which viewpoint is more convincing? Why?

3. Dore Hollander uses statistics gathered at the National Opinion Research Center at the University of Chicago to argue that many Americans still practice high-risk sexual behavior. Andrea Heiman, on the other hand, uses primarily anecdotal evidence to support her position that many people are, in fact, being more careful in their sexual behavior. Which type of evidence is more effective, in your opinion? Which viewpoint do you find more convincing? Why?

Organizations to Contact

The editors have compiled the following list of organizations concerned with the issues debated in this book. The descriptions are derived from materials provided by the organizations. All have publications or information available for interested readers. The list was compiled on the date of publication of the present volume; names, addresses, and phone numbers may change. Be aware that many organizations take several weeks or longer to respond to inquiries, so allow as much time as possible.

American Social Health Association (ASHA)
PO Box 13827
Research Triangle Park, NC 27709
(919) 361-8400
fax: (919) 361-8425

ASHA advocates increased federal funding for sexually transmitted disease (STD) research and prevention programs. Its programs include the Herpes Resource Center, the Human Papillomavirus Support Program, the Women's Health Matters Program, and an extensive publications program. The association also operates the National AIDS Hotline (800-342-2437), the National STD Hotline (800-227-8922), and the National Herpes Hotline (919-361-8488).

The Augustine Fellowship
Sex and Love Addicts Anonymous (SLAA)
PO Box 119, New Town Branch
Boston, MA 02258
(617) 332-1845

SLAA is a fellowship that helps individuals suffering from sexual and/or emotional obsessive/compulsive patterns. Based on the twelve-step program of Alcoholics Anonymous, the fellowship's program works to counter the destructive effects of sex and love addiction. SLAA publishes the book *Sex and Love Addicts Anonymous* and the pamphlets *Introduction to Sex and Love Addicts Anonymous*, *Addiction and Recovery*, and *Questions Beginners Ask*.

Concerned Women for America (CWA)
370 L'Enfant Promenade SW, Suite 800
Washington, DC 20024
(202) 488-7000
fax: (202) 488-0806

Concerned Women for America is a nonpartisan, politically active organization that advocates traditional and Judeo-Christian values. Working at both the national and state levels, CWA sponsors educational and legislative programs that address the concerns of its members. It publishes the monthly *Family Voice* magazine and the pamphlet *The Shocking Truth Behind the Government's Safe-Sex Lie*.

Courage
c/o St. Michael's Rectory
424 W. 34th St.
New York, NY 10001
(212) 421-0426

Courage sponsors the spiritual support group Encourage for homosexuals and their families. Courage advocates the Catholic Church's teaching that homosexual activity is morally wrong but believes gays and lesbians deserve understanding and compassion from the Christian community. The organization publishes the newsletter *Courage* and the pamphlet *Pastoral Care and the Homosexual*.

Desert Stream Ministries (DSM)
12488 Venice Blvd.
Los Angeles, CA 90066-3804
(310) 572-0140

DSM assists individuals struggling with homosexuality, AIDS, sexual addiction, and sexual abuse issues. Through the Christian church, DSM works to heal these "sexually-broken" individuals. The organization offers a variety of literature and tapes, including an information packet and a biannual newsletter, each on a separate topic. Newsletter titles include *Homosexuality and Truth*, *Release from Sexual Abuse*, and *AIDS Ministry*.

Family Research Council (FRC)
700 13th St. NW, Suite 500
Washington, DC 20005
(202) 393-2100
fax: (202) 393-2134

FRC is a research, resource, and educational organization that promotes the traditional family. The council opposes gay marriage and adoption rights. It publishes numerous reports on issues affecting the family, including the bimonthly journal *Family Policy* and the monthly newsletter *Washington Watch*.

The Hetrick-Martin Institute
2 Astor Pl.
New York, NY 10003-6998
(212) 674-2400
fax: (212) 674-8650

The institute is a social service organization that works with lesbian, gay, and bisexual youth, homeless adolescents, and all youth struggling with issues of sexuality. It offers individual, group, and family counseling; education about homosexuality and HIV/AIDS; and Project First Step for homeless youth. The institute also publishes numerous articles, the quarterly newsletter *HMI Report Card*, and the brochures *FACTFILE #1: Lesbian, Gay, and Bisexual Youth* and *FACTFILE #2: Fighting the Myths: Lesbians, Gay Men and Youth*.

Homosexual Information Center (HIC)
115 Monroe St.
Bossier City, LA 71111
(318) 742-4709

The Homosexual Information Center believes that the terms "homosexual" and "heterosexual" are useless ambiguities that violate the human rights and privacy accorded to all citizens. The center works to ensure that an individual's sexuality remains confidential and does not become a part of public or private records. HIC publishes a newsletter and provides information on homosexuality. To obtain these materials, write to HIC, PO Box 8252, Universal City, CA 91608.

IntiNet Resource Center (IRC)
PO Box 4322
San Rafael, CA 94913-4322
(415) 507-1739

IRC is an international organization that advocates multipartner relationships and responsible nonmonogamy. The center acts as a resource for individuals interested in multipartner lifestyles and conducts research on alternatives to the nuclear family. IRC publications include the quarterly newsletter *Floodtide* and the books *Love Without Limits: The Quest for Sustainable Intimate Relationships*, *Loving More: The Polyfidelity Primer*, and *Women Who Run with More Than One Lover or Mate: Women and Polyamory*.

Morality in Media, Inc. (MIM)
475 Riverside Dr.
New York, NY 10115
(212) 870-3222

MIM is a national, interfaith organization that works to stop illegal trafficking in hard-core pornography through enforcing state and federal obscenity laws. It seeks to alert the public of pornography's destructive effects on children and society. MIM publishes a bimonthly newsletter, the brochure *Pornography Has Consequences*, and the booklet *Pornography's Effects on Adults & Children*.

The National Association for Research and Therapy of Homosexuality (NARTH)
16542 Ventura Blvd., Suite 416
Encino, CA 91436
(818) 789-4440

NARTH is an information and referral network that believes the causes of homosexuality are primarily developmental and that it is usually responsive to psychotherapy. The association supports homosexual men and women who feel that homosexuality is contrary to their value systems and who voluntarily seek treatment. NARTH publishes the *NARTH Bulletin* and numerous conference papers.

The National Center for Lesbian Rights (NCLR)
870 Market St., Suite 570
San Francisco, CA 94102
(415) 392-6257

NCLR is a lesbian, multicultural, and legal resource center that advocates lesbian rights. The center condemns sexual-orientation-based discrimination in health care, the workplace, and in society in general. In addition to providing counseling services, the center distributes brochures, a biannual newsletter, and the *Lesbian & Gay Parenting Bibliography*.

National Coalition Against Censorship
275 Seventh Ave., 20th Fl.
New York, NY 10001
(212) 807-6222
fax: (212) 807-6245

The coalition opposes censorship in any form, believing it to be against the First Amendment right to freedom of speech. It works to educate the public about the dangers of censorship, including censorship of material deemed pornographic. The coalition publishes *Censorship News* five times a year and reports such as *The Sex Panic: Women, Censorship, and "Pornography."*

National Coalition for the Protection of Children and Families (NCPCF)
800 Compton Rd., Suite 9224
Cincinnati, OH 45231
(513) 521-6227

Formerly the National Coalition Against Pornography, NCPCF works to stop sexual victimization linked to obscenity and child pornography. The coalition stresses public education about the harmful effects of pornography and advocates legislation to prevent sexual violence. NCPCF publishes research findings and provides consultation and educational materials on the effects of pornography. It publishes the newsletter *Standing Together* and the pamphlets *Break the Chain of Abuse* and *You've Heard Some of the Myths, Now Read the Facts About Illegal Pornography.*

National Gay & Lesbian Task Force Policy Institute (NGLTF)
2320 17th St. NW
Washington, DC 20009
(202) 332-6483
fax: (202) 332-0207

The NGLTF Policy Institute lobbies for gay and lesbian civil rights and advocates legislation that would halt hate crimes based on sexual orientation. The task force also promotes education and acts as a clearinghouse for information concerning gay and lesbian issues. Its publications include the *Task Force Report* newsletter, the survey *Anti-Gay/Lesbian Victimization*, and the *Activist Alert* newsletter.

National Service Organization of Sex Addicts Anonymous, Inc. (SAA)
PO Box 70949
Houston, TX 77270
(713) 869-4902

SAA is a fellowship of men and women trying to overcome their sexual addiction or dependency. Members work toward becoming sexually healthy through a spiritual program based on the principles of Alcoholics Anonymous. SAA publications include the booklets *Abstinence and Boundaries in SAA* and *Exploring Healthy Sexuality* and the pamphlet *Three Circles: Defining Sexual Sobriety in SAA*.

Renaissance Education Association, Inc.
987 Old Eagle School Rd., Suite 719
Wayne, PA 19087
(610) 975-9119

Renaissance is a nonprofit association that seeks to educate the professional and general communities about crossdressing. The association works to dispel the belief that crossdressing is caused by a mental disorder and is only practiced by homosexuals. It publishes literature related to crossdressing and transsexualism, including the papers *Myths & Misconceptions About Crossdressers*, *Reasons for Male to Female Crossdressing*, and *Understanding Transsexualism*.

The Rockford Institute
934 N. Main St.
Rockford, IL 61103-7061
(815) 964-5819

The institute promotes Judeo-Christian and traditional family values through informing the American public about religious and social issues. It believes that a healthy family includes of both a mother and a father, and it stresses monogamy. The institute publishes the monthly monograph *Family in America* and its supplement *New Research*. In addition, it publishes the monthly magazine *Chronicles* and the *Mainstreet Memorandum* newsletter.

The Society for the Second Self, Inc. (Tri-Ess)
PO Box 194
Tulare, CA 93275
(209) 688-9246

Tri-Ess is a support and social outreach organization that stresses education about and understanding of the crossdressing community. Membership is limited to heterosexual crossdressers, their spouses or partners, and their family members. The society sponsors chapter meetings and the annual Spouse/Partner International Conference for Education (SPICE). It publishes the quarterly newsletter *Sweetheart Connection*, the quarterly magazine *Femme Mirror*, and the information booklet *What Is Tri-Ess?*

The Universal Fellowship of Metropolitan Community Churches (UFMCC)
5300 Santa Monica Blvd., Suite 304
Los Angeles, CA 90029
(213) 464-5100
fax: (213) 464-2123

UFMCC works to confront poverty, sexism, racism, and homophobia through Christian social action. Composed of more than two hundred congregations, the fellowship accepts gays, lesbians, and bisexuals and works to incorporate them into the Christian church. UFMCC publications include the quarterly newsletter *Journey*, the brochures *Homosexuality: Not a Sin, Not a Sickness* and *Homosexuality: the Bible as Your Friend*, and the pamphlet *Homosexuality and the Conservative Christian*.

Bibliography of Books

Franklin Abbot, ed.   *Men and Intimacy: Personal Accounts Exploring the Dilemmas of Modern Male Sexuality.* Freedom, CA: Crossing Press, 1990.

Margo Anand   *The Art of Sexual Ecstasy: The Path of Sacred Sexuality for Western Lovers.* Los Angeles: J.P. Tarcher, 1989.

Mary Batten   *Sexual Strategies: How Females Choose Their Mates.* New York: G.P. Putnam's Sons, 1992.

Sandra Lipsitz Bem   *The Lenses of Gender.* New Haven: Yale University Press, 1993.

Kate Bornstein   *Gender Outlaw: On Men, Women, and the Rest of Us.* New York: Routledge, 1994.

Susie Bright   *Susie Bright's Sexual Reality: A Virtual Sex World Reader.* Pittsburgh: Cleis Press, 1992.

Frank Browning   *The Culture of Desire: Paradox and Perversity in Gay Lives Today.* New York: Crown, 1993.

Vern L. Bullough and Bonnie Bullough   *Cross Dressing, Sex, and Gender.* Philadelphia: University of Pennsylvania Press, 1993.

David M. Buss   *The Evolution of Desire: Strategies of Human Mating.* New York: BasicBooks, 1994.

Patrick Carnes   *Don't Call It Love: Recovery from Sexual Addictions.* New York: Bantam Books, 1991.

Steve Chapple and David Talbot   *Burning Desires: Sex in America.* New York: Doubleday, 1989.

Christianity Today   *Marriage and Divorce Survey Report.* Wheaton, IL: Christianity Today Research Department, 1992.

Louis M. Crosier, ed.   *Losing It: The Virginity Myth.* Washington: Avocus Publishing, 1993.

Stephen Davis   *Future Sex.* Phoenix: Personal Enhancement Press, 1991.

R.F. Docter   *Transvestites and Transsexuals: Toward a Theory of Cross-Gender Behavior.* New York: Plenum Press, 1990.

Georg Feuerstein   *Sacred Sexuality: Living the Vision of the Erotic Spirit.* Los Angeles: J.P. Tarcher/Perigee, 1992.

Helen E. Fisher   *Anatomy of Love: The Natural History of Monogamy, Adultery, and Divorce.* New York: Norton, 1992.

Nancy Friday	*Women on Top: How Real Life Has Changed Women's Sexual Fantasies.* New York: Simon & Schuster, 1991.
Marjorie Garber	*Vested Interests: Cross-Dressing and Cultural Anxiety.* New York: Routledge, 1992.
Thomas Geller, ed.	*Bisexuality: A Reader and Sourcebook.* Ojai, CA: Times Change Press, 1990.
Michael Gold	*Does God Belong in the Bedroom?* Philadelphia: Jewish Publication Society, 1992.
George Grant and Mark A. Horne	*Legislating Immorality: The Homosexual Movement Comes Out of the Closet.* Chicago: Moody Press/Legacy Communications, 1993.
Dean Hamer and Peter Copeland	*The Search for the Gay Gene and the Biology of Behavior.* New York: Simon & Schuster, 1994.
Gilbert Herdt, ed.	*Third Sex, Third Gender: Beyond Sexual Dimorphism in Culture and History.* New York: Zone Books, 1994.
Janice M. Irvine	*Disorder of Desire: Sex and Gender in Modern American Sexology.* Philadelphia: Temple University Press, 1990.
Samuel S. Janus and Cynthia L. Janus	*Janus Report on Sexual Behavior.* New York: John Wiley & Sons, 1993.
Valerie Jenness	*Making It Work: The Prostitutes' Rights Movement in Perspective.* New York: Aldine de Gruyter, 1993.
Arno Karlen	*Threesomes: Studies in Sex, Power, and Intimacy.* New York: William Morrow, 1990.
Edward O. Laumann et al.	*The Social Organization of Sexuality: Sexual Practices in the United States.* Chicago: University of Chicago Press, 1994.
Linda L. Lindsey	*Gender Roles: A Sociological Perspective.* Englewood Cliffs, NJ: Prentice Hall, 1990.
Gordene Olga MacKenzie	*Transgender Nation.* Bowling Green, OH: Bowling Green State University Popular Press, 1994.
Catharine MacKinnon	*Only Words.* Cambridge, MA: Harvard University Press, 1993.
Lynn Margulis and Dorion Sagan	*Mystery Dance: On the Evolution of Human Sexuality.* New York: Summit Books, 1991.
William H. Masters, Virginia E. Johnson, and Robert C. Kolodny	*Heterosexuality.* New York: HarperCollins, 1994.

Naomi B. McCormick   *Sexual Salvation: Affirming Women's Sexual Rights and Pleasures*. Westport, CT: Praeger, 1994.

David P. McWhirter, Stephanie A. Sanders, and Machover Reinisch, eds.   *Homosexuality/Heterosexuality: Concepts of Sexual Orientation*. New York: Oxford University Press, 1990.

Robert T. Michael et al.   *Sex in America: A Definitive Survey*. Boston: Little, Brown, 1994.

John Money   *The Adam Principle: Genes, Genitals, Hormones, and Gender*. Buffalo: Prometheus Books, 1993.

Joseph Nicolosi   *Reparative Therapy of Male Homosexuality: A New Clinical Approach*. Northvale, NJ: Jason Aronson, 1991.

Joyce McCarl Nielsen   *Sex and Gender in Society*. Prospect Heights, IL: Waveland Press, 1990.

Marcia Palley   *Sex & Sensibility: Reflections on Forbidden Mirrors and the Will to Censor*. Hopewell, NJ: Ecco Press, 1994.

Robert Pool   *Eve's Rib: The Biological Roots of Sex Differences*. New York: Crown, 1994.

Judith A. Reisman   *"Soft Porn" Plays Hardball—Its Tragic Effects on Women, Children, and the Family*. Lafayette, LA: Huntington House, 1991.

Cecilia L. Ridgeway, ed.   *Gender, Interaction, and Inequality*. New York: Springer-Verlag, 1992.

Matt Ridley   *The Red Queen: Sex and the Evolution of Human Nature*. New York: Macmillan, 1994.

Martine A. Rothblatt   *The Apartheid of Sex and the Freedom of Gender*. New York: Crown, 1995.

Diana E.H. Russell   *Against Pornography: The Evidence of Harm*. Berkeley, CA: Russell Publications, 1993.

Peggy Reeves Sanday and Ruth Gallagher Goodenough   *Beyond the Second Sex: New Directions in the Anthropology of Gender.* Philadelphia: University of Pennsylvania Press, 1990.

Laurie Shrage   *Moral Dilemmas of Feminism: Prostitution, Adultery, and Abortion*. New York: Routledge, 1994.

Gerda Siann   *Gender, Sex, and Sexuality: Contemporary Psychological Perspectives*. Bristol, PA: Taylor & Francis, 1994.

Rachel Silver   *The Girl in Scarlet Heels*. North Pomfret, VT: Trafalgar Square, 1994.

Mark Simpson   *Male Impersonators: Men Performing Masculinity.* New York: Routledge, 1994.

Nadine Strossen   *Defending Pornography: Free Speech, Sex, and the Fight for Women's Rights.* New York: Scribner, 1994.

Ruth Taylor, Ann G. Nerbun, and Richard M. Hogan   *Our Power to Love: God's Gift of Our Sexuality.* San Francisco: Ignatius Press, 1991.

Lionel Tiger   *The Pursuit of Pleasure.* Boston: Little, Brown, 1992.

R.K. Unger and M. Crawford   *Women and Gender: A Feminist Psychology.* New York: McGraw-Hill, 1992.

Elizabeth Reba Weise   *Closer to Home: Bisexuality & Feminism.* Seattle: Seal Press, 1992.

Penny A. Weiss   *Gendered Community.* New York: New York University Press, 1993.

Martin King Whyte   *Dating, Mating, and Marriage.* New York: Aldine de Gruyter, 1990.

Index

abortion, 220
Adler, Jerry, 232
adultery, 68, 74, 217
*Against Pornography: The Evidence
of Harm* (Russell), 162
AIDS (acquired immunodeficiency
syndrome)
 campaign against, 162, 205
 changes sexual behavior, 217-18
 and heterosexuals, 214, 231-33
 and high-risk behavior, 214, 217,
 229, 231-34
 HIV (human immunodeficiency
 virus), 217-18, 229, 234
 and homosexuals, 88, 122-23, 181
 tests for, 217-18, 233
Alexander, Priscilla, 172, 173
Allen, Laura S., 122, 123
Allen, Paula Gunn, 90
Allgeier, Elizabeth, 211
Almodavar, Norma Jean, 167
Amazons, 89
American Association of Sex
 Educators, Counselors and
 Therapists (AASECT), 213
American Psychiatric Association
 (APA)
 on homosexuality, 140, 142-43,
 149-51
Americans
 practice high-risk sexual behavior,
 226-29
 con, 230-34
 as satisfied with sex lives, 195-202,
 213-14
 con, 203-11
 sex is becoming more casual for,
 219-25
 sex is becoming more intimate for,
 212-18
 sex changes in, 105
anal sex, 87, 89, 216, 221
Anand, Margo, 49
Anapol, Deborah M., 62
androgens, 122, 124, 128-29
animals
 and homosexuality, 88, 98, 100
 sex and bonding, 30, 223

sex for procreation, 27-28, 31, 45,
 60, 223-24
Anthony, Jane, 170
Archer, John, 115
art, sex in, 220
Augustine, Saint, 171

Babilonia, Gerineldo, 102-103
Babilonia, Mateo, 102-105
Babilonia, Pilar, 102-103
Babilonia, Prudencio, 102-105
Bailey, Derrick Sherwin, 76
Bailey, J. Michael, 125, 128, 131
Bateson, Gregory, 178
Bauer, Karla, 213
Beauvoir, Simone de, 111
Bayer, Ronald, 140, 143
Belton, Ria, 166, 167
berdaches, 89, 90, 91, 108
Bergler, Edmund, 148
Bieber, Irving, 141-43, 148
biological advantage
 as purpose of sex, 17-25
biology
 chemicals and love, 29
 determines gender, 97-105, 113-19
 evidence for homosexuality in, 120-
 29
 con, 130-34, 147
 evolutionary, 18-22
Birdwhistell, Ray, 112
birth control. *See* contraception
bisexuality
 and genetics, 132
 as normal, 88, 90-91
 and pedophilia, 80
 percentage of, 214
 treatment to change orientation, 141
Blackwell, Mr. (hermaphrodite), 100-
 101, 103
Bloom, Allan, 221
Boys and Sex (Pomeroy), 83
Boy Scouts, homosexuals in, 80
brain
 dimorphic structures in, 122
 and gender determination, 98, 103-
 105, 121

and gender differences, 122-24
and homosexuality determination,
121-24, 129
Bright, Susie, 44
Broun, Heywood, 163
Brown, Terry R., 128
Burr, Chandler, 130

Callahan, Sidney, 57
Callen, Michael, 232
Campaign Against Pornography, 162
Campbell, Ian, 186
Carnes, Patrick, 179, 180, 210
Catholic Church, on contraception,
34-39
celibacy
as a choice, 63, 76, 168
and sexual addiction, 179, 183
Chamberlain, Wilt, 209
Changing Homosexuality in the Male
(Hatterer), 148
childhood
causes for homosexuality in, 151
causes for sexual addiction in, 177,
181-83
causes for sexual dysfunction in,
206
children
adopted by homosexuals, 80
attachment to parents, 27-29, 31-32
and divorce, 70
dependency of, 27-29, 60
effect of incest on, 166-69, 171,
173, 177-78, 180-81, 107-108
effect of monogamy on, 60
effect of nonmonogamy on, 65-66,
59
gender roles learned, 109, 114-15
homosexuals recruit, 83-84
molestation of
and pornography, 153, 154, 156,
163
by priests, 220
parents' effect on sexuality of, 205,
210
in pornography, 160, 161
raising of
by homosexuals, 141
as reason love developed, 27-28
sexuality of
development of, 117-18

as learned, 88, 210
socialization of, 113-17
teaching toleration, 145
Christians
on homosexuality, 82, 88, 134
should renounce divorce, 67-72
should sometimes accept divorce,
73-78
chromosomes
and gender determination, 100, 101,
114
and homosexuality, 124-28
Clements, Mark, 212, 213
Cline, Victor B., 152
Clinton, Bill, 80
cloning, 18, 22, 23, 25
Coleman, Eli, 204, 209
compulsive sexual behavior (CSB),
149-50, 153-55, 176-83, 185-87,
209-11
condoms, 229, 231-33, 217, 221, 222
contraception, 34-39, 205
Conundrum (Morris), 110
Cornett, Carlton, 139
Cory, Donald Webster, 186
COYOTE (Call Off Your Old Tired
Ethics), 164, 172
Crapo, Richard, 84
crime, pornography causes, 153-55
cytomegalovirus (CMV), 220, 232
Davies, Nick, 160-63
Davis, Murray, 44
deSimone, Diane, 97
*Diagnostic and Statistical Manual of
Mental Disorders*, 149
Diaz, Kay, 133
Disorders of Sexual Desire (Kaplan),
207
divorce
and children, 70
Christians should renounce, 67-72
con, 73-78
as healthy, 74, 77-78
is now more common, 198
and sexual addiction, 153, 154, 157
as sin, 75
DNA
as evidence, 220
and homosexuality, 121, 125-28,
133
and proto-sex, 20, 21-22

Dorner, Gunter, 98-100, 104
drugs
  addiction to, compared to sexual
    addiction, 153, 155, 179-80, 210
  and safe sex, 229
Durden-Smith, Jo, 97

Eakman, B.K.,
education
  effect on sexual habits, 195-202,
    227
  sex
    for children, 220-21, 224-25
Elders, Joycelyn, 220, 223
Ellis, Albert, 184
Ellis, Havelock, 171
endorphins, 179
estrogen, 122
Europe, attitudes about sexuality, 87-
  89, 140
evolution
  and fathers, 30
  and love, 29-32
  and mothering, 29-30
  and purpose of sex, 18-22
Evolution of Sex, The (Smith), 20
exhibitionism, 153, 156, 177, 180,
  209

families
  changing structure of, 119
  gender roles in, 118
  homosexuality in, 121, 124-29
  homosexuality threatens, 80-81, 84-
    85
  and monogamy, 59
  and nonmonogamy, 64-66
  as product of Industrial Revolution,
    84
Farley, Melissa, 173
feminists
  and monogamy, 59
  and prostitution, 171, 174
Fernandez, Joseph, 220
fetishism, 153, 180
Feuerstein, Georg, 49
Fine, Reuben, 148
Fivush, Robyn, 113
Francoeur, Robert, 178-79
Freud, Sigmund
  "madonna-whore" complex, 208

on homosexuality, 140
on sexual health, 183

Gagnon, John H., 195
Garber, Marjorie, 109
Gebbie, Kristine, 220, 223, 225
gender
  determination of
    behavior, 98, 108, 110-12
    chromosomes, 100, 101, 114
    is biological, 97-105
      case studies, 100-105
    is biological and social, 113-19
    is learned, 100, 101-102
      con, 102-105
    and other cultures, 108-11
    and physical characteristics, 98,
      100, 101-102, 107, 109, 114
    puberty, 98, 101, 102-103, 105,
      117
    by social practices, 87-92, 100-
      105, 106-12
    and surgery, 100-102, 105, 110
  differences, 98
  not equivalent to sex, 107
  similarities between, 109-10
  and socialization, 100-105
  third category, 108-109
gender roles
  Amazons, 89, 91
  are changing, 118-19, 231
  around the world, 89-91, 108
  berdache, 89, 90, 91, 108
  and careers, 117-19
  hijra, 108
  Hyper-Feminine, 91
  Hyper-Masculine, 91
  manly hearted women, 108
  nadle, 89
  Ordinary Females, 91
  Ordinary Males, 91
  other categories, 87-92
  parents' contribution to, 109, 114-
    16
  and relationships, 117
  and toys, 109, 114
  winkte, 89
  within families, 118, 119
  xanith, 108
General Social Survey (GSS), 227-29
Giobbe, Evelina, 174

Gloria Goes to Gay Pride, 84
Golombok, Susan, 113
Gorski, Roger A., 121-22, 123
Goy, Bob, 98
Gramunt, Mark, 46
Green, Richard, 104
Gregg, Amy C., 73
Grigg, William Norman, 79
Gutin, JoAnn C., 17

Hamer, Dean H., 120, 125-27, 129, 131
Harrad Experiment (Rimmer), 64
Harris, Martyn, 158
Hatterer, Lawrence J., 148
Heiman, Andrea, 230
Heinlein, Robert, 64
hermaphrodites, 100-101
Hersch, Patricia, 141
Hickey, Donal, 20-21
hijra, 108
Hite, Shere, 48
HIV (human immunodeficiency virus), 217-18, 229, 234
Hollander, Dore, 226, 228
Hollibaugh, Amber, 174
homosexuality
    American Psychiatric Association on, 140, 142-43, 149-51
    in animals, 88, 98, 100
    as behavioral, 83
    biological studies of, 120-29
        are flawed, 131
    causes for, 141
        in childhood, 151
        environment, 131
        fear of failure, 185
        learned behavior, 147
        as psychological illness, 140, 142
            con, 140-45
    as a choice, 104, 132, 134
    definition for, 142
    education about, 83-84
    as experimental stage, 81, 84
    and family studies, 124-29
    history of, 81-83, 84
    is biologically determined, 97-105, 120-29
        con, 130-34, 147
    is immoral, 134
    as a lifestyle, 220

and Native Americans, 87-92
nonclinical, 151
as normal sexual behavior, 87-92, 139-45
    con, 146-51
parents' responses to, 90, 140
percentages of, 121, 134, 214
society should not tolerate, 79-85
society's treatment of, 143, 144, 150
symposium on, 83
and teenagers, 83-84
treatment to change orientation
    "cure" for, 104, 140
        does not work, 141-42
            con, 148-49
        as harmful, 144-45, 148
        physically, 99, 104
        psychologically, 140-44, 148-49
    twins studies on, 125, 131, 133
Homosexuality (Bieber), 141
Homosexuality and American Psychiatry: The Politics of Diagnosis (Bayer), 140
Homosexuality: Disease or Way of Life? (Bergler), 148
Homosexuality in Perspective (Masters and Johnson), 148-49
homosexuals
    and alcoholism, 149
    androgen levels of, 124
    aversion therapy, 104
    in Boy Scouts, 80
    brain differences in, 121-24, 129
    changing orientation, 80, 83, 144, 148, 149, 151
    and children
        adoption of, 80
        pedophilia, 80-81, 99
        recruiting, 83-84
    former, 132
    high-risk behavior of, 232, 233
    in military, 80, 220
    and marriage, 58, 80
    "primary," 104
    relationships of, 150
    religious positions on, 80
    rights movement, 83-85, 142, 143, 147, 150
    and sexual compulsion, 149-50
    and suicide, 149

threaten the family, 80-81, 84-85

Hooker, Evelyn, 142-43

hormones
  activational effects, 98
  androgens, 122, 124, 128-29
  and bonding, 29
  environmental influence on, 115
  estrogen, 122
  organizational effects, 98
  prenatal, 98-100, 102
  testosterone, 99, 103-104

Howard, Kenneth, 141

Hu, Stella, 125, 128

Human Genome Project, 126

Humanae vitae (Paul VI), 34-39

humans
  difference from animals, 27-28, 30-31, 43, 45, 60, 107, 223-24
  evolution of sex in, 18-25
  gestation periods of, 28

hypoactive sexual desire (HSD), 206-208

hypothalamus
  animal studies on, 121-22, 124
  and sex hormones, 98

Imperato-McGinley, Julianne, 102, 103, 105

incest
  and prostitution, 166-69, 171, 173
  and sexual addiction, 177-78, 180
  and sexual disorders, 177, 181, 207-208

intercourse, sexual
  frontal, 31, 60
  vaginal, 201

Isay, Richard, 142

Islam, and polygamy, 58

Jesus, on divorce, 70, 71, 74, 75-76

Johnson, Virginia E.
  on female ejaculation, 41
  on gender orientation, 102
  on homosexuality, 147, 148-49
  on performance anxiety, 185
  research of, 48, 204

Johnson, William R., 88

Kaplan, Helen Singer, 207

Kellogg, John Harvey, 206

King, Van L., 128

Kinsey, Alfred
  findings on homosexuality, 83-84, 104, 141, 149-50
  on women's sexuality, 205

Kolata, Gina, 195

Kronemeyer, Robert, 148

Landers, Ann, 222

Laumann, Edward O., 195

lesbians, and family studies, 125

LeVay, Simon, 120, 122-23, 131

Lewes, Kenneth, 141, 143

Lief, Harold, 208

Lindsey, Linda L., 109

Lively, Curtis, 24-25

Lloyd, Barbara, 115

Lorber, Judith, 106

love
  evolves from sex, 27, 29-32, 35
  and intelligence, 28, 29, 31
  and music, 222, 223
  as necessary to child rearing, 27-29
  profane (eros), 27
  sacred (agape), 27
  as strongest human drive, 223

Macke, Jennifer P., 128

MacKinnon, Catharine, 172

Madonna, 220

Magnuson, Victoria L., 125

Making History (Marcus), 142, 144

Man-Boy Love Association, 220

manly hearted women, 108

Mapplethorpe, Robert, 220

Marcus, Eric, 142

Margulis, Lynn, 19

Marmor, Judd, 142, 143, 144

marriage
  failure of, 72, 75
  and faithfulness, 198-99, 217
  frequency of sex in, 199
  and happiness, 68-70
  hard, 68-69
  and high-risk sexual behavior, 227-29
  historical changes in, 77
  and homosexuals, 58, 80
  monogamous, 58-61
  nonmonogamous, 63-66
  orgasms in, 200
  reasons for, 70-72

as sacred, 70-72, 74-75
similarities in partners, 197
statistics on, 196-202, 213, 216-17
types of, 63
Maslow, Abraham, 183
massage parlors, 156, 159, 209
Masters, William H.
on female ejaculation, 41
on gender orientation, 102
on homosexuality, 147, 148-49
on performance anxiety, 185
research of, 48, 204
masturbation
frequency of, 201-202
and orgasms, 42, 44
and pornography, 153-56
and sex education, 221, 222
statistics on, 216, 217
Matousek, Mark, 176, 182
McEntee, Patty, 154
media, on sex, 205, 220-23
Medinger, Alan, 146
Memoirs of a Sexual Evolutionary
(Vera), 181
men
changes in attitudes about sex, 213,
214
differences from women, 50, 119
and impotence, 215, 218
male-child bonds, 31
male-female bonds, 31
as satisfied with sex lives, 196-201
con, 204-10
Michael, Robert T., 195
Michod, Richard, 18, 21-22
Miller, Jay, 91
Moberly, Elizabeth, 151
Monet, Veronica, 164
Money, John
on cause of homosexuality, 147
on pedophilia, 80-81
on sexual repression, 208, 211
on surgical sex change, 101-102
monogamy
benefits of, 59-61
boredom in, 48-49
effect on children, 60
and feminists, 59
as necessary to society, 57-61, 85,
222
see also nonmonogamy

Moore, Constance, 205, 207
Morris, Jan, 110
mothers
attachment to children, 27-29, 31-32
and estrus, 29, 30-31
and evolution, 29-30
Muir, Charles and Caroline, 49-53
Murray, Paul, 33
Mystery of Love and Marriage, The
(Bailey), 75-76

nadle, 89
Nash, J. Madeleine, 19
Nathans, Jeremy, 128
National Association for the
Research and Therapy of
Homosexuality, 144
National Association of Social
Workers (NASW) Committee on
Lesbian and Gay Issues, 144-45
National Cancer Institute, 125, 132
National Guidelines for Comprehen-
sive Sexual Education, 220-21
National Institutes of Health
studies on homosexuality, 125, 128,
143
are flawed, 131, 150
National Opinion Research Center
General Social Survey (GSS), 227
Native Americans, and sexuality, 43,
87-92
Natural Family Planning (NFP), 34
Navarro, Bob, 153
Nearing, Ryam, 64
Nicolosi, Joseph, 144, 151
nonmonogamy
benefits of, 63-65
definition of, 63
effect on children, 65-66, 59
society should condone, 62-66
Nu, Nan, 125, 128

Ogden, Gina, 179, 181, 183
O'Mara, Peggy, 75
One Teenager in Ten, 84
oral sex, 166, 201-202, 221
orgasm
in marriage, 200
physiology of, 41-45, 200-201, 214
statistics on, 214, 216, 217
Our Sexuality (Baur et al.), 213

Out of the Shadows (Carnes), 210
Overcoming Homosexuality
  (Kronemeyer), 148

parthenogenesis, 22
patriarchy
  and prostitution, 169, 171, 174
  in society, 77
Pattatucci, Angela M.L., 125
Paul VI, 34, 37, 38
pedophilia
  history of, 81-83
  and homosexuality, 80-81
  "cure" for, 99
  and sexual compulsion, 209
Peterson, Brenda, 48
Pheterson, Gail, 172
Pillard, Richard C., 125, 131
polyandry, 63, 91
polyfidelity, 63, 64
polygamy, 58, 59, 91
polygyny, 63
Pomeroy, Wardell, 83-84
pornography
  causes sex crimes, 153-55
  children in, 160, 161
  is boring, 161
  is not harmful, 158-63
  homosexual, 82
  and prostitution, 154-56
  use escalates, 153, 155-57, 162
  use is normal, 159
  use results in abnormal sexual
    behavior, 152-57
    con, 158-63
Posner, Richard, 81-82
primates
  and sex, 30, 31
  social groups of, 107
process addiction, 179-80, 182
promiscuity, 60, 209, 227-29, 231
prostitution
  can benefit women, 164-69
  as a choice, 165-67, 174
    con, 171-72, 173, 174
  as crime against women, 173
  empowers women, 167, 169
  harms women, 170-75
  and marriage, 171
  and pornography, 154-56
  as rape, 171, 173

as victimless crime, 171, 173
proto-humans, 28
proto-sex, 19, 20-21
*Psychoanalytic Theory, Male and
  Female Homosexuality: Psychological Approaches* (Fine), 148
*Psychoanalytic Theory of Male
  Homosexuality, The* (Lewes), 141
psychotherapy, for homosexuals,
  140-44, 148-49
puberty, 98, 101-105, 117

racial sexual statistics, 196-97, 200,
  227-29
Ramsdale, David and Ellen, 49
rape
  of children, 177, 178
  and pornography, 153, 154, 156-57,
    160
rational emotive therapy (RET), 185
*Reason and Emotion in
  Psychotherapy* (Ellis), 189
relationships
  complementarity in, 76
  dyads work best, 58-60
  as hard work, 68-72, 78
  how people meet, 197-98
  multiple partner, 62-66
  passion essential to, 51
  and puberty, 117
  in religion, 76
  sexist attitudes about, 76
religion
  and contraception, 33-39
  divorce can be acceptable, 73-78
    con, 67-72
  dualism in, 77
  and evolution, 224
  heterosexism in, 76, 77
  hierarchy in, 77
  and homosexuality, 80, 88, 134
  and love, 27
  patriarchy in, 77
  and polygamy, 58
  and sex, 27, 33-39, 48, 68, 73-74
  sexism in, 76, 77
reparative therapy, 140-42, 144-45,
  148-49
reproduction
  sexual, 18-25
  and survival of humans, 27-29

256

Richards, Renee, 101
Rimmer, Robert, 64
Rogers, Sy, 146
Rose, Michael, 20-21, 22
Rosellini, Lynn, 203
Rossman, Parker, 82
Ruppel, Howard, 210
Russell, Diana, 162
Sacred Sexuality (Feuerstein), 49
sadomasochism, 153, 156, 160, 163
Safire, William, 160
Sagarin, Edward, 186
Sainsbury, Steven, 222
Satyricon, The (Petronius), 82
Schaef, Anne Wilson, 179, 180-81
Schiavi, Raul C., 206
Schopenhauer, Arthur, 27
Schumacher, Sallie, 213
sensual pleasure, as purpose of sex, 40-45
sex
  abnormal, 153, 176-83, 187, 189
  absolutist demandingness, 185-86
  abstinence from, 34-36, 222
  age at first time, 198, 234
  and aging, 218
  alters consciousness, 44, 45, 49, 63
  Americans are satisfied with, 195-202, 213-14
    con, 203-11
  avoidance of, 189-90
    con, 219-25
  as biologically inefficient, 18-23
  casual
    is becoming less, 212-18
      con, 219-25
    statistics, 205, 227
  celibacy, 63, 76, 168, 179, 183
  choosing partners who are similar, 196-97
  cloning, 18, 22, 23, 25
  clubs, 233
  compulsive, 149-50, 153-55, 176-83, 185-87, 209-11
  confusion about, 48-49
  and death, 45
  desire disorders, 204-11, 215
  disturbance, 185-87, 190
  dysfunction, 206-11
  early conditioning about, 50
  early encounters, 50, 52

education
  for children, 220-21, 224-25
  safe sex, 199, 221, 232, 234
and estrus, 29, 30-31
and evolution, 18-25, 28, 29-31
fantasies, 142, 153, 157
and fear, 44, 45
frequency of, 199, 216
group, 60, 201
healing with, 52-53
high-risk behavior
  Americans still practicing, 226-29
  Americans trying to abandon, 230-34
  multiple partners, 227-28
  and sexually transmitted diseases (STDs), 227, 229, 231-34
  who practices, 227-29
is becoming more intimate, 212-18
laws governing, 84
and loss of ego, 44-45
love divorced from, 221, 225
love evolves from, 27, 29-32
neurological high of, 179
number of partners, 198-99, 227
offenders, 153
and orgasm, 41-45, 200-201, 214, 215, 217
phone, 161, 209, 210
physiology of, 41-43
preferences, 216, 218
premarital, 197-202, 205
and primates, 30, 31
problems with, 215-16, 218
promiscuity, 60, 209, 227-29, 231
purpose of
  biological advantage, 17-25
  developing love bonds, 26-32, 206
  genetic variability, 18, 19, 20, 23-25
  reproduction, 33-39
  sensual pleasure, 40-45
  species in a rut, 22-23
  spiritual enlightenment, 46-53
and race, 196-97, 200, 227-29
safe, 43, 221-22, 229, 232
  education about, 199, 221, 232, 234
and spirituality, 34-39, 46-53, 86-92
survey of America, 196-202
tantric, 48, 49-53

257

teenage, 83-84, 196, 198, 220, 222,
   224-25, 227, 234
therapy, 204-207
time spent on, 199, 216
types of, 201
values about, 223-25
Sex Information and Education
   Council of the U.S. (SIECUS), 221
sexual addiction
   causes for, 177, 181-83
   compared to drug addiction, 153,
      155, 179-80, 210
   and incest, 177-78, 180-81
   is a myth, 178-79
   as normal human behavior, 184-90
   pornography causes, 153
   problems of, 153-55, 176-83
   signs of, 182
   treatment for, 181-83
   types of, 180
Sexual Interactions (Allgeier), 211
sexuality
   affected by social forces, 196-202
   continuum of, 88
   intolerance of differences in, 87, 143
   European attitudes about, 87-89
   society should celebrate all forms
      of, 86-92
sexually transmitted diseases (STDs),
   88, 156, 199, 220
   and high-risk behavior, 227, 229
sexual orientation
   causes for, 141
   and history, 88
   is learned, 101-102
      con, 102-105
*Sexual Recovery: Everywoman's
   Guide Through Sexual Co-
   Dependency* (Ogden), 179
Sex Work (Alexander et al.), 172,
   173, 174
Shakti, 51, 52
Sheldon, Louis, 130
Shi Peipu, 111
Shiva, 50
Small, Meredith F., 30
Smith, Janet E., 35
Smith, John Maynard, 18-20, 21
Socarides, Charles, 142-44, 147-49,
   151
society

and alternate relationships, 66
changes in condoning sexual
   practices, 190, 205, 231
and gender orientation, 100-105
patriarchy in, 77
practices determine gender, 87-92,
   106-12
sexism in, 76, 77
should celebrate all forms of
   sexuality, 86-92
should condone nonmonogamy, 62-
   66
should not tolerate homosexuality,
   79-85
   con, 145
should uphold monogamy, 57-61
Society for the Scientific Study of
   Sex, 210, 213
sodomites, 87
Spong, John Shelby, 80
Sprinkle, Annie, 220
Stafford, Tim, 67
Stayton, William R., 188
St. James, Margo, 172
Stoller, Bob, 104
Stranger in a Strange Land
   (Heinlein), 64

Tafoya, Terry, 86
tantric sex, 48, 49-53
teenagers
   codes of conduct, 224-25
   and homosexuality, 83-84
   and masturbation, 222
   sex hotline for, 220
   and sexually transmitted diseases,
      222, 227, 234
   sexual partners of, 196, 198
Teitelbaum, Stanley, 233, 234
Ternera, Amaranta, 102, 103
testicular feminization syndrome,
   100, 102-104
testosterone
   environment affects, 115
   and heterosexuality, 103-104
   and homosexuality, 99, 104
Thomas Aquinas, Saint, 43, 171
Thompson, William Irwin, 45
Tipton, Billy, 108
Tisdale, Sallie, 40
transsexuals, 100, 101, 104, 108